uncommon voyage

uncommon voyage

parenting
a special needs child

Laura Shapiro Kramer

North Atlantic Books
Berkeley, California

Published by
North Atlantic Books
P.O. Box 12327
Berkeley, California 94712

Cover photo © Milton Montenegro, gettyone.com
Back cover photo © Arthur L. Cohen
Cover and book design © Ayelet Maida, A/M Studios
Printed in the United States of America

Uncommon Voyage is sponsored by the Society for the Study of Native Arts
and Sciences, a nonprofit educational corporation whose goals are to
develop an educational and crosscultural perspective linking various
scientific, social, and artistic fields; to nurture a holistic view of arts,
sciences, humanities, and healing; and to publish and distribute literature
on the relationship of mind, body, and nature.

North Atlantic Books' publications are available through most bookstores.
For further information, call 800-337-2665 or visit our website at
www.northatlanticbooks.com.

Substantial discounts on bulk quantities are available to corporations,
professional associations, and other organizations. For details and discount
information, contact our special sales department.

LIBRARY OF CONGRESS CATALOGING-IN-PUBLICATION DATA
    Kramer, Laura Shapiro
    Uncommon voyage: parenting a special needs child / by Laura Shapiro
Kramer.
        p. cm.
    Previously published: Boston: Faber & Faber, 1996
    Includes bibliographical references and index.
    ISBN 1-55643-370-0 (alk. paper)
    1. Cerebral palsy—Alternative treatment.
    2. Developmentally disabled children—Medical care. I. Title.

RJ496.C4 K73 2001
618.92'836—dc21   2001016264

2 3 4 5 6 7 8 9 / 05 04 03 02 01

For Jay
because you are everything

acknowledgments

I WISH TO THANK Dr. Viola Frymann and the staff of the Osteopathic Center for Children, as well as, Jim Giorgi, Susan Schneider, Judith Maidenbaum, Ph.D., for their professional support and guidance. Gary Shulman and Linda Lew at Resources for Children With Special Needs lent important information. I thank Judy Dimon, Claire Roderick, Barbara Pruzan, Ben Bruno, and Syl Elbourne for their personal support and encouragement. A special thanks to Dr. Elizabeth Sharpless who sets the standard for professional dignity.

I thank my daughter Haya for being my dream come true and my son Seth for being my inspiration and love.

Author's Note

Some person's names or identifying characteristics and other details have been changed.

contents

FOREWORD My Name is Seth XI

PREFACE The Landscape XVII

INTRODUCTION Exploring XXV

CHAPTER ONE Origins 1

CHAPTER TWO Discovery 13

CHAPTER THREE Embarkation 23

CHAPTER FOUR At Sea 39

CHAPTER FIVE New Horizons 59

CHAPTER SIX The Plunge 75

CHAPTER SEVEN The Calm Before the Storm 89

CHAPTER EIGHT Shifting Currents 103

CHAPTER NINE Gyrations 121

CHAPTER TEN New Directions 135

CHAPTER ELEVEN A Whole New World 149

CHAPTER TWELVE Anchoring 171

CHAPTER THIRTEEN Haya 191

CHAPTER FOURTEEN Ashore 205

CHAPTER FIFTEEN Pathways 221

CHAPTER SIXTEEN Guides 233

Where to Turn 247

Bibliography 253

Index 255

my name is seth

MY NAME IS SETH. I am almost eighteen. I have a disability called cerebral palsy. It isn't curable, but it is something I am always able to work to improve. I have it, and I have learned to live with it. When I think about myself now, so much is different, but mostly it is the sense I have of myself growing and changing. My disability sometimes makes me think I am special. Once it might have become an obstacle, but what having cerebral palsy means is that I have to live a different kind of life than most people. I have to incorporate the life I imagined for myself with my life as it is.

This circumstance has given me many experiences, some of them difficult and some of them very happy. And I know there are more to come. One thing is I have met many interesting people like scientists, doctors, and scholars. My disability means something different to me today than it did years ago. Once I wrote that I didn't think I would change having cerebral palsy because I wouldn't be me if I didn't have it. I am not sure I still feel that way. I know I am me because of it, but if I had the choice I think I would change having cerebral palsy.

When I watch people, I think of things that other people wouldn't think about. I look at how people act and how they move. Sometimes I do more watching because I can't participate. Sometimes it's difficult to blend in or be counted in a group, and I have learned what that feels like. It hurts sometimes. It's a struggle, but I think this can happen anywhere to anyone, whether they have a disability or not. I have also learned that people like me even if I am different.

When I first see people I think about whether when they meet me they will think I'm different or how they will react to me. I think about what to do if they think I'm strange, especially when I talk. Little kids especially ask me why I am the way I am. I answer according to their ages and how I think I can make them understand. Sometimes I just walk away, or sometimes I ask back, "Why do you dress like that?" or "Why do you have that accent?" If they're older, I try to explain more of myself, but really older kids don't ask me much because they're more mature. Then we can talk about things in different ways too.

There have been people who just don't understand anything about me and think my disability is a joke. They giggle and sometimes they make fun of me. When I was smaller I got used to all of this, so now I don't say anything. I just ignore them. But if someone asked me I would explain myself to him or her. I can say why I have it, but that happens very, very rarely. In my life a stranger has never asked me anything about why I am the way I am. Sometimes I see they are wondering though. I see and feel them staring at me. The most important thing is that I don't want pity. Don't pity me. It may take me more time to do some things. But I will do them if I have time, so don't pity me.

My parents did everything they could for me. By the time I was two years old my mother had discovered "alternative" medicine. She had a back problem and finally had an operation, a "spinal fusion." She went to Carola, a woman who taught her breathing work. Carola taught my mother things to do with me. Then I went to Anat. She had a big studio with a plant in it. She did exercises with me that I didn't like. The positions she put me in hurt. I was too little to know that the exercises were going to help me learn to walk.

When I was in the first grade I knew I was different for the first time, I guess. I was too young to be afraid or worried. I think I was too young to understand much about what it all meant. Later, between third and fourth grade, I started to worry. When I saw other children doing sports and activities I couldn't do, I thought they would be leaving me behind. I guess in some ways they did. But I am there in new ways.

You need hope if you are a parent who has a child with cerebral palsy. Hope helps you. You need hope to live on. I know my parents had hope, and that's how I progressed. They believed in me, and they believed what they could do for me. You need to think about what your child is feeling. Now I want to give other people hope. I think my experience is special to who I am.

I know other people have cerebral palsy and other disabilities that make their lives very hard, much harder than mine. I still think that there is hope. My story and the story my mother tells can make them feel better. It feels right to me if we can help people have hope and believe in the future. I might be able to help others. I think of a future where I could advise parents, but at the same time give confidence to children who have special needs. I know I am lucky that I don't have serious medical problems. I want to help children who have worse situations than I do. I can be closer to them. Whatever I have to teach or help with will be more than someone from the outside.

⁓

What motivates me? Myself, mostly, but also what motivates me is my family and how much my parents care about me and are interested in getting help for me. My sister, Haya, has always been great through all of this. My good friends and teachers motivate me. My doctors help me believe in myself. They help me do things I thought I could never do. I learned to swim. A baseball player taught me how to swing a bat and climb on monkey bars. I play tennis and I sail very well. These were things I was not sure I would ever do. Because I have cerebral palsy I work harder for everything. I feel like I have an edge because I had to mature very quickly and I have learned what it means to apply myself. There are still things I worry about in my future (I hope I will drive a car), but I am very sure of finding solutions for everything.

I have two special friends, Evan and Matt. I know Evan from California and Matt from Cape Cod. They never thought it was a joke that I have disabilities. They each asked me once about it, and then we never talked about it again. They're the kind of friends who will wait for me to say what I want to say about how I feel being me. They include me and make me feel as if I can do everything that they can do. I try to do everything they do, but, as I get older, I see there are some things I may not be able to do ever.

My relationship to my parents is changing now that I am going away to college. I had a chance to live away from home a few summers, and I discovered a lot about myself and learned I like dorm life. At the same time I know my home is a place where I am accepted and loved (even if we have typical teenager/parent conflicts). I trust what my mother knows and writes about in this book. My mother experienced a lot in her body herself and did a lot of research and training. She is always very serious about my situation. I thank my mother for pushing me to see the doctors before I was as mature as I am now. I didn't always feel like going, but my mother always made me go. Today I feel differently and I am glad my mother made me stick it out. New things concern me. The future is unknown, which is always a little scary. I know I will need help—maybe with stuff I can't even imagine now. There are things about being a grown man, which are different than when I was a child. When I am nervous, for instance, it's hard for me to do simple things like pouring water. I wonder if I will be embarrassed. Then I always think I can find a way, if not to do some things one hundred percent, at least to attempt whatever it is. Nothing seems totally impossible. I can try. I can practice.

⌒

I think it's great that the treatments my mother found for me and for the whole family use nature and the mind and body. I love nature and when I do this work I can see how much nature is helping me. The new medical machines, the antibiotics, this stuff only works to a point. I don't think anything gets much better than the natural healing of the body and mind that God gave us. On the other hand, technology has greatly changed the world and especially the world for people with disabilities. I love technology. Computers make a huge difference to me because it's so hard for me to write clearly or for a long time. The Internet and email are very important also. With email I don't have to worry about anyone understanding me.

I am graduating from The Friends Seminary in June. It is a Quaker school. In September I will be a freshman at the University of Pennsylvania in Philadelphia. The Internet has allowed me to join a community of incoming freshmen at Penn without my cerebral palsy being a factor—for the moment. I want to study economics, political science, and philosophy. I want to go to Business School when I graduate. I've learned from being a student at Friends, and visiting the campus at Penn and meeting the people who will assist my transition into college, I learned that it is okay to be different. There are differences everywhere—in race, ethnicity, age, economics, opportunity, environment. I belong to one minority because I have cerebral palsy. But then no one is the same. The world is full of people with differences and I welcome them.

Dr. Viola Frymann is my doctor, and there is no other doctor in the world like her. I didn't always know this. I had to learn to accept her sessions. It took me time to discover everything. After her sessions I feel relaxed, tired, and very ready for action all at the same time. I feel immediately better. It only takes twenty minutes in her hands, and I am different. I wake up the next morning and like to lie in my bed and just experience how my body feels. The thing is about Dr. Frymann's work is I can actually feel the difference in my body and how it moves. No one makes my neck feel as easy to handle and less "spastic."

The last few times I was in California I was thinking a lot about the future without Dr. Frymann. This is about her age and my age. She is older now and I am older now. I know Dr. Frymann one day will stop having me for her patient. But I know how in touch with my body I am and how much more control of it I have when Dr. Frymann works with me. I have to think about when we no longer will be able to work together.

Last summer my breathing coach, Carl Stough, died. I had come to have a very different perspective on this work too. When I was younger I didn't like it that much and felt like quitting and thought it was a waste of time. Then I began to recognize and feel in my body what the work does. I had the understanding and importance of it. Carl's dying made me very sad, and I am still figuring things out about what to do. I still have my Homeopath and Osteopath in New York, Dr. Masiello. He has a new meaning as my doctor. When I have questions about my body, he really helps me with good answers. And I have done some Yoga with two of my mother's teachers, but I am not sure about continuing this work. I like stretching, swimming and movements that flatten out my chest from the curve that is in my back. My mother is always after me to "rise my sternum," to "work from the back body" and not to stick out my front ribs.

The best thing of all for me these days is Flexyx. I go to the Stone Mountain Counseling Center and my therapist Sarah Harber helps me the most. Just talking to her helps with having to handle lots of things. I like the work, but what makes it exceptional is the close relationship I have with Sarah. It is so important to have good relationships with therapists who you can trust to help you be yourself. When I go to a doctor or therapist I know if they really want to help or if they're just doing it for the money. I am always able to tell by the way it feels. I know by the way that they treat me. Sarah Harber, Dr. Frymann, Dr. Masiello, Carl Stough when he was alive, feel like friends.

There was a time in my life when I was sick of having people touch me. I did not want to go to any doctors. There were too many doctors, too many hands on me, too many diagnoses. They would put their hands on me, do their thing, spend half an hour with my parents, give a diagnosis, and then on another day, a totally different doctor. Maybe this wasn't exactly reality, but this is how it felt. Maybe I have a new relationship to doctors because I am more in control of my treatments; I understand them better, and I respect the treatments more.

None of this, of course, makes the disability go away, but it makes it easier to live with. Today I am a mixture of my old self and my new self. There is a Seth with cerebral palsy, and there is another Seth that cerebral palsy has nothing to do with. I am ready for the future. I know there are challenges, but I am used to that.

the landscape

UNCOMMON VOYAGE WAS ORIGINALLY created as a memoir. This expanded version is also meant to work as a resource and guide, though it remains a very personal story. After the original version of *Uncommon Voyage* was published, many more parents and individuals called me with questions; new questions, old questions. They asked me what to do, what else I knew—I am always learning more—and I found myself explaining in more detail how I found out what I needed for Seth, for me, and for our family. Everyone wants to talk and to cry. And, naturally, everyone still wants hope and encouragement. I understand. My own need for hope returns again and again. Throughout the journey the deeper questions about life keep surfacing.

The world is different today than when I first began exploring the options for Seth. Fifteen years ago we were not living in the dot-com Internet bubble. Fifteen years ago we did not think as much about how healing takes place; we were not as open to the "alternative therapies" such as acupuncture and biofeedback. We were not as willing to explore the less conventional medical options.

Writing about what transpired during these last five years since the book's first publication will I hope provide valuable information for all parents of special needs children. In the new chapters, I write about Flexyx and the work of Dr. Len Ochs in biofeedback neurotherapy, the continuing work of the Feldenkrais community, new developments in adaptive technology, the growing world of competitive sports for individuals with special needs.

This new version takes into account how Seth has changed, and how I have changed. Traveling around the country, appearing on television shows, on radio programs, at book fairs, and community centers, I met thousands of parents. Some people came to my readings with their special needs children, as if my seeing them would help them to get better. Some of these parents called me later to tell me what had happened. Information is what we all need and sharing it is essential. The more I listened the more I learned.

There are still no miracles. *Uncommon Voyage* remains a book about struggle, faith, devotion, and luck. But there have been new discoveries too, and I want you to know what has happened. Seth is going to college in a few months. This is a success story, but it goes on.

c~

What is a "special need?" Who is a "special needs child?"

A special need ranges from asthma and autism to chronic conditions and illnesses, cerebral palsy, diabetes, dyslexia, epilepsy, hearing impairments, learning disorders, mental illness and behavior disorders, speech and language disabilities and visual disabilities as well as physical disabilities.

There is a special needs child in every family; whether it is a sister, nephew, a cousin, we are all related to someone with a special need of some kind.

My book doesn't deal with each of these conditions individually but offers inspiration and information to parents of all such children. I cannot tell you what to do. I can only relate what I did and what I felt along the way and maybe it will help you make decisions differently. Perhaps you will glean something from my story and be inspired to think about your child's special needs in a new light.

When a child is diagnosed as "special," it is traumatic and confusing. There is heartbreak. It is difficult enough to attain an even keel in our emotions, never mind get information. It is hard to know what to believe about anything, especially the orthodox medical establishment, prognosis and expectations, education and rehabilitation options, special programs, immunizations.

To get information at a critical time when important decisions and immediate resolutions are needed is demanding. We are off balance, unsettled. Everything is unfamiliar, yet critical assessment and evaluations are mandatory. All parents of "special" children experience confusion, fear, sadness, and frustration. Sorting out feelings, our own and those of the people around us, is also daunting and continual. Loved ones, the siblings of our child, in-laws, spouses, are all central to the equation.

To this day I have not found collected in one place a cohesive perspective, relevant personal experience, practical information, and resources. It is all so confusing and scary. At the beginning we hesitate to explore or probe too deeply. What if there is something wrong? Then what do we do? What is the first move? Who do we trust? I am continually frustrated by this truth: there are no answers, only the right questions. The most important question is how we bring the big picture of illness into focus.

I hope you will be open to more of the alternatives. And I learned there are concrete things we can do to sort through the deluge of information and weigh conflicting opinions when they come. I trust my book will guide you in some of your decisions. I also wish to give voice to our heartfelt struggle. I want to offer encouragement and information.

My story belongs to me, but by sharing it I hope each of us will feel less alone. I want to galvanize you to think, to act, to create, enabling you to realize what can be done for yourselves and your children. The Chinese word for "crisis" has two characters: one is a symbol for danger, the other is a symbol for opportunity.

⌒

When our son was diagnosed with "mild cerebral palsy" at ten months old, I had to insist on, even beg for, the diagnosis. I was the one who kept saying there was something wrong. No one professional helped me or gave me an overview or guidelines to navigate the unknown confronted by my husband and family and me. We were alone.

When the neurologist told us that Seth had mild cerebral palsy, I asked, "What does that mean?" The image we had in our minds was of drooling kids in special vans, in wheel chairs who couldn't hold their heads up, or who walked with special sticks and often made involuntary movements.

What did it mean he would not walk for a long time or would never walk "normally?" The answers I got were vague, incomprehensible. We were surrounded by top medical professionals, yet no one ever mentioned speech. It was several months before I looked up "cerebral palsy" in the dictionary and realized yikes! there's more!

I asked, "What about physical therapy?" and the doctor answered that I could try, but I didn't know much about it or where to look.

And he offered no suggestions. I didn't know how many kinds of physical therapy existed or how to evaluate a physical therapist or a physical rehabilitation program. (At the moment of the diagnosis I could barely swallow, never mind collect my thoughts to ask important questions.)

Once I knew what Seth's circumstances were, I was propelled by a single mindedness that astonished others and myself with its force. I had a clear mission: help Seth to be all he can be. In the process I had to defy the pessimistic diagnosis and the defeatist prescriptions of the orthodox medical establishment. I had to redefine health, wellness. I had to delve deeper into an alternative and more unconventional world. I needed to uncover all the information required to help our son realize his full potential, not knowing what that potential was. In doing so, it turns out, I was also exploring myself.

Blindly, I drifted on an ocean I had never sailed before, believing that I could make right all that was wrong. It would be years before I knew anything and years before Seth walked. Today I am familiar with multiple conventional therapies, gait trainers and orthotic and orthopedic remedies, as well as neurodevelopmental treatment (NDT), neurodevelopmental biofeedback, and the Bobath method, I also have redefined my concepts of somatics. I am a practitioner of several non-conventional therapies. I am a resource for others.

My world became something it was not before. My perspective on life was profoundly altered. My voyage took me around the world of mainstream, orthodox medicine and delivered me into a completely other world, a world of "alternative" or "complimentary" therapies—Osteopathy, CranioSacral work, the Feldenkrais method, Sensorimotor work, biofeedback, Homeopathy, Yoga, and more. A multitude of new concepts, alternatives, and possibilities became part of my lexicon. I still find nothing about these options in books about cerebral palsy, or books about special needs children.

Confusion, anxiety and self-doubt remain. I agonize over what I cannot control or be sure of. I used to wish I could lie back and sail to a place where all would be well, that finally the right course would be established. Now I understand that the right course is always changing. The wind gusts and quiets. Currents change; so do tides and seasons. We must adapt. Life leads us where we have to go anyway, and it is usually while we are busy making other plans. I was on my way to a life in the theater and entertainment. Seth led me in a different direction.

My sense of mission is derived from Seth. My search for a meaningful career was resolved because of Seth's cerebral palsy. He is the reason I finally became a writer. My involvement with Resources for Children with Special Needs is because of Seth. My emotional and spiritual life was awakened and evolves and is intertwined with being Seth's mother. Even now, as he moves away from me, off to college in September and I wrestle with my feelings about Seth, I cry. And I celebrate. I am confident the separation will make way for something new in our relationship. When I receive praise for what I accomplished, when people tell me Seth's success is my success, I weigh this against the fact that I am guilty of healing myself through Seth's circumstances.

I try never to forget that Serendipity played a big role. I was and I am lucky. People say that we make our own luck. I only half believe this. Seth walks. Seth has not needed extreme medical care. He did not have seizures. We have not had to worry about money as much as some other people do. And I had the opportunity to write this book. I know I have been incredibly fortunate. I want to believe, though, that no matter what our circumstances, I would have traveled the road with as much conviction and open mindedness as I do now.

I have been accused of using Seth and his circumstances. When I ask myself if I use or exploit Seth's situation, the answer is yes if we are describing a combination of good fortune and manipulation that has propelled me forward. And defined me. Seth has learned to do this too. I hope you and your special needs child learn to do it as well.

A few years ago Seth and I were discussing the differences between the doctor who had attended me at his sister Haya's birth and the doctor who had attended me at his. It was not a discussion long on details, as I had yet to thoroughly describe to him what specifically occurred. But he knew by then that there were anomalies surrounding the labor and delivery with him. He asked me which doctor was better, knowing I would answer that his sister's was superior.

"Anyway," I said, looking into his radiant and knowing blue eyes, "I invented you."

"Oh, Mom," he responded, lying his head across my chest and letting me embrace him.

We are linked, each of us fulfilling our destiny. Was it preordained? Whatever our fate, Seth and I now are joined by a common exigency. I have a job, a mission. I need to educate myself about everything available for Seth and be sure he gets what he needs. And I have to hope I can inspire Seth to be all that he can be.

Linked, yes. And I do believe I invented him; as much as we wake up every day and invent ourselves over and over again. We all need "eyes for the 'invisibles'" to borrow a phrase of Rufus Jones. We need to know deep down that what we see, taste, touch, smell, and hear is not all there is.

⌒

Uncommon Voyage then is about all I learned, and not just what I learned that would help Seth. It is also what I learned inside because I am Seth's mother. I want to be the model and inspiration for my children. I wish them to be all that they can be as I strive to be all that I can be.

There was never any hand wringing, although I still cry. I do not deny that I have recurring feelings of sadness. These feelings contain less and less rage and disappointment because Seth is too wonderful for pity. Beyond the sorrow for what might have been, there is joy for what is. I support the integrity of Seth's experience by trying not to confuse it with my reactions, my projections.

Recently Seth has been struggling with new feelings. He is growing up and going into the world, and his emotional life is distinct from mine and from his sister and father. The anticipated separation is bringing up many feelings for all of us. It is a time of contradictions, great joy, and then pain. Rebellion is more complicated for a child with special needs.

We became the people we are because Seth is our son, our brother, our grandchild, our cousin, our neighbor, and our friend. There is a lifelong tension between trying to intervene and make the disability go away and accepting the person our son is. We hope, always, that others will accept him and love him for what he is and not reject him for what he is not. The stigma is there and frustration, and even anger sometimes. But there is also purpose and meaning and joy.

We still struggle with decisions, conflict, and lethargy. Once I agonized over whether to teach Seth sign language. Then we had to decide about surgery. Now it is about driving a car. Sometimes the battles are obvious, and sometimes they are hidden. As our special needs child becomes a special needs adult, the transition is monumental.

I have many suggestions, though only one *absolute* word of advice: Bring a notebook and pen with you everywhere. Take this notebook and pen to every appointment. Keep it by your bed and write what you were thinking or what you saw in the day. Take it to your teacher's conferences, doctor's appointments, and interviews. Memory is crucial; it is significant and it has consequences. Safeguard it. Write everything down.

∽

Many people helped me develop how I see things and what I have to say in *Uncommon Voyage*. Dr. Domenick Masiello is a constant source of wisdom. It was Dr. Masiello who introduced me to Dr. Frymann and to the work of Dr. Jim Jealous. My book is imprinted with their presence, as am I.

Like Dr. Masiello, Dr. Viola Frymann is very much a part of the equation even today. Many of the thoughts and perspectives presented here represent years of her research and teachings as they have been explained to those of us fortunate enough to learn from her.

There is no one like her. Just ask Seth and the countless parents, like me, and children who have trekked out to San Diego over and over again to seek her counsel and care. The little yellow house where we used to go for Seth's treatments is gone. There is no more waiting in the La Jolla Cove. Now there is a big Osteopathic Center for Children, spacious and busy, meeting the needs of many more children.

If you don't have the resources to go all the way to San Diego, begin by visiting Dr. Frymann's website, www.osteopathiccenter.org. Once you have educated yourself, try to find someone in your area that can help. Be sure to research carefully. There may be a doctor with Frymann's training or a Feldenkrais teacher who has studied CranioSacral work and has gifted hands. Uncover the possibilities.

While I repeat there is still no one like Dr. Frymann, I have learned there are good doctors who see the world as she does. And there are good people with a healing touch out there. I encourage you to seek them. Of course, it is important to avoid quacks and frauds. Be skeptical. Assume nothing. We must be diligent about discerning safe and reliable treatments.

One thing I know for sure: there is no one answer. It is up to us to explore. We cannot escape doing what is asked of us. And the world of special needs is not a world where you are saved by some ready-made cohesive plan. The best you can do is explore all the possibilities and take it from there.

exploring

YOU KNOW MORE than you think. That old adage, mother knows best, is true. We do know our children better than anyone. Trust this.

There is nothing like common sense. Use it. That is what it means to be smart.

No one knows your body and your habits or those of your children better than you do.

Think about what you know and then about what you may not know.

$\sim$

We often look outside of ourselves to find health. This is one of the reasons there is so much awe, so much magic about doctors, why we both revere and at the same time resent them and expect so much of them. We are looking for an outside authority to be in charge. While I know that conventional medicine is necessary and very effective in many situations, it does not necessarily have all the answers.

Of course we need to turn to people who have knowledge of specific subjects for help—especially when our loved ones are very sick. But to stay well, to sort out the information, we have to feel that what we know counts. Doctors may have information that we don't have, but the way we tell them about ourselves and our children can also make all the difference. Patients have a responsibility not to let doctors rob them of their power.

Remember: information or knowledge of a subject is completely different from wisdom. We have plenty of access to information. What we seem to be lacking is people of courage or the courage ourselves to take knowledge and apply it with good judgment and concern for the whole.

The most important health lesson of all is the awareness of the human body as a magnificent mechanism capable of healing itself.

One early morning I was at my Y for a swim, and a woman in the locker room stopped to ask me some questions.

"Do you think my friend should be concerned?" she began. "Her infant daughter holds her head to one side. Her left hand is mostly in a fist and her left eye is noticeably different than her right eye?"

"What kind of delivery did she have?" I asked right away.

"Oh she had a very bad time," she replied and then related some facts about the birth.

"How does the baby suck? Is there any trouble spitting up? Vomiting?" I stopped. Only the child's mother would truly be able to tell me.

My friend went on. "They took her for an MRI. Can they tell if she has cerebral palsy from an MRI?" she asked.

I was not certain about the answer to that. I remember Seth eventually had Cat Scans. But I did know that a trained physician, someone like Dr. Viola Frymann, would know immediately by touching this infant what was wrong, if anything. It was already clear that something was off. Obviously my friend also could tell something was not quite right, and the mother knew it too. She could see the manifestations, however slight.

I wanted to see the child, to touch her. I wanted to touch her because I feared the physician who ordered the MRI was not touching her. Touch used to be the doctor's primary diagnostic tool. Today machinery has replaced this age old laying of hands.

I told my friend about Osteopathy, about Frymann. I told her to tell her friend to search, to explore everything: Feldenkrais, Cranial Osteopathy, Sensorimotor, and biofeedback therapy, Flexyx, Yoga for the Special Child, everything I've been discovering for almost twenty years.

A few days later we talked some more in the locker room. She said, "My friend is very positive. I don't want to scare her. So far the tests show nothing wrong."

"Early intervention is the main thing," I told her. "Observing a newborn baby can provide evidence of the health of its nervous system. There are signs that indicate potential difficulties if the doctors care to look."

Two days later I saw my friend again. "What happened with your friend's baby?" I asked.

"Oh," she answered, "she took her to the doctor and there is nothing neurological."

"What does that mean?" I wondered, "am I crazy?" What is not neurological? What is going on with this child whose delivery into the world was traumatic; whose head is crooked; whose eye is small and half-closed; whose hand is in a fist?

Why doesn't the mother trust herself? She can see. I wished I could see the baby too, but I wasn't being asked. And my friend had told me days earlier that the mother was fragile. It is difficult to be the messenger. As difficult as the message itself.

～

Some time ago, after *Uncommon Voyage* was first published, Manhattan Mothers and Others asked me to be part of a panel of speakers for a group concerned with seizure disorder in children. The audience was primarily parents with children who were heavily dependent on drugs to control seizures. Most of them were at their wit's end.

The panel consisted of the Executive Director of the Epilepsy Foundation, two doctors, and me. In the audience were many children whose parents, mostly mothers, had brought them along. The doctors spoke first. Out came many diagrams and charts. I followed, telling our story about Dr. Frymann and the success of Cranial Osteopathy in seizure related conditions. Lastly, the director from the Foundation spoke. Then we opened up the floor to discussion.

Most of the stories the audience related shared a similar pattern. The children were heavily medicated, and yet their seizures continued over and over again. Afterwards, I was approached by many of the parents. Several of them took my card or Dr. Frymann's number. Some bought my book.

About a year later, we were in California for Seth's treatments with Dr. Frymann when a woman approached me in the waiting room and introduced herself. She had been at that conference a year earlier and heard me speak. She had brought her child to San Diego six months later and decided to move there after the first two treatments. At the Center, her child was being weaned from drugs, and one year later, her little girl was entirely free of medication.

The woman told me that someone else at the conference that night was also waiting to see Dr. Frymann. If her friend was as pleased as she was, she vowed to let me know. Last summer I heard from both women, as well as two others who had read *Uncommon Voyage* and brought their children to the Osteopathic Center for Children.

Evidently, they were all together in the waiting room at the Center one morning. They decided to call me long distance and reached me. I spoke to each of them individually. Every story was somewhat different, but what they shared was the leap of faith that it took to take back their child's care into their own hands. They placed it literally and figuratively, in the hands of someone who would understand the children's distress and address it.

A child's nervous system is still forming at a young age; it is still in flux. The plasticity in a child's central nervous system allows a child to recover completely or partially after an insult to the brain. The brains of very young children have a greater capacity to repair themselves than do adult brains. As long as a child's nervous system has not yet matured, there is still a chance that the child may make at least a partial recovery from early movement problems. As you read *Uncommon Voyage*, you will learn that if Seth had had Cranial Osteopathy sooner, it would have had a significant effect on him and his future.

The nervous system can be affected in many ways. We know there are subtle disturbances in motion patterns of the skull that are often symptomatic of certain disorders. Being aware of these patterns can be extremely valuable in helping to diagnose and treat developmental problems in children.

The structure of the body is intimately related to the way it functions. The principle is always the same: it is that the body functions as a whole, not a series of isolated, independent parts. The signs are easiest to read in the newborn. We just have to trust what we "see."

$\sim$

When I say *alternative*, I mean anything not allopathic (conventional). Not everything, however, that is alternative is holistic.

Holistic is derived from the Greek word *holos,* meaning whole. It is the idea that everything in the universe is greater than, and different from, the sum of its parts. Holistic medicine is an approach to health that aims to deal with the patient as a whole and not merely with physical symptoms. It takes into account the psychological state, social and environmental factors, and an indefinable dimension known as "spirit."

Osteopathy is an example of holistic medicine that straddles the worlds of mainstream and alternative care. And so is Cranial Osteopathy. Other examples of holistic medicine are Homeopathy, Chinese and Tibetan medicine, and Ayurvedic medicine.

But herbal medicine, vitamin therapy, aromatherapy, naturopaths and countless other "therapies" are alternative too. The big difference is they are not holistic. They offer no real concept of how healing actually takes place.

Finally, and most important we must recognize that health encompasses everything—our habits, our thinking, our attitude and our commitment. Maintaining our health is not about using a variety of cures. It is seeing the Spirit, Soul, Body, as a whole.

We each have to decide what kind of approach we want to health and prevention for us and for our children.

We are the key players in our health care and in the care of our children, not our physicians. To make those choices we need to be and to remain open minded.

Health is wholeness, wholeness in the most profound sense, with nothing left out.

⌒

You will not find the word "handicapped" in *Uncommon Voyage.* Although handicapped is widely used in both law and everyday speech to refer to people with physical or mental disabilities, those described by the word tend to prefer the adjective "disabled," or to be called people with disabilities.

To say that people are handicapped may imply that they cannot function on a par with others, while to say that they have a disability allows for the possibility that they can so function, in spite of having to do some things in different ways.

Some feel that there is stigma attached to the word because of its origin in the phrase "hand in cap." Actually it was derived from a game of chance, but is mistakenly believed to involve the image of a beggar.

The word handicapped is best reserved to describe a disabled person who is unable to function owing to some property of the environment. Thus, people with a physical disability requiring a wheelchair may or may not be handicapped, depending on whether wheelchair ramps are made available to them.

origins

JUNE 16, 1984, WAS A PERFECT EARLY SUMMER DAY: warm, but not yet hot like July. The sky was pure blue, the blue of Seth's sparkling eyes. The air was imbued with hints of summer's fragrance. Our family had gathered in our rented summer house in the Berkshires to celebrate Seth's first birthday. It was a Sunday. My parents were visiting for the weekend. Aunt Edna and Uncle Irving had driven up from Boston for the day. Everyone wanted to be part of the festivities for their beloved grandchild and their favorite grandnephew. He had captured everyone's heart.

My mother was busy with Seth's favorite dessert: strawberry shortcake. She stood in the yellow country kitchen and whipped the cream with an old electric beater. My father entertained Seth by working to disentangle the line of his fishing rod. Daddy already doted on his only grandson. Seth's dad, my husband Jay, arranged the presents while I decorated the table with typical birthday ornaments. Aunt Edna and Uncle Irv hung streamers, chattering incessantly about their affection for their grandnephew. Seth's dazzling smile and bright blue eyes eclipsed even the grandeur of the hills we could see out our windows.

Seth's enthusiasm was contagious. At one year old he knew how to use his incredible charm. He engaged everyone, even strangers, with his eyes, which radiated a knowing twinkle. It made everyone feel he was special. From the very beginning Seth drew people into his world and connected them to himself. We already knew he was a rare individual.

An easy baby with immense charisma, he had been sleeping through the night since he was three weeks old. He loved his baby swing. He sat cheerfully with adults in his table seat, one of those contraptions that fastens to the side of the table. In restaurants, in his stroller, at the shops and in the streets, people always stopped to

1

admire him; how handsome he was, how attractive, how charming. He never complained about anything. He basked in all the admiration.

When the cake was finished, adorned with a crown of huge luscious ruby red strawberries and appropriately engulfed by whipped cream, I carried it to the table, singing "Happy Birthday" in full voice. Seth glowed. He blew out the candle and ate his cake with gusto. Sounds of joy and pleasure emanated from all of us. The snapshots show him laughing heartily, whipped cream everywhere.

But earlier that morning, I had gone to the basement of the house, where the washer and dryer were. Alone with the laundry, standing in the dim light, I spilled the tears I had yet to cry. I hung my head, then shook my fist toward heaven, questioning. Silently, I swore my determination to defy the odds. But I was afraid of the future. Seth had been diagnosed with cerebral palsy only eight weeks before. How could this be true? What would it mean? What could I hope for now? What could I expect? The only sureness I had was that my life was inalterably changed. Nothing would ever be the same again.

When Seth was born, in 1983, Jay and I had been married for five years. Jay is an attorney with a passion for baseball. At the time of our marriage, Jay decided to go into business for himself as a sole practitioner. At the same time he supported my effort to try independent producing. Both of these quests required huge leaps of faith and even bigger financial risks. For that reason we had postponed parenting.

I was thirty-five and enjoying a small professional success and Jay's practice was stabilized, so we decided to have a baby. When we first learned I was pregnant, baby books were scattered all over the house. Once we confirmed that we were expecting a child, I thought I remembered the instant the baby had been conceived. I was blissful. I would be the very model of a healthy contemporary woman, working and remaining physically active throughout my pregnancy. I didn't smoke, and I planned to continue my regime of swimming and taking exercise classes. Although I was not as slim as I once had been or hoped to be again, I intended to stay active.

I was also at the peak of my professional life. Our child was conceived in the Berkshires, where I was producing a play at the Berkshire Theater Festival. I had just returned from Santa Fe, New Mexico, where I had produced a new musical with Madeline Kahn, and I was in the midst of casting a Broadway show—*Slab Boys*—that would feature Sean Penn and Kevin Bacon and Val Kilmer.

Looking back at the books I read at the time, I realize they were more about babies than about pregnancy. That was before the publication of *What to Expect When You're Expecting.* Years later I told the Eisenbergs, the authors of that invaluable book, how much I wish I had had their book to read when I was pregnant the first time.

My doctor was handsome and cavalier. He took a nonchalant attitude toward my pregnancy, and I let him. Jay and I did go for genetic counseling to determine the risk, the possibilities, and probabilities that our child could have genetic anomalies that might result from age, ethnic background, family history. The genetic counselor asked us a lot of questions to ascertain what we should be tested for based on our genetic history. One suggestion was that we go for a Tay-Sachs screening.

Tay-Sachs is a genetic disorder, usually found in people of Eastern European descent, especially Jews, and has serious consequences for a developing fetus. It causes severe mental retardation and some physical limitations. Babies with Tay-Sachs usually live only three to five years. The screening is accomplished by testing the blood of both parents, since both parents have to carry the gene in order for the baby to have a 25 percent probability of getting the disease. Our Tay-Sachs screening was negative.

I was Rh-negative, and Jay's blood type was positive. This combination concerned the doctor. It meant that there was a chance that the fetus would be Rh-positive, and I could build antibodies to his or her blood. Therefore, I was administered Rhogam, which is an immunoglobulin. I received the Rhogam at twenty-eight weeks, during the amniocentesis, and again after the birth. In the case of Rh-negative mothers, Rhogam is administered anytime there is the possibility of maternal-fetal blood contamination.

Twenty-eight weeks into the pregnancy I also had a test for gestational diabetes. At twenty-eight weeks the placenta begins to secrete a hormone that interferes with the mother's metabolism of sugar. The glucose tolerance test determines how the mother is metabolizing sugar over a period of time. There are various ranges of normal.

While the test was unpleasant, I was glad when the results showed my metabolism of sugar was normal. Except for a few sarcastic remarks about my increasing size (ultimately I gained forty pounds), the doctor had no other concerns. And neither did I.

The doctor prescribed a multivitamin with iron that made me nauseous and constipated. I opted not to take it. In the first three months I experienced severe headaches. The doctor told me to take as much aspirin as I needed. I took two, sometimes more, during the day if I needed them. What are the implications of the aspirin I took so easily? Today no one in our family takes aspirin casually. Mostly we rely on other remedies.

I received my first Rhogam injection, which I remember vividly, at twenty-eight weeks. The doctor monitored the insertion of the needle for my amniocentesis during the ultrasound, so I observed the fetus on the monitor. I thought I wanted a girl baby, but the moment I saw the image of the child within me on the video monitor, I knew it was a boy. I was ecstatic. Technology captured our unborn child with his little hand going to his mouth to suck. A few weeks later the hospital confirmed the male sex of our child. Our son was due June 2.

I got fat even though I continued to swim every day. I was working hard to get my show produced on Broadway, and we were in the midst of rehearsals. The show was opening at the end of March.

During the second trimester I felt fine. I had no headaches, and my only two concerns continued to be my weight and the future episiotomy. Something I had read made me feel almost "political" about not having the episiotomy. My doctor took an unconditional stance, suggesting that an early hysterectomy was inevitable if I didn't have the procedure.

Around this time Jay and I went for a tour of the hospital and began attending a natural childbirth class. My doctor took a skeptical view of natural childbirth. I was experiencing misgivings about my doctor. Jay and I went to visit him together to talk, but not specifically about my doubts. Those I continued to keep to myself. I criticized myself for not feeling more confident. After all, the doctor had a successful practice. He had delivered many babies. That was my attitude toward doctors until I recognized that I was being passive, and then I changed. But it was already too late.

In the third trimester I was waking every morning about 5:00, often experiencing a severe headache. After an hour or so I'd take two aspirin, and at 7:00 I'd usually fall back to sleep for an hour. I was tired during the day, and I liked to lie down for an hour's nap in the afternoon. When I awoke again, often I would have another severe headache. On the doctor's advice, I'd take two more aspirin.

Jay and I moved into a large duplex apartment, and I was excited and pleased by our new surroundings. After my show opened on Broadway, my attention shifted to the anticipation of our baby's arrival. Everything felt right except the headaches and early-morning waking. I dreamt that my son weighed seven pounds. My due date of June 2 came and went. I felt no change, but I began paying close attention to every shift and motion. I continued swimming daily and going to the office, but I got a later, less energized start each day. My afternoon naps continued. At the end of the day Jay and I often would go to the movies or to the theater if only for distraction. Producing a Broadway show had made me eligible to be a Tony voter, so every Broadway producer was inviting me to his or her show that spring.

Monday evening, June 13, we went out for dinner and a movie. I ate seafood. The movie was *Blue Thunder*. The following morning I awoke feeling that there was a consistency and regularity to my contractions, though they were mild. Jay remained at home with me throughout the morning, but nothing changed dramatically. We telephoned the doctor. He recommended that we go about our business for the day.

That night, again, I felt consistent, though mild, contractions. Discomfort, anxiety, excitement kept me awake. By Wednesday morning I was exhausted. My bag for the hospital was packed and near the front door, but though regular, the contractions were quiet. The doctor recommended that I come to his office for an examination. After examining me, he said that my cervix was dilated only slightly.

"It will be at least twenty-four hours," he pronounced. "Here is a prescription for Secanol. Fill it and go home and get some sleep. You'll need it." Again, I never questioned or argued with his attitude, which in this instance included the casual administration of a powerful narcotic. I even recall that when I went to the pharmacy to fill the prescription, I had to fill out a state form because Secanol is a controlled substance.

The doctor was matter of fact, unconcerned, and so sure of himself that it never occurred to me to mistrust him. And I was ignorant. If I'd known better, I could have asked for a stress test or queried whether this was prodromal labor—a precursory stage before the onset of labor—but since I didn't know, I was inclined to rely on the expert.

Our friendly UPS man woke me in the late afternoon, totally apologetic for disturbing my sleep, but bearing a gift for my yet-unborn son. My husband came home for a light dinner, and about nine in the evening we went to the hospital. Not much had changed, but some of the contractions were stronger, and by then we persuaded ourselves it was time. The baby was two weeks late. We were impatient.

After I was admitted, my doctor arrived, examined me, and nonchalantly pronounced that it would be quite some time, so he was going to get some sleep. A nurse and a doctor, both women, attended me. I wore no fetal monitor. Around 11:00 that night my waters broke. I was in a private labor room with a private bathroom and alone when the waters burst. No one fetched the waters or examined them. Had they done so, the first signs of trouble would have been apparent. It is customary to check the mother's waters for signs of meconium, a dark green fecal material that accumulates in the fetal intestines and is discharged at or near the time of birth. If the infant aspirates meconium, there are many consequences, some of which we discovered later.

As soon as my waters broke, things got difficult. The contractions were stronger and more painful. I asked for something to ease the pain and was given Demerol orally. I was writhing around, trying to find a comfortable position, summoning all I could remember from the natural childbirth classes, the ones my doctor had summarily dismissed.

Soon the nurses began to monitor the baby and insisted that I not lie in the fetal position or on all fours, the only two positions in which I felt somewhat at ease. The nurse worried that the baby was not getting enough oxygen and prodded me to alter my pose. This went on for some hours. She kept after me insistently and grew increasingly concerned, finally leaving to get the resident doctor. My cervix was still not dilated completely, and I was screaming to have the attendants "get him out of me." I wanted a cesarean.

Around 5:00 in the morning my doctor poked in and suggested that I be given an epidural. I was moved to another labor room. The epidural was not effective. I could not get comfortable. The epidural was administered again. This occurred several times. Through the haze of my fatigue, pain, and the vaguely numbing effect of the epidural, I was able to feel the contractions originating and building. I announced them to my husband, who somewhere along the way had cloaked himself in a green hospital gown. He remained with me throughout.

My obstetrician came and went, but the anesthesiologist remained in the room with me. My doctor asked the anesthesiologist to administer Pitocin. I remembered reading about Pitocin and how it speeds up contractions, but I also knew that there was some controversy regarding its use. I was too disoriented to care. I was given Pitocin. Then I was given more Pitocin.

My doctor left to scrub up. The anesthesiologist, who was left alone in the room with my husband and me, asked, "Does the doctor know the baby is crowning?" My husband and I had no response. The anesthesiologist summoned a nurse. "Does the doctor know the baby is crowning?" he inquired. Suddenly I was wheeled out of the room and into the hallway toward the delivery room.

Halfway down the corridor, from the source of my primal self, from my origins, I felt the rush and presence I knew was our baby. I announced, "Here he comes."

Out came our son, an icy blue color. He lay there between my legs on the labor table in the hallway. The clock on the wall above showed 7:00 on the dot. I was quickly shuttled into the delivery room.

Alarms sounded. A team of other doctors, with green masks and gowns, my own not among them, arrived instantly. The baby was taken from me as the cord was cut. I can't remember who performed that procedure, but my baby was whisked from the room.

"I want to see him for a minute. Show him to me. Let me touch him," I cried out.

I was allowed a cursory look as the doctors rushed out with him.

"He'll be all right," reassured my doctor, who had miraculously mate-
rialized from somewhere. "He's fine. He's breathing, and he simply
aspirated some meconium."

Maybe I had heard the term *meconium* before, but it didn't register at that moment of chaos and anxiety. I was scared, not knowing
really what was happening or what anything meant.

I was delirious with anxiety, wild. But I required a lot of stitching,
having been badly torn when our child came bursting out onto the
labor table. In the end, the episiotomy I had never wanted and so
dreaded was never performed. There wasn't time.

I was moved to the recovery room. It was 8:00 in the morning,
one hour after our baby's arrival. Around 8:30 my doctor visited me
briefly and told me that our son would be fine and that he weighed
8 pounds, 2 ounces. He said that Seth was in the neonatal intensive
care unit (NICU) as a precautionary measure and that I would be
able to see him shortly. All the fantasies and expectations I'd had of
holding my newborn child were dashed. The dream that I would
nurse him on the delivery table, cuddle him, lessen the separation
for both of us between his presence in the womb and his emergence
into the light of day, evaporated. I only wanted to know when I
would see him. The doctor seemed remote and unconcerned, again
very cavalier.

A social worker visited me. She wanted to prepare me for what I
would see in the neonatal unit. She said that Seth was hooked up
to a lot of tubes that were necessary for monitoring and feeding him.
I resisted her professional concern. I felt patronized, and I was angry.
When she said she would be available to me for further support, I
mentally dismissed her, denying any possibility that my son would
be less than perfect.

Soon I was escorted to the NICU to see Seth for the first time. I
broke down and began to cry when I saw the incubator and my
infant boy child, tubes emerging from him like the tentacles of an
octopus. Exhaustion engulfed me, though there was no way I would
succumb to sleep. I pulled up a stool and sat down next to the incubator, determined to see everything through to a happy ending. I
wanted to nurse him and directed someone to see if I could get a
breast pump in my room so I would be prepared when the first opportunity presented itself. I identified the most sympathetic nurse in the

NICU and enlisted her help. I nicknamed her "The White Rabbit." Jay, looking ashen and frightened, joined me by our baby's side.

At some point my doctor passed through the NICU to perform a procedure on another infant. He barely looked at us, never mind our baby. In the meantime, Jay and I got permission for the pediatrician we intended to use after Seth's birth to make a special trip to the hospital. Early the following morning Dr. Lee, after seeing Seth in the NICU, visited me in my room where I was frantically pumping my milk. She was very reassuring, very upbeat.

My hospital room was two floors away from the NICU, and the hospital procedure dictated that a staff member escort me there from my room. Once at the NICU, there were several procedures required before entering. All visitors, including my husband and me, had to scrub with a special soap and don a green hospital gown and gloves.

By the end of the day following Seth's birth, I informed anyone who dared to question my presence at any place in the hospital corridors or elevators, in no uncertain terms, that I was not waiting for a hospital staff member to take me to the NICU. I was going to go whenever I wanted to see my son. In the little time I spent away from the NICU and in my room, I worked desperately at the breast pump. The stitches in my torn perineum were uncomfortable when I sat. During the night I went to the NICU several times, instinctively talking to my new baby with soothing, constant words of love.

The White Rabbit was sympathetic. She allowed me to perform all of the essential tasks such as changing Seth's diaper, feeding him, and doing other maternal chores. I accomplished these ministrations through the small porthole of the incubator. When I returned to my room to pump milk, I remember walking uncomfortably through hallways, seeing and hearing other babies safely ensconced in their mothers' rooms in their mothers' arms, and feeling terribly sad.

The morning after Seth's traumatic birth, all of the tubes attached to him were removed. The White Rabbit helped me try to breast-feed. Seth was unresponsive. Because he was receiving an antibiotic, it was necessary to feed him regularly. He was already used to the bottle and the formula, and, although I was providing some breast milk, the amount was not sufficient for his feedings. So the feedings were being supplemented with formula milk. After all, he was a big baby, I told myself. I wasn't going to give up, though. Throughout the day I made one attempt after another to nurse. In between I kept pumping milk so that my milk would go into the bottle he got. The White Rabbit went off duty, and the other nurses were too busy and unconcerned to help, but I kept at it.

Seth was the most beautiful baby in the NICU, probably the healthiest, biggest, handsomest infant that unit had ever seen. One of the nurses remarked about his startling good looks. The nurses nicknamed him Don Juan and discussed how much the girls would love him. After all, he wasn't a preemie, and ostensibly after the initial scare, there was nothing seriously wrong with him. The doctors wanted to observe him for a few days to be sure that no infection developed because of the meconium fluid he had aspirated during his birth. Otherwise, not one doctor told us that there was anything to be concerned about. Seth looked 100 percent healthy. The fact that he demonstrated so little sucking motivation during my continual efforts to nurse didn't give anyone a clue about what was to come.

My attempts to breast-feed continued, as did my constant vigilance in the NICU. By the third day I was part of the surroundings, and the personnel simply expected to see me. On Saturday night, almost seventy-two hours after Seth's arrival, I made one more attempt to nurse him. The White Rabbit coaxed me into getting comfortable holding him like a football. I was at the point of desperation. I would be going home the next morning, and I was uncertain about whether he was going to be staying behind for a few more days of observation. It felt like my last chance for the bonding I craved. At 2:00 in the morning, he finally began sucking milk from my breast. Sometime around dawn I dozed with him at my bosom and later awoke to the changing shift and my nursing child.

When the resident doctor appeared, I remarked what a champ Seth was. He was thriving and handsome and functioning 100 percent without any support systems. The doctor agreed and suggested that the NICU staff would consider sending him home with me later in the morning. I was ecstatic. It was a hot muggy day, Father's Day and my mother's birthday. I prepared to dress Seth in the very same clothes I had worn home from the hospital on a July morning thirty-five years earlier.

My husband and new baby and I went home together. Seeing the waiting rocking chair and white crib, the nursery festooned with the typical accoutrements, my recollection of the nightmare I had experienced only days before was obliterated. My preoccupation with my new baby was absolute. Every aspect of his care delighted me. Changing his diapers, nursing him, holding him and talking to him gave me inconceivable delight. My joy buried all recollection of the recent trauma.

Seth was so good, always smiling, handsome, and easy, it never occurred to me to worry about the events surrounding his birth. In fact I was eager to forget them. I was not alerted by any of the hints a worried mother might have seized upon as evidence for concern.

CHAPTER TWO

discovery

THERE WAS A LOT OF EXCITEMENT AND ENTHUSIASM about Seth after his birth. He was handsome and a big baby, constantly smiling. He ate well and was alert, making marvelous eye contact from the very beginning. There seemed not a flicker of anything wrong. I wanted to show him off everywhere. I especially wanted to display him to all my friends at the Y, where I had been swimming every day during my pregnancy, where the women had been witnesses to my increasing size, to his unseen development.

Throughout the last months of my pregnancy I had had a massage once a week. The massage therapist was from Russia, where she had worked as a masseuse in a hospital for sick children. In Russia the medical community relies on massage as a legitimate treatment for disabled and suffering children. Of course I wanted her to massage Seth. Massaging your child was very au courant at the time, and the subject of numerous videotapes and books. It was encouraged as a path to bonding and promoting physical and psychological development. I wanted to take advantage of the current thinking about handling babies.

With a new baby in the house, schedules were difficult to coordinate, so Seth's first massage appointment didn't happen for a few weeks. By that time I was delirious with excitement over my child, madly, passionately in love with him. I went to the Y full of myself, bursting with pride about my beautiful son.

Seth reveled in all the attention of my friends at the Y. To this day he unabashedly enjoys being the star attraction. Anya, the masseuse, was excited to see him. We prepared him for the massage table by undressing him and playing with him. For the most part he seemed to like being handled, although he did complain some.

When Anya was finished, she startled me by saying, "He's very stiff, and you must stroke his head a lot." She demonstrated a caressing motion across the top of his skull away from his forehead.

I asked, "What do you mean?"

"He is very stiff. You must stroke his head a lot," she repeated with emphasis.

Anger engulfed me. What a stupid, horrible woman, I thought. I must be insane to entrust my son to her, a backward Russian whose use of the English language was primitive. I shut down. Seething inside from the insult, the gall that anyone would dare to diminish my son's obvious perfection, I dressed Seth and went away.

Years later, after many long searches finally led us to the rehabilitation method known as Cranial Osteopathy, I recalled Anya's advice about stroking Seth's skull. I watched a world-renowned doctor do just that in an effort to create motion and circulation inside Seth's head, and I wished I had understood what Anya had told me years before.

⁓

I met my friend Beth at the Y. We came from similar backgrounds: we were both Jewish, middle-class, suburban women who had come of age in the sixties. But we had very divergent experiences: she had married an Israeli man after knowing him only a short time and had gotten pregnant immediately; I had married Jay after a long courtship and had waited five years to get pregnant. Beth and I were pregnant at the same time, and we were each swimming every day at the Y. We became even closer friends over those nine months that we carried our sons, sharing our hopes and dreams and our anxieties for our unborn children every day. Our boys were born one week apart.

Getting together with our newborns was an emotional reunion. Jonathan was big like Seth, but huskier. During the afternoon of our visit, I was surprised to learn that shortly after he was born Jonathan had required therapeutic attention. In utero he had not periodically altered the position of his head and neck. I vaguely recalled reading that this was a fairly common occurrence. Evidently the doctor recognized the anomaly and prescribed early intervention. Beth engaged a physical therapist for regular rehabilitative sessions.

To rectify the problem, the therapist told Beth, the most important thing was to change the direction of Jonathan's head when he was lying down or sleeping to be certain that he faced in either direction at some point. Beth was almost nonchalant and unconcerned. She was sure that by addressing it early, the problem would disappear.

We had a pleasant afternoon, chatting and comparing notes. I can still picture the two infant boys, about five weeks old, in their respective infant seats, happily enveloped by the surrounding friendly talk of their loving and doting mothers. Then Jonathan reached out and grabbed one of the toys dangling above him and deliberately put it into his mouth. This was hand-eye, hand-mouth coordination exemplified; executed with aplomb.

Seth had not yet demonstrated anything approaching this developmental stage. Jonathan's action surprised me. An immense surge of anxiety welled up from the pit of my stomach. Then I suppressed it. Literally, my heart had skipped a beat. I retreated to a safe inner refuge and blotted out my intuition, vague though it was, that I had witnessed a prophetic episode. I was luxuriating in new motherhood. For the moment, the intimations of our destiny, the foreshadowing, went fleeting by. A week later our family, Seth, his dad and I, left for our summer in the Berkshires.

My clear and distinct recollection of Seth that summer is of him lying on his back, arching up as though he were looking behind himself or preparing to do a backbend. My mother also noticed this remarkably frequent act. By September, after a summer of perfect baby bliss, Seth was holding his head up, smiling constantly, sleeping regularly, and eating well. But he always held his left hand clenched in a fist. It is typical of babies to have small clenched fists at birth, but at three or four months old it didn't seem appropriate. Playfully I would smack his tiny left hand and ask, "What is this fist?" and he would laugh hesitantly.

Later in the autumn, Seth and I flew to Boston to visit my grandmother, "Honey Nana." In my photograph album there is a collection of pictures from the day: Seth lying on his belly, commando style, on a blanket atop Nana's carpet; Seth sitting supported in an infant chair with the ubiquitous offering of Cheerios before him. There is Nana beaming nearby. But her look has a shadow of concern, an undercurrent of anxiety. Seth's inability, or limited ability,

to grasp things was a topic she mentioned to me briefly that day. I
wish she had said more.

⁓

Four weeks after Seth was born I had hired Mayra Amaya to come
and live with us and help me care for Seth. She was twenty years
old and came from El Salvador. Mayra had been in the United States
for less than six months and was living with an aunt whose apartment was not far from ours. She agreed to live in our home from
Monday morning to Friday evening, returning to her aunt on the
weekends. Mayra became an important member of our household
for the next four and a half years. Her relationship with Seth and
with the therapists we eventually engaged was integral to our family's
unfolding experience. We employed Mayra at the time when I was
slowly beginning to return to work. Still nursing a few times a day,
I now began pumping my milk to store in a bottle for those feedings
that took place when I was absent. The pump went with me to the
office.

There are a lot of pictures of Seth in Mayra's arms, his left hand
still mostly in a fist, or of Seth placed standing by the side of his crib
and smiling. Always smiling. But not on all fours, not sitting independently and not even trying. At that time, Seth's routine checkups
with the pediatrician took place without so much as a whisper that
anything was wrong. The pediatrician continued to give Seth high
marks. By December I was concerned that he wasn't sitting up by
himself. I interrogated everyone—other mothers, the housekeeper,
Mayra. I began consulting baby books obsessively. I instructed Mayra
to surround Seth with cushions in an effort to encourage him to sit.
The pediatrician's reassurances were still unequivocal. Some babies
sit at four months, and many not until ten months. All children
develop at a different pace. That was her message.

On a Thursday evening in early January, on my sixth wedding
anniversary, I was nursing Seth in the white rocking chair in his
room. My concern about his not sitting persisted. It was becoming
an almost full-time mental distraction. During the feeding, as I gazed
down lovingly, adoringly upon my son, he took himself away from
the breast, looked me full in the face, and said, "Mama."

A tremor of gladness coursed through me. The sound of his voice saying an actual word was thrilling. I was smitten. The anxiety of the last weeks was obliterated by the deep connection I felt to him. He recognized me. He knew who I was, and he knew my name. I decided then and there that his motor delays were directly attributable to his cognitive development. He couldn't be growing in both realms simultaneously, and his verbal capacity, his obvious mental accomplishments, far overshadowed the motor deficiencies. Over the next weeks his words were more frequent and more varied. I relaxed.

Later in January, when Seth was well past the six-month mark, nursing changed and became difficult. He'd start out sucking fine and then would let out a wail, pulling away violently from the breast. I agonized, did some research, and decided that maybe he was teething. Nothing I did to try to accommodate him changed his extreme behavior. Very reluctantly I gave up nursing.

It was a long time before I correlated Seth's initial difficulties of sucking and the violent alterations in nursing with the neurological anomalies associated with his condition. Eventually I did acquire the knowledge to make this connection. I learned from the physician who offered Seth his greatest rehabilitative possibilities that the first question she asks the mother of any child is "How did your baby suck?"

In February, when Seth was going on eight months, Jay and I discussed enrolling him in day care at least part-time. I wanted Seth to interact with other children. Otherwise he was almost always one-on-one with me or Jay or Mayra. Jay and I visited the Bank Street program near Columbia University. We were encouraged by what we saw. There were building blocks and toys and climbing apparatuses.

On the particular morning when we visited, there were children of various ages present, but only one other child Seth's age. That boy was pulling himself to a standing position and climbing over huge building blocks meant as obstacles to reaching other areas of the room. I was surprised by his advanced motor skills.

As Jay and I rode downtown in the cab afterward, I kept asking him whether he'd seen what that other child was able to do. Fear gripped me. I had witnessed a child Seth's same age moving and handling himself in ways completely unlike what Seth was capable of doing. The child had demonstrated an ease and flexibility and ability I had never observed in Seth. At that point Seth could only stand if we put him in what we called a "walker." It was a small circular structure on wheels that allowed him to scoot about in an erect position. Eventually, this walker would become a source of controversy, but at the time it was a source of immense joy for Seth.

After our visit to the day-care center, my obsession with Seth's inability to sit, supported or unsupported, returned full force. He was due shortly for another checkup with our pediatrician, so when the time came, I went armed with a list of questions and concerns. Dr. Lee was fairly nonchalant in her responses. She said that his reflexes were good, which was a good sign. As far as sitting was concerned, she thought we should wait until he was a year old to judge. But I couldn't wait, not one more second.

My friendship with Beth continued. The needs of our infants and our other domestic and professional concerns kept us from getting together, but I spoke to her every few days by telephone. I knew Jonathan was sitting, but I didn't get to see him, so I was unaware of what else he was now capable of doing. When I told Beth about my concerns, she was very sympathetic and suggested that I consult the physical therapist she had used for Jonathan after his birth, when he'd had the head-position anomaly. The therapist's name was Amy, and Beth gave me her number.

Amy Katz came to see us on a Saturday afternoon two weeks after Seth's most recent routine checkup with Dr. Lee. It was March. Seth was an easy and happy child, so after twenty minutes of letting him get acquainted with Amy, I left the two of them alone surrounded by his toys. After an hour Amy summoned Jay and me to Seth's room. She remarked what a wonderful, happy, and amenable child Seth was, and that he had a lot of good movement in him.

"A lot of good movement. What does that mean?" I asked.

Amy encouraged us to have our physician recommend a specialist. She thought Seth would benefit from a physical-therapy program. That was all she would say.

I wanted Amy to tell us more, to elaborate. I wanted her to come back the next day and the next week, and every day until she thought Seth was doing what he should be doing. As soon as she left, I called my pediatrician. It was Saturday, but I wanted to speak to her. When Dr. Lee returned my call sometime in the early evening, I told her about Amy and what she had said.

The doctor gave me the name of a neurologist to call for an appointment. "We may as well get a baseline," she said. "After all, he was a meconium baby."

That was the first hint that she or anyone else had ever given me that meconium and the circumstances of Seth's birth might be a factor in his delayed development. By this time I had a vague knowledge of what meconium was, having asked about it shortly after Seth's birth. The truth is, though, I had no idea about what exactly a neurologist does. I just made the call on the following Monday morning to Dr. Chutorian, the neurologist Dr. Lee had recommended.

The morning of the appointment, in mid-April, Jay and I were coming from separate places, so we met at the neurologist's office in the hospital. Mayra met us there with Seth. Dr. Chutorian interviewed Jay and me before examining Seth. He asked a lot of questions about my pregnancy and delivery. Dr. Chutorian's questions spiked my memory. As I answered him, I remembered for the first time all the headaches I had had early in my pregnancy. The actual delivery was blurred, and I skimmed over it, not even mentioning the meconium Seth had aspirated.

About the night of difficult labor I said nothing. I had completely suppressed most recollection of Seth's birth. The neurologist inquired about the milestones in Seth's development, like rolling over and crawling. I told him about my concern that Seth was not sitting. We used this opportunity to describe Seth's wonderful demeanor, his easy personality.

The doctor examined Seth with me standing nearby. He took only about twenty minutes. Then he asked Jay and me to step into his consultation room. I asked Mayra to dress Seth.

Right away, the doctor said, "Your son will live a normal life. He will walk and talk and feed himself and dress himself. But he will never walk normally, and he will not walk for a long time. Your son has mild cerebral palsy." We were floored, overwhelmed. I had to catch my breath.

"What do you mean he won't walk for a long time?"

"I think it will be years before he walks," the doctor paused, "if he walks at all. He will never walk normally."

"What do you mean, 'he will never walk normally'?"

"When you see people on the street, look at them and see how they walk. He will never walk like them. Later on we can discuss learning difficulties."

I was so overcome with panic and questions that I didn't know the first thing to ask.

"There must be something we can do. Some kind of rehabilitation or physical therapy."

"You can try whatever you want, but I don't think anything will help. However, feel free."

"Will he go to normal schools? Will he swim and play tennis?"

"I can't answer these questions," the doctor replied. "This is a developmental disability. I am not going to order any invasive tests, though. The case is mild enough not to warrant CAT scans and so forth now. As things develop we will reconsider."

I didn't know anything about seizures. It would be years before I understood there were questions unasked that day.

What is a developmental disability? I wanted to ask. What is this disability? What will it mean? Give me answers. Give me a crystal ball.

I emerged from the consultation room shaking, drawing a smile on my face, almost in a trance, as I glided over to Seth. He was sitting in his stroller, smiling his ever-present smile, eating apple slices. Even then I knew that I would never look at him the same way again. The pit in my stomach was monstrous. I felt sick and anxious. I sent Mayra and Seth on their way, and Jay and I went wandering through the hospital looking for Dr. Lee, the pediatrician.

Nothing had prepared me for this revelation. None of my prior anxiety or musings had ever led me to this level of alarm or consternation. Although I had been worried for some time, it had never occurred to me that anything was so seriously wrong. And I didn't know the first thing to ask, to think, or to do.

In a flash I knew there was only one clear mandate. I had to do everything possible to make my son's life as good as it could be. Family members would need to know a certain amount, schooling would have to be investigated differently, child care might need to be reconsidered.

I had very little idea what cerebral palsy meant generally, and certainly not in Seth's case specifically. The neurologist's belief that nothing could help, that there was no course of intervention, I dismissed as hogwash. My intensely optimistic nature and my action-prone personality took over. I was scared and confused, but I mustered my energy. I would find ways of helping him. Intuitively I knew I was the starting point.

What I didn't recognize was that an altered life, a new destiny, a changed set of values, was set in motion on that April day. The diagnosis was the beginning of immense challenges—and opportunities. I struggled, failed, grew, hid, fooled myself. And through Serendipity, perseverance, and the ability to risk I mostly came through for my son—and for my husband and family. Luck is really the angel of my experience. I always think of how much worse it could have been. The truth is that time helped me with this outlook. Time and good fortune. Seth's "developmental" condition took me years to fully comprehend. Only time revealed the requirements and necessary adaptations. Time taught me the interweaving of information and circumstance. Time continues to be my master.

CHAPTER THREE

embarkation

I GREW UP THE DAY SETH WAS DIAGNOSED with cerebral palsy. Yet I was so stunned, I was unable to move normally. I couldn't feel anything. I had no idea where to begin. Jay and I wandered the halls of the hospital in search of Dr. Lee. We knew that she was on rounds that morning. Finally, standing in her small hospital office, we told her the news. She was shocked, truly surprised. I began cross-examining her, pleading for answers, for a forecast.

My craving for answers was like an adolescent's. I wanted reassurance, predictions, to know how it would turn out. She was reassuring, which endeared her to me for a long time afterward. She told us, I remember exactly, that you can tell some people have cerebral palsy only by turning over their shoe and seeing the anomaly of their gait in the imprint of its sole.

While we were talking, Dr. Chutorian strolled by. Dr. Lee invited him in to join our discussion and then quizzed him in our presence. My overriding desire was for a prediction. "Developmental" was the word I kept hearing. What did "developmental" mean? It meant that we wouldn't know what was in store, how great the challenges would be, until they developed. What did I know about a child's normal development, though? How would I gauge the dimensions of the problem as they manifested? Mothering was new. I felt a chord of primal fear.

I was scared, but the look on Jay's face gave real meaning to the word "devastation." Later, as we went down in the hospital elevator, I reassured him that it would all come out right. I was responding to my innate optimism, sure that things couldn't be as bad as they sounded. Somewhere deep down I also believed that if I said it would be all right enough times, it would be true or come true. By telling Jay, I was really telling myself. Thus began the first phase of being a mother of a special needs child. The struggle for me was to find the

fine line between trying to will things to be all better and being realistic. The struggle has never ceased.

We went together to our offices in a taxi. During the ride I kept
asking Jay what he thought, how he felt, as though his answers could
change everything. I felt fear. I felt anxious and sick to my stomach.
But I knew I couldn't show it. As much as I wanted to lay my head
down and cry, I knew it would be too alarming for Jay and our family.
There was no time for me. I had to bolster everyone around me. I
had responsibilities. My first task was to be the messenger.

I think this was the moment I recognized myself as an adult. My
husband's family, my family, and close family friends, all would need
to be told, each in a particular way. Each would have reactions I had
to be prepared for. I was still reeling, but I had to discipline myself.
True to my nature, I decided to do everything I could, to take charge,
and to get things rolling.

At the office I sat at my desk taking deep breaths, and then I called
my father. At first I couldn't tell him that the diagnosis was cerebral
palsy. I skirted around the words, describing instead the expectations
as presented by the doctor. I told him I couldn't answer empirically
what the neurologist had used for the diagnosis. Finally, I confessed.
Yes, the label the neurologist had used was cerebral palsy. I begged
Daddy not to repeat it. It was a label. And I had no real understanding
of its meaning.

After speaking to my father and getting my bearings, I phoned
the physical therapist, Amy, who had encouraged us to seek the neurological diagnosis. She was unable for personal reasons to take over
Seth's case, but she recommended a therapist she had worked with
during her hospital years. The therapist, Susan Scheer, Amy warned
me, was hard to get, busy, and much in demand.

I also phoned Annie Black, my physical therapist who had become
my friend. Annie's open-minded, receptive attitude to treatment for
my lower back pain had convinced me she knew things. When I told
her what we had learned that morning, she agreed to use all her
resources to get the best recommendation for a therapist. Without
consciously knowing it, I was already becoming resourceful and
preparing to advocate for Seth.

⌒

So began one of the most significant aspects of my relationship to Seth's needs: the diary of my own experience and the discoveries of what I need for my own body's health illuminates the path to take for Seth. First I preview; exploring for myself the efficacy of treatment. Then I parlay this information, using it as a resource and jumping off point. Inevitably, my searches for solutions for my own physical challenges have led me to innovative solutions. Whenever the results are meaningful, I am excited about the possibilities for Seth.

Annie Black's inquiries also led to Susan Scheer. By the afternoon of the day of the diagnosis I had left a message for Susan. I was still stung by disbelief and anxiety, but I wasn't paralyzed. And I was going to be sure that my son would not be either. Not that I didn't have feelings; I just didn't have time to indulge them.

At the same time that Annie gave me Susan's name, she also mentioned the Feldenkrais method. She was training in this method of bodywork and suggested that it had proved very successful in treating people who had sustained insults to the nervous system. In the past, whenever Annie started talking about "alternative therapy," I listened halfheartedly, feeling vaguely resistant to anything New Age, wanting to latch on to only the old tried and true. This remained the same that day.

⌒

Meanwhile Jay's parents had to be told something, but not "cerebral palsy." Planning our approach to them was paramount. In the case of my own mother, I knew she would be calling me as soon as my father spoke to her that evening. On the one hand, I wanted to lay my head on her shoulder and weep and beg for reassurance about the future. Realistically, I knew she would be wringing her hands and needing me to alleviate her anxiety.

Reassuring everyone else and bracing everyone with "think how much worse it could be," went a long way to prop me up. The attitude I adopted for everyone else's benefit came to be my own salvation. Repeating the phrase like a mantra rescued me from self-pity then and still does today.

Hearing the words of the neurologist on that April day set my head spinning. I had gone to the consultation not really knowing what a neurologist was and not expecting to hear anything like what he told us. Even though I had been anxious for months owing to intuition and ultimately Amy Katz's observations, I never thought that cerebral palsy would be my reality. Maybe I should have been better prepared to ask questions. But about what? Until that moment, my child was the most perfect child in the universe.

Where to begin? Everyone's style is different, but mine necessitates action. Others may need to explore first, or go to a library, or call experts. I needed to act. While I investigated getting a second opinion, the most important thing was to get Susan Scheer into the house as soon as possible. I wanted to "fix it," and she was the person who would know how. I needed an expert with tools.

Susan Scheer became the primary caretaker of Seth's rehabilitation and my principal point of reference for the next twenty months. After doing an initial evaluation, she came to the house three times a week for one-hour sessions with Seth. Susan was trained in the "neurodevelopmental" method of physical therapy (or NDT), also known as the Bobath method. This method is the one most commonly used for infants and children with cerebral palsy in the United States. Karl and Berta Bobath, a husband and wife introduced it in the 1950s from England, and it is considered very mainstream.

The NDT approach helps prepare the child's posture and movement to permit the development of "functional skills" or those skills needed for feeding, dressing, and bathing, the skills that are basic to living independently. Treatment focuses on encouraging the child to use normal rather than abnormal movement patterns and on preventing deformities or muscle patterns that make developing movement skills more difficult.

Susan was very positive about Seth's prognosis. She was always upbeat and balanced in our home, enchanted by Seth, while remaining professional. At the same time, she could throw me off balance completely because instantly and unconsciously I made her the authority and the barometer of Seth's future. Anything she said was loaded for me.

For a long time after the diagnosis, the overriding sensation was of being out of control and depending on others: other people's information, other people's predictions, other people's experience, other people's abilities. It was not a comfortable position to be in. Nobody was ever so reassuring that I was able to calm my anxiety. No one offered an overview, precise answers, or specific solutions. I could not depend on anyone to follow through the way I would. My problems were my problems, and there was no professional or friend who would take them as seriously as I did. At the same time, I was not an expert. I did not have the tools to do without anyone's help.

Of course, that happens to all parents of children with problems. We are dependent on so many other people besides ourselves. We have to be. They are the experts. They have experience in the realms that affect our children, and they know what can make a difference in our children's lives.

Our relationships with these people are complex. We need them. We desperately hope that they will succeed. Maybe we also believe that if they like us—the parents—they will help our children more or be able to achieve more. We want miracles, magic. And these professionals hold the promise of those miracles. We make them into gods.

In my case, Susan could make the most casual, offhand comment and it would either encourage me for days or devastate me to the point of obsession. Her most frequent statement was that she was working for "quality." That was reassuring. I wanted Seth to have quality, and nothing persuaded me he wouldn't. Of course, quality was integral to the Bobath philosophy.

Susan demonstrated patterns or activities she wanted us to practice with Seth. I had Mayra observe the therapy sessions and carry out all Susan's instructions, as well as practice with and encourage Seth as much as possible. Mayra was much better at it than I was. At the end of my day, I wanted to come home and simply love my baby. I didn't want to do physical therapy with him. I barely wanted to worry about his situation, even though I did to the point of mania at times. Watching Mayra, I learned how to encourage better movements for Seth. I continued to have faith that things would be all right. But I kept asking Susan about things like tennis and downhill skiing, as though she would be able to tell me everything I wanted to know about the future.

In June we traveled to Boston, to the Children's Hospital to consult with a celebrated neurologist, Dr. Michael Bresnan, and get a second opinion. My parents live in Boston, and Dr. Bresnan had been recommended to us through my mother's contacts in the hospital world. My father accompanied Jay and Seth and me to the interview. Dr. Bresnan characterized Seth's problem as "moderate" as opposed to "mild." I asked which was worse. "Moderate" was worse.

Dr. Bresnan illustrated what he predicted Seth's gait would be by walking across the room with a perceptible scissoring action, knees knocking together, his legs dragged forward by swaying his hips one at a time. We were stunned. I looked across the room at my father and knew in his forlorn gaze that he was desolate. I vowed then and there to do all the interpreting of any firsthand observations. From then on everyone would get their information only through me.

Needless to say, we did not feel cheered by Dr. Bresnan's diagnosis. We spent that afternoon with my grandmother, my "Honey Nana," before returning to New York. Nana kept telling me not to worry. "He has a good head on him," she repeated many times that afternoon. She told me that every time I spoke to her until she died eighteen months later. I knew what she meant.

When I looked into Seth's eyes, I knew how smart he was. I knew he had mental acuity, and that this was one of his strengths. And I knew this capacity would get stronger because of the challenge in his life. Time brought that intuition more and more into focus. Go with the strengths. Develop them and use them to support and improve what's not as strong.

We spent much of the summer in the Berkshires. The small, rented French-style farmhouse, with its large, leaded bay window, was our family's first weekend home. Friday afternoons Seth and Jay and I would pile into our two-door compact car. Waving good-bye to Mayra, the three of us would then travel the two and a half hours to West Stockbridge, singing songs or conversing in baby talk. Seth never complained on long car rides. He amused himself or us, giving us an early glimpse into his amenable nature. He was an incredibly cooperative and happy infant. The pain of his circumstances had not yet become entwined with his psyche.

To the outside world Seth seemed like any other one-year-old. Nothing was obviously amiss to the casual observer. On close observation, though, many prophetic movements and postures were already in play. For example, Seth continually held his left hand in a small, tight fist. There are many photographs of him being held by one of us, and his left fist is in this characteristic ball. I used to playfully slap his fist and ask him why he did it. Not too many years later I learned the value of stimulating his fist in this way. So while intuition already governed many of my responses, learning to trust my instincts was another matter.

The way Seth liked to lie on his back, arching as though to look behind him, always drew a comment from my mother. Later I learned that this tendency, too, is characteristic of the kind of cerebral palsy Seth has. Ironically, the photograph I treasure most from this summer is one of Seth in a red, one-piece short-sleeved cotton suit lying in this exact pose. He is lying on the sofa under the bay window in the living room of the farmhouse. Had I had experience with another child, I might have known right from the beginning that Seth's tendency to lie in this position was a major indication of his neurological condition. It wasn't until four years later, when I handled my infant daughter, that I recognized the extreme stiffness, the almost brittle nature, of Seth's body.

That summer of 1984 was a summer of continual consultations and interviews. It was a time of engagement. My whole life focused on Seth and his care. Susan Scheer was a new entity in our family life. Mayra was probably present more of the time during Susan's sessions than I was. Her interpretation of each of Seth's sessions was of great importance for me. Mayra adored Seth, as did Susan. The same appeal that was apparent in the NICU hours after he was born was at work for Seth already. It continues to serve him today. His innate intelligence and charm assisted him then as now and is a strength he draws upon.

Susan Scheer recommended that we get a pediatric orthopedist to evaluate Seth. She said that the growth of his bones needed monitoring. When I consulted our pediatrician, Dr. Lee, she concurred. The "best" as far as Dr. Lee was concerned was the same doctor Susan Scheer wanted us to use: Dr. Alfred Grant, chief pediatric orthopedist at the Hospital for Special Surgery, a very reputable institution. We made an appointment.

What vaguely disturbed and unsettled me, even at this early

juncture, was my increasing awareness that I was doing all the initiating. No one was giving us an overview, especially not our pediatrician. Dr. Lee had been casual about Seth's progress. I had consulted Amy Katz without the pediatrician's encouragement. I was the one who had gone to the doctor and said that we wanted more information based on Amy Katz's observations. Only then had Dr. Lee suggested a neurological consultation. I couldn't determine whether it was because she felt sanguine about Seth's prognosis or whether she didn't know much more than I did.

Again, here I was doing the initiating, asking for another doctor. What if Susan Scheer hadn't suggested such a consultation? I asked myself. Who was there to guide me? Dr. Chutorian had said that I could try physical therapy for Seth if I wanted to, but he hadn't suggested anyone, and he certainly hadn't provided any explanation of the different kinds of therapy, and neither had Dr. Lee. I felt I was floundering. The happenstance, random nature of acquiring information troubled me. There never has been anyone to help me chart an overall course of treatment for Seth. Different professionals offered various prognoses and insights, but none of them helped me map out steps and goals. When I realized no one was going to help me in this task, I felt abandoned and alone. Coping with this isolation burdened me with a sense of responsibility that at times felt very scary.

When I finally dared to look in the dictionary for a definition of "cerebral palsy," I got another jolt. I read, "a disability resulting from damage to the brain before or during birth and outwardly manifested by muscular incoordination and speech disturbances." Speech! No one had said a word about speech, I realized. Muscular incoordination seemed benign. But speech, an entirely new sphere, loomed. I felt exactly as I had on the day when Dr. Chutorian had stated his diagnosis and as I would each time I encountered a new piece of information: lost in the unknown, flailing and spinning, asking myself, what now?

A few days later Susan Scheer agreed that we should definitely consult a speech therapist. She recommended Phyllis Fabricant. I knew a woman who was a speech pathologist, and she recommended that before doing anything else I should get Seth's hearing tested. So I had two upcoming appointments: the orthopedist, Dr. Grant at the Hospital for Special Surgery, and Jane Madell, Ph.D., at the New

York League for the Hard of Hearing. Coincidentally, the League for the Hard of Hearing was located in the same building as United Cerebral Palsy (UCP), a place I was never directed to and never wanted to go.

How do I remember all of this, all the names, the chronology, and the results? Because it is all written down in journal after journal. Although not too much had occurred in Seth's care up to this point, we had had the neurological consultations and diagnoses. We had Susan Scheer. So I decided to keep a diary of Seth's progress and record information as I received it.

Keeping this record has been one of the most significant aspects of my experience as a mother of a child with special needs; it is a helpful practice with any child, for that matter. To this day I also keep a journal about my daughter and all her medical visits and school conferences. I record random thoughts and observations about both children as well as all their little illnesses. How did this happen? True, I am a writer and keeper of journals. But someone else suggested this particular mindfulness.

A friend had told me about her recent health problems. She said that in her search for a remedy, she had had to consult many specialists and inform them accurately about her condition. The only way she was able to keep everything straight, to remember everything, was to keep a detailed diary. She recorded her own health status as well as everything the doctors told her. Listening to her, I knew I needed to do the same for Seth.

July 3, 1984, was our appointment with the orthopedist. Seth was not even thirteen months old. I remember waiting for Dr. Grant an inordinate amount of time in a waiting room full of cigarette smoke. I was angry about being treated as though I had nothing else to do in life but wait for a doctor. Furthermore all of us in that waiting room, a pediatric environment, a room full of parents and children, were breathing air full of cigarette smoke.

From my notes, I see that I learned more about cerebral palsy from Dr. Grant than I had up until that point, although I might have availed myself of even more information had I tried. He said that cerebral palsy is a perceptible motor problem.

Medical professionals hesitate to use the term "cerebral palsy" when first diagnosing the condition because it implies a prognosis.

Because of the "plasticity" of a child's central nervous system, there
is always the possibility that a child will recover after an injury. The
brains of infants and young children repair themselves more frequently than do those of older children. As the nervous system orga-
nizes over time, motor abilities are affected differently. If a brain
injury occurs early, the undamaged areas of a child's brain can sometimes take over some of the functions of the damaged areas. As Seth's
treatments evolved, we certainly subscribed more and more to this
theory of the brain's capacity.

Dr. Grant gave us a definition of Seth's kind of cerebral palsy: static
encephalopathy. While the phrase had appeared in the reports of
both neurologists, I had read them very cursorily and with great
resistance. The book *Children with Cerebral Palsy: A Parents' Guide*,
explains the term "static encephalopathy" to mean an abnormal brain
function that is not getting worse. Other terms used in this context
are "motor delay"; "neuromotor dysfunction," or delay in the mat-
uration of the nervous system; "motor disability," indicating a long-
term movement problem; "central nervous system dysfunction,"
which is a very general term to indicate improper functioning of the
brain. When used as a label, "cerebral palsy" refers to a disorder of
movement and posture that is attributable to a nonprogressive abnormality of the brain. The basic distinctions of cerebral palsy are the
age of onset and the lack of progression. This static nature of cerebral palsy, its lack of progression, means that the disability itself does
not worsen.

But *Children with Cerebral Palsy* had not been published when Seth
was small, and I had not consulted any books except the dictionary
after Seth was diagnosed. What Dr. Grant was telling us was all new
information, and it was specifically about Seth's condition. He repeated
something Dr. Lee had told us the day of the initial diagnosis when
we stood in her consulting room at the hospital.

Dr. Lee had said that "cerebral palsy" is a "wastebasket" term, a
broad label that encompasses many different disorders of movement
and posture. Later I also learned that all such disorders are caused
by a brain injury that occurs before birth, during birth or within the
first few years after birth. There are pregnancy risk factors, delivery
risk factors, and neonatal risk factors. The causes of cerebral palsy
are unknown in 20 percent of the cases. The injury does not damage

the child's muscles or the nerves connecting the muscles to the spinal cord, only the brain's ability to control the muscles.

One of the chief diagnostic signs of cerebral palsy is the persistence of primitive reflexes. However, even a child with the mildest form of cerebral palsy has difficulty performing the continuous changes in muscle tone that are required for normal walking.

Depending on its location and severity, the brain injury that causes a child's movement disorders may also cause other problems, including mental retardation, seizures, language disorders, learning disabilities, and vision and hearing problems. The part of the body in which the child experiences abnormal muscle tone depends upon where the brain damage has occurred. The one common denominator is that all children with cerebral palsy have damage to the area of the brain that controls muscle tone.

Children with *increased* muscle tone are said to have *high tone, hypertonia,* or *spasticity.* Because their muscles are tight, movement is tight and awkward. These children love to stand on their legs, but they stand on their toes or scissor their legs. Scissoring, which is the most common gait disturbance, occurs because of the increased tightness in the muscles that control adduction and internal rotation of the hips. Children with increased tone can be identified by the ways they arch their backs and roll over. At first I thought that Seth fell into this group. But all children with cerebral palsy have problems with movement and posture.

Children with low tone or *decreased* tone are said to have *low tone, hypotonia,* or *floppiness.* It is difficult for children with low tone to remain upright against the pull of gravity. Sitting, for instance, is difficult. Low tone also influences a child's ability to keep his trunk stable enough so that he can use his arms to reach and to grasp. When low tone affects a child's abdominal and respiratory muscles, it can hinder the development of speech. Seth seemed to fit into this category too, but as I learned more I found that there was a third classification.

Fluctuating or *variable muscle tone* describes children who have a combination of high and low tone. For instance, Seth has low tone while at rest but high tone with activity. Increased tone helps to stabilize a position such as sitting or standing, but it may end up making other movements difficult or impossible because it may cause the tightening of muscle groups in other parts of the body. "Muscle tone" was a term I heard repeatedly. I had recognized early in Seth's development that Seth's body was different than other children's, but I hadn't known enough to identify these "tone" characteristics as indicators that anything was wrong.

My resentment about waiting for Dr. Grant was ameliorated when the doctor suggested that although one can't make accurate predictions, there were predictors, and they looked good for Seth. At best, the doctor said he wouldn't even rule out downhill skiing. (He was wrong.) He said that Seth would need either surgery, inhibitory casts, or braces. He X-rayed Seth's hips and said that there was only the slightest flaring. All the bones were okay. Because he was so positive and seemed to appreciate Seth's personality and humor, we liked Dr. Grant very much.

⌒

It is strange, looking back, that someone who prides herself as much as I do on thoroughness and action took such a passive stance regarding my son's devastating diagnosis. I relied wholly on the professionals—the neurologist, my pediatrician, Susan Scheer, and Dr. Grant. I would bounce along from one expert to the next, heeding their advice for some time to come. I did no research. I barely read the neurological reports, and when I did, I skimmed. I never contacted United Cerebral Palsy. I didn't go to the library. I was too scared. I wanted to believe Seth's condition was so mild that the early intervention I was orchestrating would be enough to ensure his normal development. The thought of something more severe was out of reach. And I wanted to keep it that way.

Why wasn't I paying attention? What was I avoiding? I was what psychologists call "in denial." All the parents I've met and interviewed say that they responded as I did during some phase of coming to terms with their child's special needs. We cannot blame ourselves. Who wants to hear that your child is not perfect, never mind possibly impaired, ill, or in danger? Such concepts are so difficult to grasp and to live with—to say nothing of explaining them to others.

It took several years before I was able to open the channel of memory, but I finally did have a startling recollection of a childhood experience with two disabled children. There are many layers of feeling when I think back on these two central figures in the landscape of my childhood summers on Cape Cod. My best friend Patty's youngest sister was "mongoloid"—we call it Down's syndrome today—and our neighbors had a young son, Jimmy, who had severe cerebral palsy.

I spent long days at the beach playing "mother" to Patty's sister or to Jimmy. My friend's sister was with me almost daily, and I seized every opportunity to be with her. She came from a large family of ten children, so I slipped in easily. We had long, varied days together swimming, building sandcastles, and taking walks.

Jimmy used a wheelchair and was on the beach infrequently, and he visited only briefly. So my time with Jimmy was more specific. Jimmy was severely impaired. He was unable to support even his head. It drooped over to one side, his chin grazing his collarbone. He drooled, and his speech was slurred and unintelligible. There were no motor functions he performed himself. But he was sweet and smiled, and I loved him. Jimmy visited his mother in the summer for a few weeks. Afterward he returned to the Fernald School for the Handicapped, a state institution in the Boston area, close to our winter home.

Jimmy's mother, Mrs. Townsend, was my parents' good friend and neighbor. She had her hands full. Because of a congenital condition, her husband, Jimmy's father, was also confined to a wheelchair. Most of the time he was in a constant-care facility, but Mrs. Townsend had him visit accompanied by a nurse's aide while their son was visiting home, too. It was work for her to care for two extremely needy individuals simultaneously. Consequently, my doting on Jimmy delighted Mrs. Townsend.

Tending to Jimmy, keeping him entertained, occupied, fed was my occupation for two weeks every summer. Jimmy's intelligence was limited, but I saw that he knew me and responded to my care. I felt important and capable. I patted myself on the back for loving someone seemingly so discarded. After all, his parents had no place for him at home, and society was certainly not welcoming him into its midst.

For many years, while I was eight and nine, ten, and eleven, my summers included the company of these two "retarded" children. I had many other friends and activities, but Patty's sister was a constant companion, at least during the day, every summer. Jimmy's visit was a centerpiece each July. It felt natural to be nurturing, patient, and understanding. I liked it. Did I have an inkling of my future? Were these clues?

When I was growing up in the 1950s, words such as "retarded," "mongoloid," and "handicapped" were commonplace. The child with Down's syndrome was identifiable by certain unmistakable characteristics. I remember a doctor friend of our family visiting us and instantly noticing Patty's sister on the beach. I watched him come up to her, look curiously, take her hands in his, and turn them over to examine her palms.

In the months between September and June, I gave only fleeting thoughts to my two favorite summer companions. Until I was twelve. That winter, at Christmas time, Mrs. Townsend came to visit us. The plan was for me to go to her home for an overnight and bake Christmas cookies. En route, she spontaneously suggested that we stop at the Fernald School and make an unannounced visit to Jimmy.

The school had a policy of not allowing children under sixteen in to visit, but I looked very mature. We walked into Jimmy's ward. I was confounded by what I saw. A room the size of a gymnasium was full of severely disabled young boys. There were children with hydrocephalus, their heads the size of watermelons and their bodies like midgets; there were boys with cerebral palsy in wheelchairs; boys with Down's syndrome; autistic boys lying on beds looking vacant or encased in straitjackets. The spectacle was devastating.

Presumably, I handled the visit well—I didn't break down or run away. But afterward I obsessed about people who had overcome great obstacles. Helen Keller was one individual who intrigued me. I read obsessively about her and others who had surmounted difficult odds. People who were disadvantaged, but nevertheless realized notable achievements fascinated me. And I read voraciously about their mothers; about parents of children with special needs. I remember the shelf where I parked myself in our town's public library to pore over these books.

My parents barely spoke to Mrs. Townsend again, angry that she was so careless and exposed me, a child, to the vastness of the physically disabled, engendering in me an inner world of dark anxiety. Like many little girls, I was forever thinking about babies and being a mother. Now I worried intensely that I would have a child with cerebral palsy. I wrote about it in my diary, wrote stories about it.

Eventually my parents moved to another summer home in another neighborhood, and I don't remember the last time we saw "Mrs. T." My concerns faded as I grew into adolescence. Elvis, the Beatles, the Vietnam War occupied me. I went to college thinking I wanted to study anthropology or psychology, and instead I was absorbed by the arts, by theater, dance, film, art history, literature. I moved to California to study and to work. I was distracted by and immersed in new aims and interests. Somewhere along the way, I recall being told that Jimmy or his father or both had died. By then I rarely thought about Jimmy or my friend Patty's little sister.

Three years following Seth's diagnosis, when my passage to this memory opened from nowhere, the only curiosity was that it had taken so long. I was still in an early stage of coming to terms with Seth's disability. Looking back now I realize that I was doing my best just to get the help I needed, to overcome the lack of direction from the primary-care physicians. Yet, I must admit, this denial, this tendency to acquiesce in the presence of "authorities," had led me to stick it out with my ob-gyn during my pregnancy even though I had doubts. It had led me to postpone earlier intervention in Seth's care even though I intuited that something was not right. The understandable tendency to accept the status quo would come into play significantly again and again in my responses to various situations along the way.

CHAPTER FOUR

at sea

AS THE SUMMER WANED AND FALL BECAME INTOXICATING, we spent more time in the City on weekends. Our neighbors had an adopted Korean daughter, Kara, and they were expecting to adopt another little girl from Korea any day. Kara was six years older than Seth, and the two played together all the time, Kara delightfully acting the part of older sister. It was a warm September, so the children were often in bathing suits splashing in a small inflatable swimming pool.

Seth's inability to ambulate is obvious in the photographs from that autumn. Kara is busy propping him up or tending to him much as I must have tended to Jimmy and to Patty's sister years earlier. Seth is full of smiles, obviously content to be waited on and assisted like a little prince. The twinkle in his eyes never diminished, and the bond between Kara and Seth was so strong that even Lia's arrival a few months later did little to fray it.

In September of 1984, on the front cover of my first journal, a blue-and-white hardback diary, I affixed a typed list of the specialists involved with Seth's care, their addresses and phone numbers. Looking at it today evokes an ocean of memory.

The list begins with Dr. Lee, the pediatrician. Today she no longer treats Seth or my daughter, Haya, but it took a lot of time before we let go. (As I recall her casual attitude toward my initial concerns in the early months, her failure to educate me about the risks of immunizing Seth, her inability to offer anything but empty praise, I am embarrassed that it took me so much time to decide to stop seeing her.) Since Dr. Lee constantly applauded my efforts on Seth's behalf, it was hard to resist her. I gloried in all I was doing for Seth, and all the recognition she gave me. After a great deal of thought I came to understand my weakness, but also to see that I was responding in a very human way.

Praise is a wonderful feeling. I realize now I was on a perpetual quest for love, some damage left over from childhood. Dr. Lee's admiration bonded me to her. But it clouded my ability to decipher good advice or to feel entitled to aggressively question her or other professionals. As I gained insight into my psychology, I was more able to separate myself from this yearning for love. I recognized my need for affirmation, but I stopped it from interfering with my getting information or results. It remains an ongoing struggle, though.

The second name on the list is the neurologist, Dr. Chutorian, who provided the initial diagnosis. We went back to him only one more time. Although a third neurologist besides Drs. Chutorian and Bresnan would examine Seth the following year, it would be five years from the original diagnosis before Seth got a complete neurological work up, in 1989, at the Spitz clinic in Philadelphia.

Dr. Alfred Grant, the orthopedist, is the third name. Three or four more consultations over the next two years made us reconsider Dr. Grant's suggestions.

The three therapists who were treating Seth every week were Susan Scheer, who came three times a week; Peggy Smith, an occupational therapist who came twice a week; and the speech therapist, Phyllis Fabricant, who treated Seth every Friday. Phyllis's sessions were sometimes conducted with Susan Scheer's participation. I have a file full of these therapists' intermittent reports, requested by me or by the various doctors. Phyllis also wrote a short weekly report, which she left with me every Friday. It greeted me when I arrived home at the end of the week and influenced my state of mind every weekend. I had an abundance of feelings about each of these people. So did Seth. They dominated our lives.

Susan Scheer was definitely the "captain," although Peggy Smith's outlook and approach predominate to this day because Peggy was extremely prescient. She did many things that later were encouraged in the more unconventional treatments. She rolled Seth around playfully and hung him by his ankles. She stimulated him with various modalities and games, using shaving cream, applesauce (which would play a big part later on), and water. Peggy mentioned the Feldenkrais method occasionally during the first few months, as Annie Black had, but I didn't investigate it. It sounded too "far out," and I was hanging on for dear life to what I thought was tried and true.

Peggy discussed stimulating Seth's lungpower, getting him to scream and sing and make loud noises, an insight that proved prophetic. Until recently a voice/breath teacher has been the primary caretaker of his speech issue. This has worked very successfully. Peggy's sessions were vibrant, comprehensive encounters unlike anything else in Seth's life at the time.

Seth's life was one long therapy session when we factored in Mayra's participation. Everyone was working at his rehabilitation. I was reassured, believing in the power of these influences to make everything all right. We purchased a therapeutic bolster and a huge ball for Seth's sessions with Susan and Peggy. Phyllis also used the bolster to position Seth during some of her work with him. To this day we are on the mailing list of the company that sold us the equipment. The catalog arrives three or four times a year. Its cover always depicts a child either in a wheelchair or using other orthopedic devices, reminding me of what I haven't had to face. Our whole family uses the bolster for one thing or an other, and I still encourage Seth to sit on it whenever he can.

In sharp contrast to Peggy's sessions, according to Phyllis Fabricant's accounts, her sessions with Seth were nettlesome, and that state of affairs only escalated over time. Although, as I look over Phyllis's reports, I see that she often wrote, "Seth did well," it always felt as if there was some qualification. In one report she wrote, "Seth had an excellent session. I hear a variety of sounds. He imitates many words. Try to continue to have him say a word before he gets what he wants. He is a great pointer, and we don't want that to be his main mode of communication. I asked Mayra to put out his clothes in the morning, and he must say each piece before it is put on."

But most of Phyllis's reports were not so upbeat. Seth didn't like the sessions with her. He especially resisted when she tried to work in his mouth with a little stimulus tool, and his reaction would upset Phyllis. At the time, I didn't make the link between the discomfort he had had when nursing months earlier and his difficulties in his mouth. Phyllis encouraged Mayra to use a toothbrush in his mouth, too. He hated it, and I think Phyllis almost hated him for his adversity. Years later, when another professional asked me why Seth had so much reluctance and sensitivity to overcome in his mouth, instantly I knew why.

Like many people with cerebral palsy, Seth's sensory experience is different than mine or Jay's or Haya's or most people. One place he experiences increased sensitivity is in and around his mouth and tongue. As my awareness and knowledge grew, I learned that the tongue is often at the center of function, especially movement. The tongue is a fleshy, movable, muscular organ. It attaches in us to the floor of the mouth. It is the principal organ of taste, an aid in chewing and swallowing, and our primary organ of speech.

The movements involved in every action of ourselves affect every other aspect of our organism. Our sympathetic nervous system consists of two large nerves on either side of the vertebral column. All these nerves have their roots coming out of the thoracic and lumbar regions of the spinal cord. Here the tongue has genuine power and influence, and these dimensions are only partially recognized. All of Phyllis's prodding and pushing in his mouth increased Seth's anxiety and resistance.

As Thomas Hanna wrote in one of his numerous and lucid essays, we must think of ourselves as being controlled not from without but from within. What is more within than the tongue? Movement is the best clue to life. In Mr. Hanna's view we have from birth until death a loop of four elements: skeleton, muscles, nervous system, and environment. I believe the tongue links all of these elements.

Soon after Phyllis began treating him, and when Seth was only fifteen months old, she said she wanted to teach him sign language. Susan Scheer concurred. I was shocked. What! Did that mean that he was not going to talk? Would we all be signing? How could they know at fifteen months? Was he expected to make words fully comprehensible already? Frantically I began consulting baby books about normal sound production and the expectations regarding speech development. Since I had no point of reference, I was in a complete dither. When I asked Dr. Lee, she felt that it was premature to make an assessment, but she was uncertain. Jay was unalterably opposed to Seth learning to sign.

I felt I was in charge, that I was being very capable and responsive, but I also had doubts, nagging anxieties. The debate over teaching Seth sign language, as well as my level of anxiety, persuaded me to search for a pediatrician who specialized in developmental disabilities.

I thought that such a person could educate us, provide some per-spective and an overview on Seth's condition, and give us some guid-ance in making decisions. Coinciding with the conundrum about teaching Seth to sign and the beginning of our search for this pedi-atric expert, Susan Scheer persuaded us to consult Dr. Larry Price, a podiatrist, about Seth's feet.

Susan Scheer wanted us to consult Dr. Price because of Seth's poor feet and ankle alignment. She believed that an orthotic device would preserve the bony alignment of his feet and the integrity of his joints. She thought that the orthotic adjustment would mean a stable base for his feet while weight bearing, distributing the pres-sure more evenly over the surface of the heel and border of the foot. She communicated this to us directly and by letter to Dr. Grant, a letter that I kept in my file. In her letter to Dr. Grant she wrote that there was no need for an extension of the orthotic apparatus over the ankle. We were all thinking in terms of a device that would fit easily into Seth's shoe. However, when it came time to stand by that assessment, Susan backed down.

Seth was not standing independently and was not pulling him-self to a standing position, although he loved being placed in a standing position. He adored his "walker." There are tons of pictures of Seth in this contraption. In every picture he is wearing a broad smile. The walker gave him mobility, allowing him to move about from place to place just like the other children of his age who were already walking and getting about independently.

I was vaguely aware of some disagreement about the advisability of walkers. I knew that Peggy believed, for instance, that a child should stand only when development allowed for standing and not before, otherwise the feet would be compromised. On the other hand, it was Dr. Lee who had first recommended the walker and pooh-poohed the criticism of its efficacy. Susan Scheer had had no objections to it.

The walker made life easier for us. It helped Seth get from place to place more quickly and independently. He was fifteen months old, the age when most children begin to walk, and he was getting heavier to carry. He would get even heavier before he could walk independ-ently. In the meantime, for better or worse—and later we learned that it was for worse, much worse—we let him use the walker and have the joy of getting about as though he were walking. We were about to make another ill-advised decision as well.

In my diary I noted that the office visit to Dr. Price was the beginning of a pattern of my having to rehash the very painful events surrounding Seth's birth. The nurse received Jay and me, and, while Seth played nearby, we had to answer many questions regarding my pregnancy and delivery. I still did not link Seth's condition with the nightmare of the delivery. Was I sleeping? I became emotional when I recounted the events of Seth's birth, but I was too absorbed by his daily care and his future care to make connections.

Later, when I did let it all register, it was because it was necessary to face myself, too—a difficult thing to do. The same qualities that prevented me from getting rid of my ob-gyn and getting rid of Dr. Lee also prevented me from making those links. The lesson I've learned is that you need to be aware so that you can take responsibility. And the mandate is to keep the doctors and professionals human, not to elevate them. This means giving constant, ongoing attention to health-care providers in both the mainstream and alternative worlds of medicine.

Dr. Larry Price, the podiatrist, advised us to put Seth into "inhibitory casts." These were removable plaster casts that covered his entire foot and ran up to his knees. He wanted Seth to wear the casts most of the day and always while he was in a standing position. Unlike Susan Scheer, Dr. Price thought that an orthotic device was an "under treatment." He was glad that Seth could get his heel on the ground when standing. He felt that we could experiment with helping Seth while he was still an infant by putting him in the inhibitory casts.

Dr. Price believed the casts were better than braces because the braces increase "tone" and diminish the sensory experience of the foot on the ground. He said that the inhibitory cast would decrease tone, as for instance a hiking boot does, keeping the alignment of the foot neutral. "Tone" was becoming a familiar word.

But, while the doctor was talking about decreasing tone, I wasn't thinking about whether these inhibitory casts would influence Seth's sensory experience. Insecurity, a sense of having to deal constantly with the unknown yet having to make important decisions, was becoming a familiar circumstance, though not a comfortable one.

Later the question of sensory experience became paramount, radically altering the whole course of Seth's therapy. Eventually we realized that only the contact of Seth's foot on the ground is a sensory experience; casts, braces, and orthotic devices interfere with the tactile experience. But I didn't have this information then. I had to discover it as part of my own education. For the time being, I relied on Dr. Grant for guidance in making the decision about the casts.

Dr. Grant said that the issue of inhibitory casts was still being debated. There were those who believed that the casts decreased tone and those who said that they did nothing. He told us that he was in the middle. Although the casts occasionally helped to decrease tone, neither he nor his colleagues believed that the devices eliminated or reduced the need to cut the Achilles tendon. He insisted that we were still going to face surgery. (I couldn't begin to contemplate that possibility for the moment.)

At fifteen months Seth was not a candidate for surgery anyway, so the casts couldn't hurt him, Dr. Grant said. He insisted, twice, that in his experience a time would come for surgery, that the physical therapist would object, and that we could get twenty-five other opinions and still have a painful decision to make. But he went along with putting Seth into the casts. In the meantime, many years have passed, and surgery has not come yet.

Encountering conflict, confusing information, mixed messages, and differences of opinion, forecasting the future, having to decipher and choose: this was my life. I spent my time following through, checking everything, and trying to filter all the information. In the meantime, Dr. Grant also urged us to use his clinic for Seth's rehabilitation. I wanted to stick with the status quo. It was familiar when everything else wasn't.

The therapists in Dr. Grant's clinic were not trained in the neurodevelopmental treatment (NDT) method of the Bobaths. I told Dr. Grant that I objected to making a change in the kind of therapy Seth was receiving. I wanted to continue using therapists trained in this Bobath method. He told me that he had had enough of the NDT people. They were coming out of his ears, and he objected to my insistence on this kind of therapy.

At the same time, Annie Black was urging me to make an appointment with a Feldenkrais teacher in our neighborhood, Charles Bonner.

Afraid of offending her and alienating someone, who might be a potential source of information or a valuable link, I agreed and scheduled the appointment.

We were on a voyage to heal, to care, calling on all doctors, spending all our money, searching everywhere, everyone, searching each other. My time alone with Seth had sanctity beyond anything I had previously known. Aside from my husband, I had never adored anyone so completely as I did my son. I felt close to him in a sacred way. My instinct to nurture was aroused tangibly.

Sometimes I would look into Seth's twinkling blue eyes, feel the contact of our two souls, and say aloud, "Seth, my darling boy, my love, my life, I need guidance in making the right decisions for you." He would smile. I felt that he answered me with complete trust. His look gave me the faith that I was making the right decisions.

Seth had a busy calendar. In September we had him fitted for his casts. That involved an appointment where he had to be mildly sedated; the prospect caused me no end of anxiety. I scheduled the time to meet with Charles Bonner, the Feldenkrais practitioner. There were also routine checkups with the orthopedist and the pediatrician.

We finally located a developmental disabilities expert, a pediatrician at New York Hospital/Cornell Medical Center, Dr. Daniel Kessler, and scheduled a series of interviews with him. The three therapists were coming for a combination of seven visits every week. We were also considering some kind of day-care environment where Seth would be exposed to other children. We were setting up interviews and visits to make that happen.

Thinking back, I ask myself, what if I hadn't been self-employed? What do the parents of other special needs children do about time away from work? How do their employers treat them? What allowances are made? I was also lucky to have Mayra. Her assistance was invaluable. Mayra absorbed the therapists' messages and kept up what I never could have done, providing Seth with constant, vigilant intervention. I always felt that she was my greatest hope. Her continued optimism and devotion to Seth was a bulwark.

We could barely afford all the medical care and consultations. The insurance company lagged in reimbursing us for the therapists and doctors, all of whom wanted to be paid immediately. They resisted paying for any speech therapy, so that cost was our responsibility entirely. The issue of a "preexisting condition" was about to arise with the insurance company. We eventually resolved the issue of the preexisting condition, but in the meantime bills began to mount up.

Self-employment was fine for the latitude it allowed in the way of time, but I had to generate business. In order to do this I was going to be away in Los Angeles for ten days every month. I was developing several literary properties for the motion picture studios and television networks, and the meetings with writers and studio executives took place exclusively in Los Angeles. I arranged ten days each month to be in Los Angeles to accomplish what I could in one fell swoop. Mayra's presence took on a new dimension.

In October Seth's hearing test proved he had no substantial auditory difficulties. He responded well to low frequencies, which include people's voices. Dr. Jane Madell at the New York League for the Hard of Hearing observed that only high-frequency sounds had to be significantly louder in order for Seth to respond. This was not unusual in children with cerebral palsy, she said. Although there was no significant hearing problem, a loss of high frequency meant that the fricatives—*f*'s, *sh*'s, *th*'s, and *z*'s—would be harder to hear.

What I couldn't know then was that the fricatives would also be harder for Seth to say. Saying his very name, "Seth," would become one of my son's daily struggles. Announcing himself by name-whether it be on the telephone when he calls a friend, when he walks into a new situation, a new classroom, when he is asked, as we all are so often, who is calling—is his everyday chore. It is the constant reminder of who he is and how he struggles.

The hearing test was very important. An estimated twenty one million Americans have some degree of hearing impairment. Hearing affects a wide range of skills, including the development of language and learning abilities. (You will read a lot about this in later chapters.) We were glad to learn that Seth's hearing was intact.

In early October we were on our way to consult with Dr. Daniel Kessler. As with so many other things in our experience, Serendipity played a major role in our finding Dr. Kessler. We learned about Dr. Kessler in a casual meeting that led to my reading an article. In the article I found Dr. Kessler's name, so I tracked him down. I kept thinking how one chance encounter had led to another, as we wended our way along circuitous paths to a suite of offices in an attic in New York Hospital. These "random" instances of good fortune combined with my dogged determination and tenacity often brought results. Yet there was much more I could have investigated, and this is still a continuing theme I play out in my mind. Vigilance is the watchword of parenting a child with special needs, but it is tiring work.

Dr. Daniel Kessler was a protégé of Dr. T. Berry Brazelton, the Dr. Spock of my generation of parents. When I was pregnant, it was Dr. Brazelton's books I thumbed most often. After Seth was born and before he was diagnosed, Dr. Brazelton's books seemed to offer the clearest guidance.

Dr. Kessler was our dream doctor. He was a pediatrician with a small group practice whose specialty was children with developmental disabilities. Not only did he pick up the phone and talk to me at length the first time I called; he was willing to consult with another doctor on either a short- or a long-term basis. He had no clinic, so there was no agenda about using his physical therapists. Eventually he offered the most comprehensive perspective. His competence in the field prompted me to consider using him as Seth's primary-care physician, a decision over which we agonized for months. In the end, we decided to use him only as a consultant.

The testing Dr. Kessler wanted to do was not scheduled until late November. But before our first face-to-face meeting in October, he read the existing neurological reports and discussed with us by phone the importance of environmental influences and current assessments regarding Seth's cognitive problem-solving abilities. I asked him many questions about casts, the orthopedic versus physical therapy conflicts, the issue of the urgency of Seth beginning to learn sign language. I also had questions about playgroups.

New psychological questions were cropping up, for instance, how much to let Seth struggle and how much to help him (another recurring theme). Dr. Kessler's responses were very helpful. I liked his unsanctimonious perspective on his own medical profession. He struck me as extremely instinctive, exceptionally bright, a promising beacon of insight. And, most important, I felt like he was listening. I had someone to talk to.

In the meantime, because of Annie Black, I took Seth to see Charles Bonner, the Feldenkrais practitioner who worked down the street from where we lived. Mayra went with us. Charles Bonner asked a few preliminary questions and then spent an hour handling Seth. Seth seemed to love him and didn't object to being handled. This changed later.

Afterward, Bonner was very reassuring. He specifically said that all of Seth's functions would come in, and he was convinced that Seth would be fine. Bonner thought that Seth was very strong and that Seth's favoring one side over another was normal, and that Seth's flexion was good. He did not think that Seth would have difficulty walking. He said that his "fantasy" was that Seth would have absolutely no perceptible difficulties. He said that Susan Scheer was doing everything he himself would do, and that if he took on Seth as a patient, his work would be overlapping with what she was doing.

Naturally, I wanted to believe everything Charles Bonner said. I was buoyed by what I heard, and he immediately endeared himself to me with his positive outlook. Bonner also said that if Seth's feet developed okay, there would be no hip problems. That prediction helped me counteract the image the neurologist, Dr. Bresnan, had given the prior spring when he demonstrated what he imagined Seth's gait would be. Bonner's insights were the beginning step in my education about the body's structure. The childhood song about the ankle bone connecting to the knee bone, connected to the hip bone would take on greater meaning for me soon.

Bonner thought that Seth would follow his own distinct patterns, which would parallel normal patterns. The one thing that caused Bonner alarm was Seth's failure to realize when he was at risk of falling. Bonner believed that Seth's biggest teacher in the end would be gravity.

The prospect that Seth could be injured in a fall brought up the issue of helmets and protective headgear. The brochure for the company where we bought the bolster illustrated children in different kinds of headgear. By this time I knew that Seth's falling was due to his lack of a reflexive action to protect himself rather than the result of a lack of balance. The nagging theme of how much to protect him, when to intervene, when to leave him alone, raised its head once again. That was not the last time we thought about helmets.

How can I tell you now how prescient Charles Bonner's insights were? After years of practicing Yoga and other bodywork, and from what I have gleaned from the doctors who have worked with us over the last seven years, I am now aware of many things about the development of bones, the differences for all of us in our two sides of the body, and the master part that gravity plays in all our lives. But I didn't know then what I know now. I only reacted to the positive sense Bonner gave me, at least in the beginning.

The reality and the ordeal of being a first-time parent of a child with special needs induce paralysis and confusion. I've cried out so often the refrain, "if only I had known." Hindsight hits all of us at different times in our lives. With this particular kind of parenting challenge, the words take on new significance. Our children are diagnosed, but we aren't offered much besides the labels. If we only had access to more information and greater perspective, we could make wiser choices, if not more informed ones. Our relationships to the professional and medical communities are fostered in a narrow and dependent atmosphere. We don't trust ourselves to question, probe, challenge, and investigate. Parents have developmental stages just like children do. And for parents of special needs children, the stages are more complicated.

It had never occurred to me, for instance, that I should question whether or not Seth should be immunized. How could I have known to even ask such questions when Seth was getting his first diphtheria-pertussis-tetanus (DPT) shot? Years later, when I met other parents of children with developmental disabilities, I learned about the vast studies that discourage the immunization of children with any neurological anomalies.

Now, because I have read *A Shot in the Dark* by Harris L. Coulter and Barbara Loe Fisher, I know that in large field trials conducted by Britain's Medical Research Council to assess the efficacy of the pertussis vaccine in children from six to eighteen months old, children with any personal or family history of convulsions, epilepsy, hydrocephalus, mental defect, as well as any child who had been recently sick, were excluded. The authors and others have recommended that the pertussis vaccine be withheld from patients with any neurodevelopmental defect, because they are considered a high-risk group.

Coulter and Fisher report that in 1981 the National Childhood Encephalopathy Study conducted in Britain gave the following contraindications to pertussis vaccination: "a personal or family history of epilepsy or other neurological disorders, evidence of developmental neurological defects," and so on. Most doctors have been taught very little in medical school about reactions, contraindications, or the permanent neurological damage that can be caused by the pertussis vaccine. I remember the adage, "There are no answers, only the right questions." How does one begin formulating these questions? How many American parents are aware that their child could die or become brain damaged after a serious reaction to a DPT shot?

I was ushered out of the darkness by a guest on Oprah Winfrey's TV show. This woman's son had gone to the pediatrician a happy, healthy child and gotten a DPT shot. He began to have convulsions and seizures within hours of receiving the shot. The child is now permanently brain damaged, living part of each day on life-support systems, in and out of the hospital for treatments. Very few Americans know that some Western European countries have stopped recommending mass immunization with the pertussis vaccine because they have decided that the risk of vaccine damage is greater than the risks of catching the milder form of whooping cough that is prevalent in developed nations today. Certainly we should have been informed of the vaccine's potential hazard and controversy before Seth received the pertussis vaccine.

c~

Our knowledge about risks and options is limited by a powerful orthodox medical society that shields us from exposure to possibilities outside the conventional. But there is a huge alternative world out there that includes mainstream, sometimes nonorthodox, medicine, alternative therapies, as well as the practice of various Eastern disciplines such as massage, Yoga, acupuncture, and Ayurvedic medicine.

For instance, the *Reader's Digest Family Guide to Natural Medicine* says that Ayurvedic medicine, which arose in India at least 2,500 years ago, is considered the first organized approach to health care based on natural phenomena as opposed to magic and superstition. Its emphasis is on preventive health care. It prescribes an individually designed diet and a unique daily routine and activities that will help each individual maintain balance. Texts dating back several centuries attest to the skill of Ayurvedic practitioners in a variety of major and minor surgery procedures. Those familiar with traditional Chinese medicine can trace the lineage of pulse diagnosis and the importance of keeping energy forces in balance to Ayurvedic medicine.

The *Reader's Digest* guide points out that along with many other holistic health practices, Ayurvedic medicine contrasts sharply with the simple (and perhaps simplistic) cause-and-effect thinking of modern orthodox medicine known as allopathic medicine. For instance, the Indian medicine deals in an integrated way with body and mind. Although Ayurveda and Yoga come from the same ancient roots, they have for some time been considered distinct. Nowadays there is a trend toward bringing the two back together. Patients who learn specific Yoga postures, meditation, relaxation, and breathing are able to maintain their health and manage themselves using these tailor-made combinations.

The guide also suggests that the Ayurvedic philosophy of medicine may be an excellent integrating perspective for bringing together different holistic therapies. It is perhaps the oldest system in use today and easily accommodates therapies and treatments as diverse as Homeopathy, Osteopathy, antibiotics, surgery, nutrition, massage, meditation, and acupuncture.

But most of us are scared to seek out alternative treatments. What do we know compared to the experts and specialists? We want to do right by our children, to help them in every possible way. How can we go about discovering a method of thinking so that these alternatives are at least considered? We need to share information amongst ourselves. There are many networks for accessing information, but trying out one group or another may feel like just another thing to do, another responsibility.

Where does one start looking? Who has time? From my current vantage point I believe I have much to tell others about what I know. Yet I often find that when I offer my experience, my divergent view is not well received, even by parents who are searching for answers.

We have lots to do in our own lives as well as in the lives of our children. With Seth I didn't even have many of the problems that other parents have. He was not as impaired as many other children are. He wasn't terminally ill or hooked up to life-support systems.

He wouldn't need a wheelchair or other functional help (such as help with toileting). When he was still small we didn't have another child to worry and care about yet. I had much to be grateful for and much more time than others to explore.

And still I didn't do everything I could have. I wasn't in touch with United Cerebral Palsy, because I was still avoiding reality. I didn't spend all my spare time reading up on cerebral palsy or therapeutic responses. I hadn't written to any organizations or contacted any of the networking opportunities that existed.

Instead I kept thinking about how much I was doing. And I heard it from everybody else too. I can't count the number of times that other parents or friends or total strangers said something about what a good mother I was and how much I was doing for Seth, how lucky he was. I tried to demur and be graceful. After all, what else would I do?

As Pearl S. Buck writes so eloquently in *The Child Who Never Grew:*

> *Driven by the conviction that there must be someone who can cure, we take our children over the surface of the whole earth, seeking the one who can heal. We spend all the money we have and we borrow until there is no one else to lend. We go to doctors good and bad, to anyone, for only a wisp of hope. We are gouged by unscrupulous men who make money from our terror, but now and again we meet those saints who, seeing the terror and guessing the empty purse, will take nothing for their advice, since they cannot heal.*

Or even when they can, they refuse money from those who cannot really afford it. We eventually met healers who did this.

Growing up in China, Pearl S. Buck was exposed to people with many deformities and challenges. Chinese society openly accepted people as they were, believing that any affliction was part of one's destiny, ordained by heaven. Yet Ms. Buck hid her mentally impaired child from the world even as her own fame grew and more about this great writer's personal life became known. There was shame and embarrassment. People were cruel.

I have been a witness to this in Seth's life. By now he has more than a dim knowledge that he is not like others. He and I have learned a lexicon of responses when questions are put to one or both of us.

I recognize the unkind glances of others, their overt and implied ridicule, and I fear for my son. He is managing, although there are dimensions that have not yet been revealed and experiences yet to occur that we cannot yet imagine.

I always have to think about how lucky I am, too. There were professionals who were both accessible and affordable, and I had the good sense and an inclination to use them. I was fortunate to live in a city where there was a wealth of talent to choose from in the "alternative" world. I myself was the product of an upbringing that had offered fine education, and had fostered in me a belief that I could influence my circumstances. My husband was supportive and encouraging and continues to be. Although he needed reassurance, Jay still never got depressed or stopped being a helpmate.

Looking over all my notes and diary entries, I see that Charles Bonner's appointment with Seth occurred before Seth began wearing the inhibitory casts. We met with Dr. Kessler in early October, but his testing was not completed until the end of November. Meanwhile the two therapists, Susan and Phyllis, were keeping up the pressure on me to teach Seth sign language. I investigated other therapy settings. The information I gathered continued to be haphazard and conflicting. I talked extensively with someone at the Developmental Disabilities Clinic at Roosevelt Hospital where there was a school program. In the course of that conversation I was informed that the staff physiatrist was inalterably opposed to inhibitory shoes.

In the meantime, Seth visited Dr. Lee a few times because he had a persistent rash. At every visit she told me that Seth was gorgeous and that whatever I was doing was working wonderfully. I also took Seth to see Dr. Grant, the orthopedist, for a routine follow-up visit. Dr. Grant told me that Seth's neurological ability was improving, that he was making great strides, but that his hip cords and ankle cords were a little tight. He told me he thought that the anticipated inhibitory casts would help decrease tone, but that if the muscles were going to be tight, they'd remain tight anyway.

The doctor kept saying that the question we needed to ask was what we should do after the casts. (We hadn't even gotten the casts yet, but we were already having to be worried about what to do after them!) He said that we ought to be thinking about clear plastic braces since Seth would have to have braces for stability. He also kept saying that bone surgery was probable between the ages of four and eight, and that Seth would need to wear casts until his growth was complete, probably at fourteen.

Soon after this visit with Dr. Grant, we went for the tests at Dr. Kessler's clinic. Dr. Kessler's office was in an attic, but his clinic was in the basement of New York Hospital, and I noted in my diary that it was rather an unpleasant place. Seth was not thrilled to see Dr. Kessler, especially his white coat, so the doctor removed it right away. The staff wanted to weigh and measure Seth but, seeing Seth's anxiety, I discouraged them, and in the end they forgot all together.

The conclusion of the tests matched my instincts. Except for the gross motor achievements such as walking, Seth was considered "age appropriate," though he was on the "low" end of the sound-production scale. His cognitive and small motor achievements fell in the normal age range. The staff told us to relax and enjoy him, that he would absolutely be in the mainstream and would go to school with other "normal" children. They did observe, however, that Seth was an appealing child and how eager everyone was to eliminate frustration for him. They cautioned that we should let him be a little frustrated, that frustration stimulates learning.

The ramifications of their suggestion would thread their way through the rest of Seth's life, my life, and this book. Questions about when to intervene and when to leave well-enough alone occur on every level. Just seeing Seth struggle with his shoelaces makes me want to jump up and tie them for him. Just hearing a question put to him about why he talks the way he does, prompts me to answer.

By the end of 1984, eighteen-month-old Seth had seen two neurologists and was being treated by three physical therapists for a total of seven sessions per week. A pediatric orthopedic specialist was following him with routine visits and series of X-rays. A pediatric podiatrist was treating him, and he was wearing plaster inhibitory leg casts. A developmental disabilities expert, a hearing specialist, and a Feldenkrais teacher had all diagnosed him. He was going for routine pediatric checkups as well as visits for minor pediatric ailments.

It took me years to recognize the extraordinary number of people who were examining, handling, and diagnosing Seth. Together we

were on a voyage to heal, to cure, calling on all doctors, rehabilitators, spending our money, searching, searching each other and other's
experiences, looking into the faces of the healers and facilitators for
a glimpse of the future.

One big issue that loomed was one of speech versus sign language.
As Dr. Kessler explained to us, children at about eighteen months
begin to make logical connections between two ideas. Articulation
problems don't become a concern until three years of age. The question for us was whether sign language would give Seth greater independence? Children are capable of learning several languages. How
could it hurt him? Seth already seemed to have developed his own
sign language. How would this option affect his motivation?

Peggy Smith always remarked how wonderful Seth's motivation
was. She said that he had no perceptual deficit and a strong automatic desire to use both hands together despite the disability. As his
occupational therapist, she was pleased with the changes in Seth's
shoulders, where he was initially very sensitive around the neck.
She thought his hands would change, although it would take time
because he was beginning to sit up. She had complete confidence in
him.

When she, or others, used words and phrases such as "perceptual
deficit," it was hard for me to ask what she meant. It's part of my
personality not to want to seem ignorant. But I was ignorant. In this
case, she was referring to a deficit in visual perception, not the ability
to connect two ideas.

The question of intervening, of either helping Seth or allowing
him to remain frustrated, seemed part of the equation in the dilemma
about signing. If we taught him sign language, would he ever learn
to talk, or would we have eliminated a motivating frustration? Dr.
Kessler, whom I trusted so much, supported Phyllis the speech therapist, while Dr. Lee and Jay were opposed to the sign language. I
called Dr. Madell at the New York League for the Hard of Hearing,
and she, too, was opposed to the signing.

We entered January 1985 with a full appointment book and an
immense mixture of anxiety and hope, two emotions that seem to
go together in all our experiences with Seth. They are joined to pride
and joy these days, but the anxiety and hope are never absent, the

fingers of these two powerful emotions endlessly intertwined with each other.

During a routine visit to Dr. Price, the podiatrist, we learned that the tone in Seth's legs was "dramatically reduced," and that he was standing beautifully. Dr. Price built up the inhibitory casts so they fit better. We went back for a reevaluation at Dr. Kessler's clinic in March. The report was good. Although Seth continued to have some difficulties in gross motor function, there had been marked improvement in recent months.

In the personal-social area, Seth was capable of imitating housework, was able to remove at least one garment, but he was still unable to put on any items of clothing. Dressing him was very frustrating for me at this time. Mayra took over during the week, and I tried to grow into it on the weekends, but often I left it to Jay, who continues to be his fashion consultant-valet to this day. Seth could scribble spontaneously, build a tower of two cubes, and was capable of dumping a raisin from two bottles simultaneously. He was functioning near an age-appropriate level. His vocabulary consisted of approximately thirty words, and he was capable of expressing two wants.

It was less than a year after the initial diagnosis, and I was confident and hopeful some days and nervous on others. I still didn't know what to expect. Seth wasn't walking, so I knew I couldn't consider a conventional kindergarten. A long-time member of the Health and Fitness Center at the 92nd Street Y, I was aware of parents coming and going on the elevators to the nursery school three floors above the gym. There were certain weeks during the year when the school conducted interviews of prospective candidates for this much sought after school and parents would be weighing their children's options for kindergarten after "graduating." I overheard the anxious talk of mothers, mostly as they contemplated aloud the odds for their children being accepted into the program.

Dual emotions snaked through me while I listened to such talk. My perspective on the priorities of life was shifting. While these parents worried about the status of their children's early education, I was thinking about whether Seth would ever walk at all. Repeatedly, I was reminded that my agenda was different from theirs.

Surprisingly, I was also relieved. At least I was spared the excruci-ating anxiety over the position and rank of Seth's schools. He had cerebral palsy. What I was looking for had nothing to do with pres-tige or reputation. Of course, years later when our daughter, Haya, was getting ready for kindergarten, my thinking changed once again.

Then in April an unforeseen circumstance inaugurated a new phase in Seth's care. The events of the next six months had more to do with me than with Seth, but ultimately the course of all our lives was changed.

new horizons

OVER THE YEARS I HAD HAD BACK PAIN, but for five years it got worse. It was unbearable. I tried everything. Always active, swimming, practicing Yoga, dancing, I was open to any path to fitness, but nothing seemed to relieve my discomfort.

During a difficult episode, one of the women at my gym had recommended a group of physical therapists where I initially met Annie Black. When Seth was diagnosed, I had turned to her for resources, and she was a great help. Annie had a good touch, and we had talked often during my sessions with her. She described a wide gamut of physical rehabilitation methods that interested her.

She talked about CranioSacral therapy, the Feldenkrais method, and other unconventional methods. She wasn't encouraged to use these alternatives in the group practice, but she described them. I listened a little. Then I began listening a little more. I recognize the resistance most of the medical establishment had to the kind of therapies Annie was describing. I was resistant myself.

Annie's work helped, but I got to the point where I could no longer get comfortable, and I was always in pain, sharp pain. Annie wanted me to try Robbie Ofir, a therapist who was a Feldenkrais practitioner as well as a physical therapist. She had met him the summer before when both of them were participating in a Feldenkrais "training" in Canada. He could come to my house. She thought I should give him a try because I wasn't getting better. Her insistence about the benefits of the Feldenkrais method had led me to take Seth to Charles Bonner the previous fall. She often mentioned a Feldenkrais practitioner, a woman named Anat Baniel, and wished out loud that Anat were available to see Seth.

In her book *The Magic of Touch,* Sherry Suib Cohen, discussing the Feldenkrais method, reports that the violinist Yehudi Menuhin, the theatrical director Peter Brook, the anthropologist Margaret Mead,

Karl Pribram, director of the Neuropsychology Laboratories of Stanford University, and even the basketball star Dr. J—Julius Irving—have revered Feldenkrais and his methods. The Feldenkrais method is an almost impossible to describe neuromuscular education and reorganization program designed to promote better posture through self-awareness of stance and movement.

Moshe Feldenkrais was a Russian-born Israeli scientist with a black belt in Judo, (the first European to hold the black belt), an electrical and mechanical engineer, and a mathematician. He also worked as a researcher on the French atomic bomb program. Having watched his videotapes and encountered his students and disciples, I believe he must have been a difficult, contentious person. Be that as it may, he believed that one can break age-old self-destructive patterns of movement, influence the brain to change hurtful body movements, and improve one's quality of life and functioning through body movement awareness and skill. Feldenkrais believed that the emotional and nervous systems can be "taught" to heal the physical person. This process is known as "sensory reeducation."

All of these ends are accomplished with special exercises that reorganize and stimulate parts of the brain and initiate new learning. Students learn from their own sensorimotor experience by using the process of "childhood organic learning." Learning comes from doing and is greatly dependent on the unconscious functioning of the nervous system. Learning itself is seen as a powerful therapeutic and self-actualizing force.

The Feldenkrais method is an educational system, not a therapeutic system. The exercises are designed to improve function rather than correct it. Learning is engendered not through moving, but through awareness of the *process* of moving. Feldenkrais believed that nervous structures look for order, that movement is the most efficient means for achieving this order in the mobile, changing world. Repetition is necessary to facilitate learning.

There are two aspects to the learning. One phase is known as functional integration. It is accomplished by a one-on-one relationship between the therapist and the student. The therapist gets the student to repeat ordered, prescribed body movements and manipulations, using his or her hands to skillfully influence, pace, and suggest possibilities to the student. Specific exercises open the nervous system to new potential. An intimate relationship develops, similar to the one between a physical therapist and patient. The technique is basically nonverbal and hands-on, geared to those students requiring individual attention.

The other aspect to the learning, taught in groups, is called Awareness through Movement (ATM). ATM is a learning process that makes self-direction easier. In both methods the student *learns to learn* how to attend to his or her particular movements with greater awareness. The student learns to refine the details of his or her actions.

Eventually, I benefited from both aspects of the teaching. I discovered old habits and explored previously unused muscles and patterns of movement, and in the process I developed greater balance, more control.

Robbie Ofir, the Feldenkrais practitioner/physical therapist Annie recommended, came to see me in early March. Amused, he watched me as I demonstrated various positions I had learned over the years for relieving my back pain. I showed him the movements that bothered me now. Then he asked me to lie on my back and close my eyes. He gently, very gently, manipulated my head and then my legs in small, imperceptible ways. Maybe I breathed more deeply. I know that when I got up after the treatment, I felt changed.

A new therapist was now added to the parade, except this one was for me. I scheduled Robbie's treatments on the afternoons when Seth wasn't having his sessions. From the beginning Robbie was interested in Seth, his diagnosis and his current prognosis. Robbie encouraged me to read the Feldenkrais literature and bragged about the incredible success Feldenkrais had had with children with cerebral palsy.

One especially well known book in Feldenkrais circles is *The Case of Nora,* about the challenging case of a young girl whom Feldenkrais had treated. I read this book and saw videotapes of Feldenkrais working with children. These tapes eventually persuaded me to teach Seth how to ride a horse. But more on that later.

Like Annie Black, Robbie also spoke often about Anat Baniel, Mr. Feldenkrais's protégé, an Israeli woman known for her exceptional talent for rehabilitating children. Before his death, Moshe Feldenkrais had led many large seminars and demonstrations all over the world, and Anat, then a young woman, had assisted him. She was his last

personal disciple and pupil, and apparently Feldenkrais had passed
on much of his knowledge to Anat before he died.

Anat was at the forefront of the Feldenkrais Trainings that were
currently being offered throughout the world. The seminars were
lengthy, sometimes running for six weeks, and were held several
times a year. It took over three to four years to train in the Feldenkrais
work. Up until the 1970s only thirteen people had been trained to
practice functional integration. Then in 1975 Feldenkrais accepted
an invitation to establish a three-year training program in San Fran-
cisco for some sixty-five students. With the completion of the program, the Feldenkrais Guild was formed, representing the more than
seventy-five people then capable of practicing functional integration.

The Feldenkrais therapy was very helpful to me. I was always
better after the treatments. Not only was I without pain immediately
following the sessions, I was acquiring a new sense of my physical
self. I was gaining awareness of my breathing and patterns of movement, and this influenced how I felt. But I was impatient. In the long
term I felt frustrated by my back's limitations and discouraged that
the pain recurred when I engaged in my regular daily routines.

Robbie wanted me to give things more time. He began treating
me in March, but by early April I was restless and eager to resume
my old activities. My quest for a "fix" urged me to seek help within
the "establishment." On the recommendation of my personal physician, I consulted an orthopedic surgeon. After a CAT scan and examination, the doctor recommended that I have a spinal fusion. In April
I went into the hospital to have my third and fourth lumbar vertebrae fused. This was a very serious surgery, and in my typical way I
didn't ask many questions. It seems remarkable that I passed through
this momentous surgery with no idea of its importance. I was in the
hospital almost four weeks. Again, I wish I'd known there were other
alternatives to the surgery. But I didn't. I still believed in the
Feldenkrais work, however, and wanted to integrate it into my
rehabilitation.

Seth was going to be two years old in June, and he was wearing the
casts on his legs most of the time during the day. He loved the fact
that they allowed him to stand with some apparent stability, although

not independently. He would stand next to something like his crib or a table, where he could hold on, grinning widely, thrilled by his vertical stance.

He did, however, prefer his sneakers for crawling. He would loudly insist upon wearing his Keds or his L.A. Gear sneakers if we were going to be anywhere that didn't have apparatus to help him stand. In February, when Dr. Price built up the inhibitory casts so they fit better, he also fit Seth for an orthotic, which Seth could wear in his sneakers while crawling. Dr. Price believed that Seth would need to wear the casts until he was "cruising." "Cruising" describes what children do when they are beginning to walk and need to "cruise" from one support to another until they are more secure. Cruising was something Seth never did.

We were still struggling with the issue of Seth's speech and whether to teach him sign language. We took Seth for a reevaluation with Dr. Kessler, the developmental disabilities expert. Dr. Kessler and his staff were impressed and encouraged by Seth's progress. They reiterated that he seemed "age appropriate" except for his motor skills. As far as Seth's speech was concerned, they thought he was following the normal development of a child who combines gestures prior to speech. They didn't push the sign language.

We were relieved to hear everything the experts had to say, since, as you can imagine, every appointment for Seth was loaded with anxiety for us. The outcome dictated our mood and outlook. At that juncture I felt relieved about the prospect of not having to keep Seth in a bubble. I hoped for normalcy. Of course, over time I learned that normalcy had many different hues and shades.

⁓

In the interim, my back situation absorbed me. I left the hospital at the end of April and immediately resumed the Feldenkrais sessions with Robbie Ofir. He came to the house twice a week. He continued to have an ongoing interest in Seth and often wanted to see him when he came to treat me. Just after surgery I was very limited in my activities, although this did not in any way affect my therapy. There was residual pain from the surgery, but after my sessions I felt completely comfortable and at ease. I was learning a great deal about myself.

Does it sound fatuous to describe getting in touch with my breathing, my capacity to concentrate and differentiate small movements so that when I lifted a glass of water to my mouth, I learned not to lift my shoulders too? I was increasingly aware of the power of touch, of the effects of one person's hands on me with a "light" but significant pressure. I began listening to Robbie when he said how much this Feldenkrais work could help Seth. I began thinking about touching Seth myself.

We took Seth to see Dr. Grant, the pediatric orthopedist, in June. Seth was almost two years old and long overdue for X-rays. The doctor thought the left "boot," the plaster cast, was taking on the shape of Seth's foot, but he also thought that Seth's hips looked better than they had a year earlier. He observed that Seth was making strides with "balancing reactions," which was important because stability is essential, especially at the beginning of walking. He repeated the questions about inhibitory casts and whether they eliminate the need for surgery later. He mentioned the clear plastic braces again. He asked us to consider a future operation to cut the Achilles tendons on Seth's feet.

Then Dr. Grant said something that has continued to resonate through my entire experience with Seth, especially in recent years. He emphasized that the twenty-one-year-olds, and the young adults he has treated, whether they walked or not, had told him that they valued speech and upper-extremity dexterity and ability more than anything else. Today his words echo significantly as I witness the difficulty in Seth's fine motor skills.

At the time I didn't know if he was indirectly addressing our conundrum about Seth's speech. Now I understand the truth of his message fully. Today Seth's frustrations center on his inability to easily execute fine motor tasks like buttoning his clothes, tying his shoes, cutting his food, using a key. Seth's speech and fine motor difficulties present the most significant challenges. But I wasn't able to imagine what Grant meant at the time. I was only worried about whether Seth would walk independently.

Peggy Smith and Susan Scheer both wrote reports about Seth during this time. I asked Peggy to describe to me how she saw Seth.

"Oh, he's wonderful," she said. "So bright and attentive. He has real self-motivation. Self-direction. You are very lucky he is so bright. I expect his own motivation will see him through wonderfully."

"But will he do everything other children can do?" I asked her, as I asked everyone constantly, as I asked myself invariably. "I mean, will he be like other children? I mean, I know, not exactly. I know all children are different, but will he seem different in a major way?" I was holding my breath.

She said, "We are doing many tasks designed to develop motor coordination skills, and he's come a long way."

But I saw there was still extreme deviation on the left side of Seth's body. He held his left arm, left hand, left shoulder, left leg, and left side of his trunk differently than the right side of his body. The actions on the left side of his body were less precise and more spastic.

When he played, he needed to stabilize his shoulders and trunk for building with blocks or fitting the pieces of a puzzle together. The increased tone in his neck decreased his ability to vocalize. The volume of his voice diminished. Any major effort for Seth put a strain on his lungpower, on his diaphragm.

We could see that while playing rudimentary games like tossing the ball he was tense through the neck where the vocal cords reside. He drooled excessively. While he worked to remain stable and upright, even when doing simple tasks like pushing a small toy, the tension in his upper trunk put further strain on his body. We could see the exertion on his face by the involuntary actions around his nose and mouth. He made funny expressions like a little chipmunk, but of course they weren't deliberate.

Most important to us were his diminished body-righting reactions. The slightest jarring or unfamiliar noise would cause him to fall over. We were constantly worried about this, and it became a greater concern when he started his schooling. Playgrounds can be dangerous places. I knew that helmets were often a consideration for children with cerebral palsy.

Years later the extent of the threat of this problem was graphically illustrated one evening when we were standing on a corner in the West Village with pizza to take home for dinner from our favorite New York pizza parlor. I was holding the boxes, and Seth was standing beside me on the curb while we tried to get a taxi. It was dusk. Suddenly a mammoth truck passed by and honked its horn. Seth fell right over, completely prone, onto the street. The loudness and suddenness of the noise had caused him to lose his balance.

Peggy wrote in her report that Seth had good basic perceptual awareness and had shown a tremendous increase in tolerance over the last weeks. He was more willing to allow Peggy to handle him. She said that he possessed a wonderful memory, especially when it came to their created play. Seth was beginning to "bunny hop" crawl; whereas up until then he had only "commando" crawled. The focus of the therapy was to change his motor patterns and alignment and to develop motor control that supported skill acquisition.

Seth demonstrated continued improvement in most areas of gross motor development. He was able to sit up on the floor by himself. Unfortunately, he preferred *W* sitting, which means sitting with the knees forward along the floor in front of the trunk and the feet behind the buttocks. Although the *W* sitting allowed him the greatest degree of trunk stability and freed his arms for play, it reinforced the already strong abnormal pattern of his hips and feet. I heard myself and others—Mayra, Jay, the therapists—say, "Seth, don't sit like that." I still hear myself issue this order to this day.

By summer Seth was creeping independently on both hands and knees as his primary mode of locomotion. During creeping, his left hand often remained in a tight fist; while the right-hand fingers were only slightly flexed, but flexed nonetheless. He was also "kneel standing." He was beginning to kneel walk, a mode of ambulating that would see us through the next few years. (We never could use his pants for hand-me-downs; they were always worn out in the knees.)

∽

The summer of 1985 brought a significant demarcation, however. The Feldenkrais work was becoming a powerful influence for me, and I embarked on two explorations that changed me even more. I met and began working with Carola Speads, and in June I enrolled in a seminar with Anat Baniel.

When I had first taken Seth to consult with Charles Bonner the previous fall, Bonner had mentioned Carola Speads. Carola was a woman in her late eighties who taught "Physical Reeducation and

Movement" on the Upper West Side of Manhattan. Born in Germany, Carola had begun her professional career in Berlin, where she later had her own school. Carola had taught for many years with the pioneering movement teacher Elsa Gindler. Since 1940, Carola had been teaching her techniques to groups and individuals in New York and in workshops throughout Europe and the United States. The benefits of Carola's instruction program of gentle exercises, or "experiments," as she called them, were incalculable.

Singers, dancers, other performing artists, bodyworkers, psychoanalysts and their patients, victims of multiple sclerosis, asthma, arthritis, among others, were her students. She had worked in the fifties with Fritz Perls, the psychoanalyst, and she considered physical reeducation to be like psychoanalysis: you had to live through it. Like Feldenkrais, she believed that the emotional life and the physical life of a person could not be separated and were greatly influenced by the nervous system. Whereas in the Feldenkrais method the work was accomplished with exercises and through one-on-one contact; Carola's work was accomplished by breathing.

Breathing! Admittedly, I was skeptical, but I was in the mood to explore. My surgery had confined me to home, and I had more time on my hands than usual. I was wearing a large plastic brace, which surrounded my entire torso. I couldn't sit comfortably, which is typical for people who suffer back pain, and it was a condition I wanted to remedy as soon as possible. I recalled Charles Bonner responding to my concerns about Seth's sitting by mentioning Carola and some of her techniques.

Jay, Seth, and I would be spending most of the summer on Cape Cod, and Mayra was going with us. I was concerned about my progress and Seth's development. Before we departed I wanted to investigate some of what I had been hearing about. At the same time, I was aware of how dependent we were on others. I wanted to expand my role in Seth's rehabilitation, to be more directly, more differently, involved with Seth's care and to be more in charge. Although my new self was still unformed, I was getting in touch with a new dimension inside.

Robbie Ofir also knew about Carola Speads. He had read her book, *Breathing: the ABC's* (now titled *Ways to Better Breathing*) and was curious for me to find out more. During the summer, Robbie was

planning to participate in the last session of a Feldenkrais training
in Canada as part of his official Feldenkrais certification. Susan Scheer
had planned a vacation, and both Peggy and Phyllis would not be as
available during the summer months. My anxiety about being on
my own propelled me to act. I called Charles to get Carola's address.
It turned out that her classes were being held near our New York
apartment.

Nothing in my experience prepared me for Carola and the environment of her teaching. In my high-powered, fast-track, super dis-
ciplined life, I never imagined that in the middle of the day, in the
middle of New York City, in a light, airy apartment, anywhere from
ten to twenty people could be assembled for "experiments" in
breathing. The students constituted almost a new breed of people
who placed an emphasis on themselves that was new to me.

There was Carola sitting lithely on the windowsill. Piled in the
corner of the room was a collection of mats, poles, juggling pins,
balls, wooden hoops, straws, Japanese tappers, and rolling pins. Every
"lesson" would begin with Carola saying, "Now, be very open-minded.
Let the changes come through."

Over the years I became a serious student of Carola's. I grew aware
of the quality of my breathing, the state of my inadequate respiration. I achieved an increase in circulation, a lessening of tension, and
I realized the "manifold interdependencies between breathing and
the various organs of the body." But that evolution took time and
many classes over many years. Later I even went to class twice a
week. For the time being, however, I benefited from a half-dozen
lessons before we went away for the summer.

I was completely unaware that opportunities for self-discovery in
both the mental and physical realms even existed in this context.
This unfolding took place within and without. I felt different after
each class, although it took me time to develop the patience and concentration for the work. There were a variety of sensations related
to breathing in the experiments. I recognized my "unawareness" of
my poor breathing.

My back pain began disappearing even though I was sitting for
long periods on the floor. There were no set routines because breathing
is so individual. But through the experiments I began to see an

immense variety of approaches to successful breathing. I learned the importance of breathing and how it is part of the religions of many diverse cultures. I realized that among my own ancestors, the Hebrews, the word for "wind," or "breath," was the same as the word for "soul."

The other significant event at this time was that Anat Baniel was visiting New York from the West Coast. She was teaching a two-week seminar for people unfamiliar with Awareness through Movement (ATM). I knew I had to go. Again my eyes were opened wide to another universe. In a large room, during ten early-summer evenings, up to 250 people gathered to try the movements Anat directed.

We began by lying on the floor, eyes closed, doing a body scan. How did each part of our bodies feel? the skull? the rib cage? the shoulders? spine? pelvis? legs? arms? We initiated a range of motions. We did head rolls and eye rolls. We did arm circles. We lay on our stomachs. We lay on our backs and sides. We moved with our legs, hips, feet. We stood, walked, bent, swayed.

How many of us feel our feet on the floor, how our toes are resting when we stand? Even in this moment as you read my words or I write them, do either of us have any sense of our breathing, where our sit bones are placed, how our sternum is positioned? Too New Age? Try again.

Are we breathing into our side ribs? Are our shoulders resting on our torsos? When we reach for the telephone, step on the escalator, answer the door, are we breathing? Can we feel ourselves? Are our legs really under us when we stand? Where is our head and chin?

My awareness grew. My body was different, though not entirely comfortable. I often felt—and sometimes still do after intense sessions of any kind of bodywork—as if I was wearing new clothes that didn't quite fit.

The few classes I'd taken with Carola that spring and Anat's seminar revealed a radically different range of possibilities. It never occurred to me that there were so many people involved in these studies. I felt I was part of a new culture, exploring new terrain. I was making new contacts, new friends. I was in a fantastic new orbit of experience. Seth's cerebral palsy and my recent surgery were measured and received in an unprecedented manner. We left for the

Cape as I was awakening to this new world. I was committed to use the little I had already learned. And I felt I wanted to experiment with Seth and see whether I could help him as well as myself.

Seth was in his casts all summer, and I was in my brace. I tried to practice daily a little of what I had learned from Carola's few classes, what I had gleaned during my seminar with Anat, and what I had been learning in my sessions with Robbie. I made great strides in my rehabilitation. I was healing very fast. By early July, only eight weeks after the surgery, I was able to swim small distances in the ocean. I was walking on the beach, began driving again, and took up most daily routines quite freely. When I went to the surgeon for my checkup, he was genuinely amazed by my progress.

Mayra, Jay, and I were vigilant with Seth all summer. We encouraged the movements Susan and Peggy had taught us. We created play that invited him to develop more motor control. On the beach I had Mayra bring buckets and sand toys. She helped me haul buckets of water, which I encouraged him to dump on the dry sand and then pat the wet sand into shapes. I could see his fingers working, especially the ones on his left hand, which were always held so tightly. On rainy days I made cookie dough, and he helped me roll it out. Together we cut out the cookie shapes. These activities encouraged him to coordinate hand and eye movements.

Mayra and I constantly intervened when we observed him *W* sitting. I initiated small touches, and he liked them. On the beach, while he was barefoot, I played with his toes and the soles of his feet. I rubbed his hands gently in the sand. If he was lying on his back at any time, I played with him to mimic the movements we had tried in Anat's seminar. "Let's roll from side to side, Seth. Let's shake our legs in the air. We'll lie on our tummies and crawl like animals; turn our heads from side to side looking for our prey. We can roll our eyes all different ways. Touch our left foot with our right hand and our right foot with our left hand. Breathe, sweetheart, breathe. Don't hold your breath."

Whenever I could, I touched him around his diaphragm and rib cage as I had learned to touch myself in Carola's lessons. I easily observed the changes in his respiration and the increased ease and softness that occurred in his body when I touched him in this way. I began looking at him differently. The little I had already learned helped me assess him and react to him with entirely new responses, new awareness—*new eyes.*

ᐟᐧᐧ

In September, when we returned to New York, Seth could still barely pull himself up to stand. His legs were not capable of bearing his weight without help from his arms. He could be helped into standing from half-kneeling, and he could be placed in a half-kneeling position, but he could not assume the position himself. He was able to kneel walk, but his balance and tone were very poor. When he stood without the inhibitory boots or without the shoes with orthotic devices, his pelvis locked, and he showed excessive hip and knee extension. There was terrible rotation of his ankles inward and downward; while at the same time he was "fixing" in the shoulders; they were taut and rigid. He had no balance. I was appalled.

Seth's upper body was well developed, but his left hand lacked discrete control, and his shoulders were often involved in keeping him stabilized. We noticed that his drooling was even more extreme, and it was more pronounced when he tried harder at new things that were difficult. He had many more words, but he was still frustrated when he was unable to communicate his wants and needs. Nevertheless, he demonstrated above-average receptivity to language.

As explained in *Children with Disabilities* by Mark L. Batshaw and Yvonne M. Perret, if speech is the act of producing words, language implies having something to say. A usual consequence of early brain damage is a developmental delay in language, rather than a language disorder. Children with a "receptive language disorder" have difficulty understanding what they hear; it's not that they can't hear. When there is a receptive language disorder, there are also accompanying cognitive deficits, problems with social interactions, and a lot of difficulty with communication skills. Fortunately, we were not encountering any of this in Seth.

We were thinking about expanding Seth's environments and started to explore play school or preschool settings. This new step presented real challenges in our emotional life. We faced a new reality, new concerns, and new fears. Seth was over two years old and still was not walking.

A year earlier, in September, Susan Scheer had encouraged us to find "socializing" environments for Seth. She wanted a teacher or trained professional involved to encourage his cognitive skills, to help him learn how to influence his environment. Looking back, I think she probably had so much hope for Seth, such confidence in Seth, and was so excited by the possibilities of his development that she was pushing ahead prematurely.

Susan had asked me to explore a preschool setting called Basic Trust. The school focused on bringing the child into the mainstream. Jay and I went to look at it. Basic Trust consisted of two large rooms with bars on the windows in the basement of a rundown brownstone on the West Side of Manhattan. It wasn't at all what we had in our minds or in our dreams for our firstborn child. We decided our own time with him, the ongoing care Mayra provided, and getting him to the park where there were other children was enough for the moment. I also looked into Red Yellow Blue & Glue, an art program at the 92nd Street Y, but he was still too young. We waited.

New York City is a unique place. The competition and drive that exists in the City is so great, so all-encompassing, that it is easy to lose perspective. Parents of two- and three-year-olds are well into the quest for the best preschools that will move their children into the best nursery schools that will ensure the children entrance into the best elementary schools and so on to college. I admit I was relieved to miss this experience, *for the time being.* Later I got caught. For the moment I kept a quiet distance whenever those discussions occurred, which was often. My thoughts still centered on whether my child was going to walk, or even go to school with other "normal" children.

Seth was over two years old and couldn't walk or stand independently. Many of his upper-body movements were unusual or not well accomplished. He always needed someone with him. He was toilet trained, but he needed assistance with his clothes. He ate independently, for the most part, using regular utensils and glasses, but his motions were more than clumsy. Aside from involuntary action, he could not handle many aspects of feeding. Dressing and undressing, toileting, eating, these were the daily routines for which he required constant help.

We needed a place where the presence of someone else with him all day would be accepted. We didn't want to underscore his differences by sending him to a place where he alone would have a caregiver. We were confident that he would ultimately learn to walk, but in the meantime he was still in his stroller. We never used the word "wheelchair," but his stroller functioned much like one. He was getting too big to carry, and the casts were a factor as well. We were facing our son's disability with new perspective.

We were interested in a Jewish school, so we went to talk to the director of the nursery program at our synagogue. It made the most sense to explore possible alternatives for Seth within our own faith. The school had a very fine reputation. I remember the interview well. We toured the facility, which was large and impressive and housed many classes. We described Seth's limitations, and the director asked us why we didn't consider a wheelchair. I was mute. My son was going to walk one day, maybe not normally, but independently. We decided to wait on nursery school.

In the meantime, I returned to Carola's classes and resumed my therapy with Robbie Ofir. My brace was removed, months earlier than expected. The progress of my rehabilitation produced great awe in my surgeon's office. After I told him about my course of therapy, though, his reaction was different. As soon as I began explaining Carola and the Feldenkrais work, his eyes glazed over. The response of Dr. Lee, Seth's pediatrician, some time later, was even more extreme. She called the treatment "witchcraft."

Every visit to Dr. Lee began and ended the same way. Seth and I arrived, either for a routine checkup or for a visit for a minor sore throat or ear infection or some kind of baby rash. Dr. Lee oohed and ahhed over Seth. He was so handsome. He was so sweet. He had such a wonderful smile. I was such a wonderful mother. I was doing so much for him. It was so amazing. I was the apotheosis of the devoted, searching mother. My actual response to Dr. Lee and everyone else was always the same. I was doing what any mother would do. I was lucky. I was hopeful. I declined admiration, remaining incredulous that any parent wouldn't do as I was doing.

We visited Dr. Kessler during September. One of my new concerns was how much Seth overheard our discussions about him, especially when Susan or Peggy or Phyllis came for his sessions. While arriving or leaving, they sometimes wanted to talk, and I wanted to hear their spontaneous reactions. But I was unsure.

On the one hand, I didn't want Seth to feel that we had things to say that he shouldn't hear, but, on the other hand, I thought that some conversations should take place without him around. I worried about conversations he overheard between Mayra and the therapists, too. Mayra was young, and though she loved Seth, Seth loved her, and we loved her and valued her enormously, she didn't have the discretion I knew was needed in these circumstances. I wanted professional guidance on how to handle the professionals. I wanted insight about how to protect my child.

I was becoming a juggler and tightrope walker, trying to handle Seth's disability and the legions of professionals involved with it. I was sorting and sifting advice and input, managing the feelings of everyone around me, especially my husband's and son's, but also my family's and helpers'. I was learning to be political. I was trusting my intuitions and not searching out more empirical information, but I was also tuning in to new possible treatments as a result of the bodywork I was doing for myself.

As I pursued the Feldenkrais work and studied once a week with Carola Speads, I couldn't ignore the remarkable change in my body, in my physical self. I had to acknowledge the value in the work. As September moved into October, I felt more and more that Seth's progress was stymied, that maybe I should be thinking differently about his care. He was still wearing the casts. His therapy sessions continued, but I saw few changes. The routine was comfortable and safe, which was reassuring, but I was nervous.

Robbie's and Annie's words, my visit with Charles Bonner, my own experience haunted me. I was primed to plunge into something new when the opportunity presented itself. In mid-October Robbie told me that Anat Baniel was coming to New York to live and work.

CHAPTER SIX

the plunge

JAY URGED CAUTION, BUT I JUMPED to connect with Anat. Jay was open-minded but more prudent in his enthusiasm than I was. I was already benefiting from firsthand experience both in the hands of Robbie and from Anat's seminar in June. My mind was also filled with possibilities that I was gleaning from my work with Carola. It is true that I am not Seth. The source of my difficulties was not totally rooted in my nervous system, although they became embedded there. But my experiences showed me there were possibilities for Seth here too.

Because of my relationships with Robbie Ofir and Annie Black, I had met Anat personally during her seminar the prior June. She was quite intimidating, a real star. She is Israeli. Her style is provocative, testy. My own professional life was centered in a celebrity world, but Anat was like no other luminary I had ever met. She possessed confidence and exuded presence only people who are completely comfortable and secure physically, mentally, and professionally have. She is striking, with beautiful cascading auburn hair and the lithe body of a dancer. She moves with more ease than anyone I've ever known. She is commanding before a large crowd, very charismatic.

The nature of Jay's and my work meant we were often in the company of movie stars or famous writers. I was traveling every few weeks to my apartment in Los Angeles, and this also attracted Anat to me. In June we had spoken about Seth only in passing. But she was aware of him. Like many people, she was more concentrated on what seemed like my glamorous life.

Jay and I together project a dynamic aura. There is glamour and style about us because of his entertainment practice and my history as an independent producer. But when it came to our son, his struggles and his difficulties, we were innocents and did not feel as capable as we may have seemed. The difference between our public persona

and our private one was huge. Bridging this void, using our promi-
nence to attract and maintain what we required socially or for business yet remaining involved in the actual needs of our son, was and
is a major challenge. We were always trying to bridge the gap between
what we could make happen in the world of Broadway and Hollywood and what we could not make happen for Seth.

Our circumstances played out with Anat on a big stage. We wanted
her to be drawn to us, and knew that our social connections would
accomplish this. At the same time, we wanted her to recognize us
as ordinary parents desperate to do whatever we could to help our
child.

Anat was using another therapist's office on the West Side of Manhattan. We played phone tag for some time before I finally reached
her. We talked at length about Seth. I knew my participation in the
June seminar was a plus. It demonstrated my serious intentions, and
Anat is a serious person. I told her everything we were doing for
Seth. I described the other therapists, Susan, Peggy, and Phyllis, and
their work. I described the casts. She asked me many direct, pertinent questions. She wanted to know only a little about the birth history and about the neurological diagnoses. I told her about the hearing
test, his eyesight, his intelligence.

When Anat finished asking all her questions, she said, "You'll
have to let everyone else go." I was flabbergasted. "And you'll have
to throw away the casts. He will never learn to walk as long as he
wears them."

Now I was speechless. She hadn't even seen him! This assessment
had taken place by telephone. I made an appointment to bring Seth
to see her.

Why did Anat insist on the disposal of the casts when Charles and
Robbie hadn't? Because Anat knew more than anyone else and was
sure enough of herself and her facts to act on them. Anat taught the
teachers. She was at the forefront of the training of new and old
Feldenkrais practitioners. She was generally acknowledged as one
of the therapy's greatest practitioners and as Feldenkrais' heir. And
she was known to be just as difficult and ornery as he had been.

I tempered my nervousness about her for Jay's sake. I wanted us
to go to the first appointment with open minds. I told him about the

phone conversation, but I was casual. Nothing was written in stone. We were exploring. We were both anxious about Seth. He was two and a half, beautiful, bright, good-natured, and we doted on him, but he was not walking.

Anat's office was difficult to locate in the labyrinth of a large apartment complex. As we wandered around, I became anxious and frustrated. I didn't want to be late. I knew from the June training that Anat could be late but we couldn't—a carryover of Mr. Feldenkrais's style. Many of the practitioners I met who were students/disciples of Feldenkrais maintained testy, contentious personas. We arrived not a moment too soon at Anat's office. There were two rooms, a small reception room and a very large studio that contained a therapy table, a giant ball, and a huge potted plant. Wonderful big windows made everything bright and airy, but the room was stark, all business.

Anat removed Seth's casts immediately. She said she wanted him to go barefoot as much as possible. The walker was an absolute no-no. She rolled Seth around on the floor, playfully, but with purpose. She picked him up by the back of the neck. She dangled him from his ankles. She put him on the table on his back, rotating his hips, feet, and arms. Seth complained loudly during the session. This was work, not play. The session reminded me a lot of what Peggy, the occupational therapist, did with him, but there was new content.

Without fanfare or speeches, when she was done, Anat laid out her treatment plan. Seth was to come to see her three times a week. No casts. We were to pay for all three sessions, at ninety dollars each, every week, at the time of the third session. Payment was expected whether Seth attended or not. Except for a death in the immediate family, she expected him to appear. Mayra could bring him to the sessions, but she had to remain outside, and Anat wanted to speak to Jay or me at least once a week. In order to be reimbursed by the insurance company, we needed an M.D. who would examine Seth and prescribe the therapy. In order to accomplish this, Anat needed to submit forms to the allopathic physician, but she wasn't promising anything. There was no other discussion.

Anat's confidence in herself, her unequivocal presentation of the terms of her involvement left no room for argument. We were either going to do it or not do it. We couldn't equivocate either. We understood without doubt that if we didn't, there were plenty of other people ready to use the time she was allotting for Seth. We accepted her offer and set up appointments for the following week.

We left Anat's office and sent Seth on his way with Mayra. He was animated differently than I had ever remembered seeing him. Jay and I took some big breaths and then talked. The reality of what we were doing began to sink in gradually. What would we tell everyone? We felt awkward about informing Susan Scheer and the other therapists that they were no longer needed after all this time and after all their loyalty and devotion.

There was also the big question of how to explain ourselves in the world. What would we tell the doctors? In addition to Dr. Lee, there were Drs. Grant, Kessler, and Price, as well as the neurologists. Then there were our parents and friends. No mainstream medical community recognized Anat's work. Her work was not acceptable in conventional terms. Feldenkrais work! I could just hear the reactions. Most people couldn't say it, never mind spell it. The insurance company was not going to accept her credentials as valid for reimbursement without the sanction of this doctor she referred us to.

Jay supported my instinct to try Anat. There was plenty to recommend her work, both in my own personal experience and from what I was reading about children with cerebral palsy who had been treated by Feldenkrais. Witnessing Seth in Anat's hands gave us enormous confidence. I wasn't without misgivings and anxiety, but my willingness to be a renegade myself probably encouraged me to try something outside of the mainstream for Seth. Jay's trust in my choices for Seth probably overrode any reluctance he felt. But he was also impressed by what he had seen in Anat's office. And we were both desperate for progress.

My conversation with Susan Scheer was difficult. I told her our intentions, what we wanted to try. She wasn't exactly skeptical, but she expressed disappointment and reservations. She was sad about having to say good-bye to Seth, and there was coolness about her departure. I felt anxious.

My misgivings retreated some when I spoke to Peggy Smith. She was enthusiastic. She knew about Anat, knew her reputation, and believed wholeheartedly in the Feldenkrais work. She expressed optimism about Seth's future.

I spoke to Phyllis by phone. She and I had never stopped struggling over the sign-language issue, and I had remained slightly uncomfortable with her. Seth liked his sessions with Phyllis the least. And
there were always those little handwritten notes at the end of every
week to influence my state of mind. The power these people had!

As far as the doctors were concerned, I felt no urgency about
calling them and announcing my plans. I assumed that the information would come out naturally. Our family and our friends were
another matter. I was quiet for the time being.

By November Seth began regular sessions with Anat. We also
enrolled him in an early-childhood program at the Studio Elementary School. Serendipity again! When a woman at my gym had overheard me talking about my difficulty finding a mainstream setting
appropriate for Seth, she had piped up about the Studio School. What
was special about Studio Elementary was that it required that a parent
or a baby sitter be present for each child. So Seth would be like all
the other children, even though Mayra always had to be there with
him.

The Studio Elementary School approached child development in
completely psychological terms; it was their primary lens on all issues.
I paid attention to this philosophy only later. I chose the school
because it met a unique requirement for Seth. Typically, I grabbed
onto the aspect that met my primary need, never looking any further. I only did half my research. It was in the neighborhood, Mayra
could go, and they wanted him. He remained in the school from the
fall of 1985 until the spring of 1987.

For two-year-olds and three-year-olds the school day was 9:00 to
12:00 in the morning, which left plenty of time for him to go to his
sessions with Anat. It was wonderful for him to have the daily company of a group of children. They were totally accepting of him, and
he was participating in a structured environment of play and learning.

The other monumental change was that Seth now *went* to therapy.
Until his work with Anat, everyone had come to the house. His sessions had been in his room, on his turf, so to speak. The change in
the therapy environment had a dramatic impact. Mayra was not per-
mitted in the sessions. She waited outside in the reception area,
something Seth resisted ardently at the beginning. He put up a big
battle with Anat at every session. He was testing who was in charge,

and he didn't like the results. He was as angry, riled, and aroused as I'd never known him to be. Anat's reports in the early weeks focused solely on her power struggles with Seth. These struggles were a centerpiece of their relationship and what she saw as a primary part of his therapy.

Anat's position was that she was in charge, and that Seth needed much more discipline and order. He could not dictate the terms. If he didn't want to cooperate during sessions, Anat simply went about other tasks and made him wait it out in the therapy room until the session was over. Her approach was to treat the whole child, his personality as well as his neurology. She felt that Seth needed to have an ordered, respectful relationship to her and the work they were doing. He needed to see the therapy as work and comprehend the gravity of the effort. At two and a half!

Anat spoke to Seth directly, telling him clearly that she and she alone could teach him to walk. She had rules he was required to obey. She wanted him to do unusual things with his body, things he wasn't used to trying. He was very resistant to start. For example, Anat put a lot of emphasis on Seth's tongue. She wanted him to practice putting the tip of his tongue into each corner of his mouth. She dabbed applesauce, which he loved passionately, on the corners of his mouth to encourage him to practice. When he failed to cooperate, she insisted that we take away applesauce at home. She wasn't kidding. This was not a friendly, chatty relationship. This was professional and demanding work. As much as I respected Anat, even idolized her and knew the value of her work, I worried over my little boy.

We adored Seth. He continued to be outgoing with a twinkle in his blue eyes and an exceptional intelligence. I loved talking about Seth and hearing how wonderful he was. After several sessions with Anat, I called her to talk about Seth. When I got her on the phone, Anat said, "He is a very manipulative, angry, and spoiled young man. Full of expectation." I was in shock; not sure if she knew whom she was talking to.

"Seth is a prince," she went on. "He insists on getting his needs gratified immediately. Laura, you and Jay are too doting, too indulgent. He needs to ask clearly for what he wants and to wait, too. He needs to struggle. Helping him in every little way, with his dressing, his feeding, anticipating all his needs, is nothing but disservice."

"But I find him so easy," I replied. "He is such a happy boy, always a pleasure, easy to take everywhere. He never complains."

"Why should he? You do everything for him. He needs frustration. He needs the experience of his limitations. He needs to become motivated to do what's necessary to overcome his circumstances."

It was very difficult for me to accept these lessons for my child, a child so young, my firstborn, my only baby who was always smiling at me and giving me so much joy. I thought Anat's attitude was harsh. I didn't see Seth in this light. I spoke to Mayra about it.

She agreed with many of Anat's insights. "She's right, Mrs. Kramer. I mean, we all love him very much, but we do everything for him. He doesn't like to wait for anything. Like a big boss. He is very demanding."

Admittedly, I was uncomfortable and not entirely open to these observations. It was hard for me to understand that Seth could be as wonderful as he was and still have these unattractive streaks, traits that were undermining his progress. And traits that would not serve him well in life. Later Seth's other facilitators also perceived these difficulties in him. Dr. Frymann, his Osteopath, has told me many times how manipulative Seth is and how little he cooperates. Charles Bonner complained about his power struggles with Seth. Today I often experience for myself the truth of these people's insights. Time has proven all of them correct.

I tended to do less for Seth than Jay did, partly because of the difference in our personalities, but also somewhat owing to our different abilities. My surgery, my small size, my lesser strength made it impossible for me to carry Seth around or lift him from one place to another. I was more inclined to get Seth to do things for himself. And I am more selfish than Jay, lazier. Sometimes I didn't want to get up from the chair to get what Seth needed, a tendency that may actually have benefited Seth without my consciously knowing it.

The other reason was psychological. My sadness about Seth's circumstances, the horror of his birth, my anxiety about his future, all were channeled into being responsible for his rehabilitation. I was the prime investigator and instigator of his care. Jay relied on me in this context, although we discussed everything. Jay was very busy making a living and generating the money we needed to meet the enormous financial burdens of Seth's situation. The therapy Seth had been receiving was only partially covered by the insurance company, and we were always battling with them. Now we were totally insecure about whether they would reimburse us for any of Anat's therapy. Meeting Anat's bills each week put tremendous pressure on our cash flow, but we did it. The strain was enormous, so other bills were sometimes set aside.

The financial burdens were staggering. Jay made a good living by anyone's standards, but not only did we live in Manhattan, but the expenses for Seth's treatment continued to be exorbitant. Mayra cost, Anat cost, all the speech therapy was completely out of pocket, none of it reimbursed, and the Studio Elementary School was expensive. There had been the casts, the orthotic devices, Drs. Kessler, Price, and Chutorian. We had been married just five years when Seth was born, and we were trying to establish ourselves in the world. My work was not lucrative, yet there were many expenses associated with it. And we made many business mistakes that had financial consequences.

Jay, too, was silently trying to reconcile his fantasy of a son—the relationship he imagined he was going to have when his boy child was first born—and the undefined reality of Seth's circumstances as it unfolded. Jay was wondering whether he was ever going to play sports with Seth, whether they would ever toss a ball around in a field together. Up to this point, his devotion to Seth was an outlet for his distress. It still is. He has done a lot for Seth. He still does.

Three times a week after school, Mayra took Seth to Anat. On Fridays I sent along money. We sent our money every week, but Anat did not fill out the insurance forms regularly. I was annoyed. I felt I was in my own power struggle with her. By sending Seth and my money regularly I was demonstrating my level of responsibility, my seriousness. I wanted it reciprocated. The physician signing the forms for the benefit of our insurance company needed Anat's paperwork. The lag in her getting forms to him made our insurance claims more tricky.

And I wanted to be part of her inner circle. I knew she thought that my contacts in the entertainment industry could promote the workshops she was planning. I thought that being her special friend would help Seth advance more quickly. A few times we made plans to get together for a coffee in the evening, and every time she canceled, usually at the last minute. Once I went to the appointed place only to have her not show up. Though she had a completely plausible explanation, I was not happy. I tend to be very precise, very organized, and I value my time immensely. I was juggling work, a husband, a son with special needs, a home where three meals a day are planned and served, and I was still almost always on time.

Anat and I finally had lunch together. I lent her some books, and it took a long time to get them back. We both had busy schedules. Aside from her private practice, Anat was teaching several ongoing classes that were heavily subscribed. She was planning an accredited Feldenkrais training to begin the following year and was often committed to speak or teach elsewhere in the world. I was traveling extensively. We communicated mostly by answering machines or by my writing letters.

In November Robbie informed me that a change in his professional life meant he could no longer treat patients in the City. I was going to need a different therapist. Charles Bonner was still in the neighborhood, so I called him. We planned some sessions. In the meantime, I considered participating in a Feldenkrais training myself. Mia Segal, one of the original thirteen Feldenkrais students, also Israeli, was planning to begin a three-year course that would meet in the City.

My work with Charles Bonner was progressing nicely, although it was different from what I had experienced with Robbie. I saw Bonner once a week and attended Carola's classes regularly. I continued to pursue the idea of Mia Segal's training and, when the May segment was announced, I enrolled. In the meantime, my relationship with Anat was strained. Her forgetfulness about the insurance forms irritated me. Some of the time allotted to speaking about Seth each week was absorbed by my going over what forms she needed to send us.

That winter Seth told us, "I am going to learn to walk, and Anat is teaching me." It was February. Seth had been going to Anat since October. Things had been quiet for a while. I had heard no complaints from either Seth or Anat lately, and Anat was away teaching.

It was a Sunday evening, and I was brushing Seth's teeth. I had him propped up on the counter around the bathroom sink in front of the mirror. He made a motion with his tongue into the corners of his mouth, a movement that Anat had been insisting he practice. He grinned at me with his totally ingratiating smile. Then, with a twinkle in his baby-blue eyes, he asked for applesauce. With great sobriety, I told him I needed permission. His persistent lack of cooperation with his tongue during his sessions had meant that Anat had decreed that Seth be given no applesauce at home.

"I have to get permission. Mayra will ask Anat tomorrow," I told him.

"Yes, Anat," he told me. "Where is Anat?" he asked. I told him, and he launched into a discussion about Anat being his teacher and learning to walk. At the end, he sang a song, "Anat, where are you?"

Seth was changing. He was feisty, and he was stronger. He was talking, and his speech was much clearer. I understood everything he said, and Mayra did, too. He was even using his legs to stand. By the spring, he could stand behind his stroller and use it for balance, pushing it as a way of moving. He got tired easily, but it was remarkable to see him upright. Everyone commented about his progress. I knew from my intermittent chats with Anat that she was beginning to be pleased with his progress, too. Their struggles were subsiding. Sometimes she was able to "walk" him around the room, holding him only by the back of the neck. We were very excited.

We were not alone. Others noticed the changes. Up until this point, our decision about the Feldenkrais work had met with extreme skepticism. When I took Seth for a routine pediatric checkup, Dr. Lee was startled by the differences in him. She asked me what we were doing. I saw her eyes glaze over when I began to tell her about the Feldenkrais work. She responded with her typical speech of admiration for all I was doing, but it sounded empty. Our parents, both sets, although informed differently about Seth's circumstances, noticed his progress too. At school the teachers said that they perceived not only increased motor development, but also a psychological change in Seth. We continued to be reassured by what they said about his intelligence.

I took my upcoming training with Mia Segal very seriously and even wrote to the Feldenkrais Guild to check that the classes would count toward accreditation. At the time of Mia's training there were many political hassles among the various factions of Feldenkrais personnel in the United States, and how accreditation should be accorded was under some dispute. There was a Feldenkrais Guild and a Feldenkrais Association. Who controlled what aspect of Moshe Feldenkrais's heritage was being hotly debated. I wanted to be sure that Mia's training afforded me the best chance of accreditation.

Anat was planning her own training, but it would be taking place at some distance from New York. For the moment, there was nothing definite. However, I know Anat believed that part of the experience of the training was being sequestered. That was fine for some people, but I had a young child and a husband. My intention was not to become a Feldenkrais practitioner, only to be better informed about the work.

As the spring progressed, so did Seth. There was a visible difference in him. All of his upper-body dexterity was improving. His posture and carriage improved. He was not drooling as much unless he was trying hard at something. We were more than encouraged. As we approached his third birthday, our hearts were filled with more hope than we had had for a long time. Anat said he would learn to walk, and I finally knew deep down that this was true.

My relationship with Anat grew even more strained. We weren't getting reimbursements from our insurance company, but we weren't giving up our fight with them. We hoped to prove the efficacy of the therapy, and we wanted the paperwork from Anat for record keeping. The insurance company questioned the allopathic physician about the type of treatment. They took the position that because Feldenkrais therapy was not a recognized orthodox form of treatment that there were only a limited number of sessions they would pay for. The insurance company set an arbitrary cutoff for benefits. The doctor argued with them, but we lost in the end. During this controversy Anat's records were even more essential to us. Then Anat mixed up some appointments, and we argued about whether we were financially responsible for her mistakes. Although I informed her well in advance of a time we would be absent with Seth for a family event in Boston, she forgot and held us responsible for the sessions. She was difficult. I had known this about her, but I was exasperated.

Mia Segal's Feldenkrais training started in early May on a Thursday and ended twelve days later on a Sunday. There was only one day off, and the class began at 9:30 in the morning and ended every day at 5:00 in the afternoon. There was a two-hour break for lunch. About thirty people attended, most of them complete strangers to me, although I had seen some of them at Anat's seminar in June of the previous year. It turned out, of course, that I met people who knew people I knew, and I felt very comfortable.

Among those participating, there were bodyworkers, physical therapists, and Alexander teachers. Alexander teachers are students of the Alexander method, a therapy for changing posture and movement to allow newer, far better physical function. It is a method of adjusting body posture to relieve chronic pain or muscle tension, and to increase range of motion. Through massage and gentle verbal commands, Alexander teachers help students bring about an improved ability to move, to eliminate common problems like slouching and hunching.

There were also psychotherapists, marriage counselors, musicians, actors, and teachers. They all wanted training in the Feldenkrais method. A woman named Connie was there, as I was, to do research for her own child. Connie's daughter had been in a car accident and used a wheelchair, without speech or any chance, as far as the orthodox medical establishment was concerned, of ever resuming a normal life. Connie had come all the way from Ohio to the training and planned to have her daughter join her so that Mia could treat her. I also hoped that Mia would treat Seth once or twice.

Mia was difficult. She was invariably late for class in the morning but was annoyed if anyone arrived later than she did. She played favorites, creating an inner circle of people who got more attention than anyone else. The classes themselves, however, were fascinating and revelatory. I learned something every day about myself and about the body.

The work was mind expanding. From the first class, I felt different, but not just in my body. I noticed that my memory was expanding. My brainpower was different. I concentrated better outside of class, felt more alert, more present. I had some Spanish-speaking people in my life, and I discovered that my Spanish fluency was increasing. I made the mistake of not writing things down during this first segment of the training, but I learned. During the later segments I took copious notes.

As far as my body was concerned, I was experiencing myself anew. I felt my feet on the ground differently. My gait altered. My shoulders relaxed, the neck tension lessened, and I felt my head resting atop my torso differently. My back was soft. I was in an altered physical state. I was also exhausted, not of energy, but of enthusiasm. The days were consuming, and I didn't feel like doing anything after class. Nothing. My mood was good, although small, seemingly unimportant things easily irritated me. It was as though I was floating, and the mundane disturbed my equilibrium.

Over the next three years I established strong bonds with a few of the people I met during the training. One, Brian, a physical therapist from New Jersey, specialized in a technique called "Trager." Trager work is the innovation of Dr. Milton Trager. The technique known as Trager Psycho Physical Integration focuses on the subconscious routes of muscle tension. The treatment involves a variety of movements that are meant to promote relaxation and increase range of motion and flexibility.

Brian was very interested in Seth, and he was also curious about my back surgery. Neither Seth nor I ever used the Trager technique directly. Brian also spoke often about a bodyworker from Lithuania who had helped many ballet dancers. He thought that I should go myself and also take Seth to see him. Over time Brian and I became enduring friends.

Then my universe blew up. Two weeks after Mia's workshop ended, I had an irreparable falling out with Anat. There was another mix-up concerning Seth's appointment. It had to do with a doctor's appointment and a change in time for his session with her. Also, during my week with Mia, I had neglected to send Anat her money on the appointed day. Mind you, I was still not getting my insurance forms from her regularly, if at all.

Anat and I had a very nasty telephone conversation. She told me to find someone else to treat Seth. She didn't care to deal with me anymore. I was devastated. I felt terribly guilty. The shock of her abrupt and severe attitude silenced me. We were through, abandoned. Worse, I didn't know what to tell Seth, how to tell him that the person he pinned his greatest hopes on for learning to walk would no longer be there for him.

It was the end of May. We were going to Cape Cod at the end of June. Where would I begin? What would this mean for Seth? He had come the longest distance in such a short time. Anat had only treated him for seven months, yet there was real hope that he would be walking independently soon. He had matured immensely in a short time. Being in school had benefited him, and the standards Anat had set for his behavior had meant great strides emotionally for him and for us.

I was paralyzed, but only for a day. Then I pushed myself into action. Abandonment is an opportunity for redemption, I decided. I knew Charles Bonner was available and had loved Seth when he first met him. I called him to see what his fall schedule allowed and whether he could see Seth a few times in June. I thought Seth needed a periscope on the autumn. I reassured myself. I had acquired new information from attending the workshop with Mia Segal and had made many contacts, and I knew it would all still be there when we returned from the Cape in the fall.

In September I was planning to resume another leg of the Feldenkrais training. In the meantime, the insights I had gleaned from Mia and the ongoing work with Carola fortified my intentions to work on Seth myself over the summer.

Seth, Jay, Mayra, and I packed ourselves for the Cape. I took with me a renewed, if shaky, faith that I could influence Seth's development and a commitment for Seth to continue the Feldenkrais work when we returned in September. Jay took a sheaf of paperwork. We were initiating a malpractice suit against the doctor who had delivered (or hadn't delivered) Seth, and against the hospital. Jay was overseeing the case with seasoned malpractice attorneys. We left in June. There were many significant changes that summer. Not the least of them was that when we returned in September, I was pregnant with our daughter.

CHAPTER SEVEN

the calm before the storm

TOUCHING MY LOVED ONES, MY CHILDREN AND JAY, my close friends and family, frequently, casually, seems a natural part of my life. I always held my babies close, carried them around until they were too heavy. To this day, I brush their foreheads lightly or stroke their backs gently as I put them to sleep. A caress is always my response to affectionate feelings. But something happened during the summer of Seth's third birthday, the summer after we were abandoned by Anat. Touching acquired a new dimension. The thoughtfulness I was learning in Carola's classes meant that I put my hands on Seth with new attention. The knowledge I had acquired about stimulating my breathing translated into an awareness of Seth's breathing. The awareness I was acquiring in the Feldenkrais work awakened me to the power of touch.

I became aware of my ability to influence Seth's progress that summer. Every evening, when it was time for him to go to sleep, I would sit on Seth's bed and quietly work on his torso. I would begin at the base of his spine, on one side or the other, and gently gather his soft baby skin into my fingers, lifting it ever so slightly away from his center. Holding it a moment until I witnessed breath filling the space, I would then let the skin fall back toward his body.

These "skin-fold experiments," as Carola called them, facilitate inhalations and exhalations. As she describes in *Ways to Better Breathing*, this technique works the same way as when we loosen a too-tight belt. We immediately feel relief, drawing a big breath of freedom. What you do is grasp a double portion of skin with your thumb and index finger or with your thumb and four other fingers. Or you can grasp a skin fold with both hands simultaneously, but don't pinch. Hold the skin off its base until a deep breath gets through.

The reactions are clearly visible as well as palpable. When I rested my hand on the area where I had just taken a skin fold on Seth, I could feel the softening reactions of his body underneath. I would work over one specific area for a long time before going on to another area. You can grasp the same skin fold several times. I had to skip areas that were too tight to grasp easily. Soon there were fewer of these.

I would work for at least half an hour every evening, always beginning where it was easiest, where there was the least tenderness and the most looseness. I tried to begin at the small of his back then work up from the rim of the pelvis to his shoulders. The reactions were instant and dramatic. Seth wiggled and lengthened his trunk, often yawning widely. He stretched out his entire body along the length of the bed. He inhaled hugely. He loved it.

This was my nighttime experiment. At the end of half an hour his breathing was wide and steady. I could see the sides of his rib cage visibly expand, the breath filling out his entire torso. To this day I can produce this result in Seth and in my daughter, Haya, as well as in myself. Haya's friends, my nieces, and other family members always ask me to "do my back." I have never met anyone who doesn't enjoy this experiment. It feels unbelievably wonderful.

In the daytime I incorporated many of Carola's other lessons into Seth's play. Tapping experiments were the easiest. Tapping influences the condition of the body immediately. I tapped Seth's chest cage with my hand cupped slightly. I never stayed on one part, but covered as much of him as possible.

His breathing responses were remarkable. I tapped his back and his breastbone. I know how this affects me, and he had the same response. He yawned and stretched and took deep breaths. This is the best way to wake a sleeping child. Today whenever I go to wake my children, I tap them lightly all over. They stretch and yawn, lengthen themselves, and arise with pleasure. Try it.

I did what Carola calls "pressure experiments" on myself and on Seth. These are done very lightly by applying gentle fingertip pressure to the breastbone and the area between the ribs. I did this casually while playing with Seth and tried never to make it "therapy." Especially with the pressure experiments, I limited the time because of the impact I experienced when I did it to myself. Sounds crazy? Try it as you sit and read this. You'll be yawning and gulping breath quickly. In Seth's case, the tightness around his rib cage and abdomen would fade, and an increased elasticity and softness would envelop him. I saw him sleep more calmly. I thought the clarity of his speech improved. These subtle experiments appeared to have profound reverberations. There were no professionals; there was no formal therapy, yet these touches left him in a state of complete well being.

When we were on the beach, I played many "imagination" games with Seth: we lay on our backs and imagined that we were lying on glass so we could see ourselves from below and above. Then we "painted" ourselves with black paint. We "painted" the length of our bodies, our legs, our arms, in our imaginations. He loved these kinds of mind games, and we did many variations. During this kind of play I also saw changes in his breathing.

We played rolling games. Lying on our backs with our knees up, we rolled our knees from one side to the other. Sometimes we rolled all the way over, sometimes not. Or we counted. I counted all the little knobs (vertebrae) on his back; he counted the knobs on mine. We rolled our eyes. Can you move your right eye to its corner? Back to center? Back and forth? Can you keep your left eye still when you do this? Let's trace our eyebrows with our eyes. Slow and fast. Or make full circles with our eyes, slowly, now quickly. And more. Anyone can experiment with these exercises. We all respond differently and with different abilities, but the actual experiments change us.

All summer I "worked" on his feet and hands using many of the techniques and experiments I had learned in Mia's training. I played with each of his toes, each of his fingers. I knew from the training that if I wanted to learn something, I needed to be comfortable. I reached for this with Seth. I wanted him to be at ease and feeling what he might not have felt before. I was always talking to him, trying, playfully, to bring his consciousness to his body. I still do this today, now more directly, reminding him to soften his tongue, or to think about his big toe. The big toe! Within two years, with my understanding of the importance of the big toe, I could have written a treatise. What I continually learn about the big toe is astonishing. Just wait and see.

I presented these exercises as games, as amusements. Smile, I always told Seth. Be happy in the throat. Smile. Smile. These insights had been gleaned from Mia's training, and they made the summer

eventful. Although we didn't witness major steps that summer—
Seth didn't suddenly stand up and walk around—we noted a significantly new freedom of movement, of naturalness. More than
anything, I felt connected to him. I was experiencing a new capacity
in myself and loved my new relationship with Seth.

~

In September we returned to New York and confirmed that we were
going to have another child in late April. I was ecstatic. There was
no question that Jay and I wanted another child. We believed in
having more than one child. We were both happy we had siblings.
We wanted Seth to have a sister or a brother he could turn to when
we were no longer around.

But I was also nervous. Seth still wasn't walking, and I worried
that we were going to need a double stroller. Everything I knew
about cerebral palsy made me feel calm about having another child.
I didn't believe that Seth's circumstances were a result of a preexisting condition or a problem with my pregnancy. However, the experience of Seth's delivery put me on alert. This time there were certain
unequivocal requirements as far as I was concerned. I wanted a
woman doctor. I wanted a doctor who was going to be present during
the entire delivery. I did not want Pitocin.

I continued taking classes with Carola and sent Seth to Charles
Bonner twice a week. The second section of Mia's training began the
first week of September, right after our return, and Seth resumed
his days at Studio Elementary School. We had a pattern, a convenient and flowing routine. We were also lucky that Mayra would be
staying with us for at least one more year.

There were no major disturbances, except that Charles Bonner
also began reporting a struggle for power with Seth. But that was
nothing new. I needed a rest from Seth's rehabilitation. I did nothing
that fall to pursue other Feldenkrais teachers or other kinds of rehabilitation. I did no research. I made no doctor appointments, consulted no orthopedic people. The casts were long gone. Sometimes
Seth was able to stand for a few seconds independently, but he was
still using his stroller to walk. He took no steps independently, and
he was now over three years old. But Charles was optimistic. I com-

forted myself with what everyone always told me: Seth would walk independently one day.

My professional life absorbed me. I felt tremendous pressure to accomplish something concrete before the birth of our second child. The nature of independent producing was nebulous, elusive, at least for me. Acquiring a literary property or coming up with an idea is the beginning of a long process of development. I had no financial backing. Jay and I covered all the expenses of traveling and working with writers to prepare our projects. There were meetings with many celebrities, writers, directors, as I tried to attract them to my projects. Sometimes they would say yes one day and no the next day. I often had promising reactions from the motion picture companies and television studios, but up until then I was unable to get any concrete commitments from them.

I was giving the producing one last chance. Two of my projects were of interest to important writers and one movie star. I was commuting to California once a month for ten days to meet with the writers and studio personnel, to do the "Hollywood Shuffle," as I called it. I was making many entries and reentries into the lives of my husband and son because of this coming and going. Early Saturday morning, they would wave as my taxi pulled away from the curb, Seth ensconced in his father's arms. Mayra didn't stay with us on the weekends, so the "boys" would be on their own until Monday morning when she returned to work.

My being away brought about a shift in the relationship between Seth and Jay. Up until then, I had been the central overseer and instigator of Seth's rehabilitation. Jay always spent time with Seth, more quality time than I in many ways did, since he had the leisure to just play with Seth without the responsibility of supervising the therapy. But when I was in L.A., he was left to deal with Charles Bonner and the Studio School and whatever else cropped up during my absence.

And there was another major development that changed Jay's relationship to Seth and profoundly influenced Seth's future. We had initiated a lawsuit regarding the circumstances of Seth's birth. The defendants were the doctor and the hospital. Jay's leadership role in our efforts made him feel as I felt about Seth's rehabilitation: that he was doing something that would help Seth directly and in a practical way.

Two years earlier, my uncle, a malpractice attorney in Boston, had told Jay that the statute of limitation on our right to begin a malpractice case was running out. The statute of limitations was two and a half years. He persuaded Jay to at least explore the merits of a case, reminding us that we needed to keep in mind financial concerns regarding Seth's future. Even if we made enough money to meet Seth's continuing needs, Seth, himself, would need to be independent of us at some point. My uncle wanted us simply to investigate our case.

We had had no contact with the obstetrician after Seth was diagnosed. Although he had taken a cursory, callous, and nonchalant attitude about the events surrounding Seth's birth, I had consulted the doctor routinely during the postpartum period. In April 1984, when Seth was first diagnosed, ten months after his very bumpy arrival into the world, I still owed the doctor a small balance, an insignificant sum, for one of the last visits. His nurse called to remind us. It was in the middle of a busy business day, but Jay took the call. Jay told her to inform the doctor that he was on his way over to the office. As Jay reported to me, he told the doctor about the neurological assessment we had received days earlier. Supposedly, the doctor was shocked. Jay informed the doctor that we planned to take no action against him.

Later, we changed our minds. After our preliminary discussions with my uncle, Jay engaged a reputable New York firm to examine the merits of our case. Following Jay's initial contacts and discussions with the lawyers at the firm, I had several conversations with one of the junior attorneys. At this point I had not yet made any connections between the nightmare of Seth's birth and his present circumstances.

Whenever I had described the events of Seth's birth, usually as part of giving his medical history during the intake process required by the doctors before they examined Seth, I had never put two and two together. Talking about it had always been an emotional experience, nothing more. In the context of the legal setting, while recounting the events of the birth, they acquired new dimensions. Recalling the horror of that night, the concern that the baby was not getting enough oxygen, the doctor's absence, my baby emerging on the labor table in the corridor en route to the delivery room, his blue

color, the aspiration of meconium, made me see how all those circumstances were connected to Seth's disabilities.

Ultimately the attorneys counseled us to bring a lawsuit against
the doctor and hospital. So we filed the necessary papers. Jay was
in the forefront of the lawsuit, supervising and organizing the lawyers.
Just as I was able to channel much of my energy into a mission for
Seth's rehabilitation, Jay's responsibility to supervise the lawsuit
helped him relieve his own sorrow. The momentum of the case was
building just as I discovered I was pregnant. Although it had taken
almost two years, the lawyers were getting ready to move full speed
ahead.

During the fall that Seth started with Charles Bonner, cousins
from South Africa sent us an article about a South African neurologist based at UCLA who was doing laser surgery on the spines of
children with cerebral palsy. The procedure was called a selective
posterior rhizotomy. The traditional surgical procedures for children
with cerebral palsy are all orthopedic surgical procedures. However
the selective posterior (dorsal) rhizotomy is a method of reducing
muscle tone using neurosurgical procedures, operations on the nerves
and brain tissue. This new approach involves selective cutting of the
nerves of the spine to reduce the spasticity of muscle groups in the
upper or lower extremities or trunk.

The success of the surgery depends upon certain neurological factors. Children with spasticity are considered for surgery, but children
with low trunk tone or the involuntary, purposeless movements of
a certain type of cerebral palsy are not considered good candidates.
Although I instinctively recoiled from the idea of surgery, I was
instantly energized by the hope of a cure for Seth. With Jay's help I
got information from the neurologist at UCLA and the name of a
New York neurologist who could assess whether Seth was a good
candidate for the procedure. In December we went to see the new
neurologist, Dr. Sandra Forem.

As I read Dr. Forem's report today, it is at once informative and
amusing. In it she concludes that Seth was not a candidate for a selective posterior rhizotomy at the time. The doctor feared that such a
procedure might "unmask" an underlying "dystonic/athetotic" component, bringing on weakness of the hip girdle, and that the operation would offer little functional gain. Dystonia is a slow, rhythmic

twisting movement of the trunk or an entire arm or leg. Dystonia may also involve abnormal postures such as severe rotation of the trunk. Athetosis is slow, writhing movements, especially in the wrists, fingers, and face.

We weren't going to take any chances. But the report also makes note of Seth's motor achievements since he "began the Seldencrest [sic] physiotherapy." She attributed his improvements in speech, standing, the initiation of independent locomotion to "Seldencrest therapy." She also noted that although we had previously reported that Seth was hypersensitive in his mouth, now he brushed his teeth and had much less difficulty swallowing foods. "Seldencrest therapy" was responsible, the doctor surmised. But her complete ignorance about Feldenkrais work, her inability even to spell the name properly, alienated me.

More and more I saw my relationship to the orthodox medical world unraveling. I could not imagine telling Dr. Forem about my breathing work and how I practiced with Seth. There was no common ground. She advised us to take Seth to an orthopedist who would follow the development of his bones. She suggested that we consider another orthotic device. I didn't follow through with anything she recommended. I didn't have enough rapport with her to have confidence in anything she told me. Increasingly this was my experience in dealings with doctors.

Seth was going to Charles Bonner twice a week and spending a four-hour morning at Studio Elementary School. I had little direct contact with Charles Bonner, relying on Mayra to tell me about each of Seth's sessions. I consulted with Seth's school routinely, but visited there infrequently, again relying on Mayra for reports. It was as though I had checked out. Lethargy had set in. I was tired after three years of constant vigilance. Jay was busy with the lawsuit. He was helping prepare me for my deposition, which was scheduled for later that winter.

I worked as much as I could, though I was being very careful during my pregnancy. I wanted to stay slim. I went swimming three or four times a week and started race walking, having given up running while I was pregnant. My interest in bodywork did not wane. The third section of Mia's training was planned for December. I was excited about participating. I was attending two of Carola's classes every week. I had faith that Carola's work would enhance my growing child, and Carola was very encouraging, telling me what a wonderful, healthy baby I was going to have. Although I gained only twenty-one pounds during this pregnancy, Carola kept saying that the baby would be very big.

I was going to two of Carola's evening classes each week and was diligent about my attendance in Mia's training, but I wanted more. Following the December section of Mia's training, I wrote to Anat seeking to enroll in her weekly beginning/continuing classes. Because of my due date I was going to miss the May segment of Mia's classes. I thought that it would be good to fill in with Anat's classes. Anat was also advertising workshops, but I thought a weekly class would be better for me during my pregnancy.

Looking back on this correspondence, it is interesting that apparently I harbored no grudge against Anat, felt no reluctance about studying with her. When it came to increasing my understanding and knowledge, I wanted the best. I knew from attending Anat's June seminar two summers before, and from my summer experience with Seth, that Anat was in a league of her own. I even trusted the "abandonment," believing that things have a way of working out for the best.

What I hadn't counted on when I tried to hook up with Anat was Anat's big personality. While I tried reaching her several times by phone, our busy, divergent schedules prevented us from making contact. I finally wrote to her, enclosing a deposit for a month or two of classes, explaining I was pregnant but still participating fully in Mia's training. Our daughter was due in April. I mentioned in my letter to Anat that I knew Feldenkrais recommended doing the work right up until the day of delivery. Anat's secretary wrote back, returning my check.

In her letter she said that Anat had asked her to write to me because Anat felt that this time in my pregnancy was not a good time to be taking Feldenkrais method classes. Evidently Anat thought that even the beginners class would be uncomfortable for me, requiring agility that would be difficult. The class was almost full, and Anat wanted to offer the place to someone who could get the full benefit from every lesson. I was disappointed. I felt rejected. And angry. It's funny to me that until recently I remained on Anat's mailing list, but this 1987 correspondence finally severed all direct ties to her.

Seth had adjusted to working with Charles Bonner. Over the summer that intervened between Anat and Bonner, I had talked Seth through the separation from Anat. The fact that I was more connected to Seth than ever during that time helped him weather the loss of Anat. I also felt that Anat's separation had made room for me to work with Seth. I asked myself whether I would have used that summer to begin to work with Seth if I had known that Anat was there.

The most important thing was that Seth believe in his potential, that he be secure about his possibilities. I wanted Seth to know Jay and I believed in him, and that we were calm. I wanted him to know that we trusted ourselves to get whatever he needed to help him. What he saw reflected in us would send the most important message.

⌒

Through study I have learned that the unconscious is central to the Feldenkrais work. Many Feldenkrais practitioners have subscribed closely to the work of Milton Erickson. Both Feldenkrais and Erickson believed that the widening of awareness through movement occurs unconsciously. Learning happens to a large degree through the unconscious functioning of the nervous system. It is the nervous system that has the life experience of the individual available to it, as well as the biological wisdom gained through the process of evolution. The learning process is the important thing; it should be aimless.

Milton H. Erickson was acknowledged as the foremost authority on hypnotherapy and brief strategic psychotherapy. He surmounted enormous health problems throughout his adult life. Confined to a wheelchair, color deficient, practically quadriplegic, he retrained himself in everything. But he believed that it was these very challenges that were the best teachers about human behavior and potentials.

Along with both nonverbal and other verbal techniques, he used stories, especially anecdotes, to suggest, to communicate powerful messages. Erickson believed that our unconscious mind knows more than we do. The conscious mind is our state of immediate awareness. The unconscious mind is made up of all our learning over a lifetime, much of which has been forgotten by the conscious mind but nonetheless serves us in our automatic functioning. In other words, our brain cells are so specialized that we have literally a brain cell for every item of knowledge, and they are all connected.

Erickson believed that the power to change is something that lies dormant within the individual and needs only to be reawakened. He was a proponent of the idea that therapy is anything that changes the habitual pattern of behavior. I try to keep in my conscious mind what I know about Erickson's teachings when I deal with Seth (or anyone, for that matter). I stress the positive as much as possible.

My seriousness about the Feldenkrais work and many other studies including Carola's, the work of the pioneer hypnotherapist Milton Erickson, the anthropologists Ashley Montagu and Gregory Bateson, and the psychotherapist Alexander Lowen still fascinates me as I look back today. I am reminded of how much I invested in the pursuit of greater information and insight into the healing arts. I studied the writings of Alexander; the work of Ida Rolf, the trailblazer of deep tissue therapy; Gestalt therapist Fritz Perls; and many others including the extensive lexicon of B.K.S. Iyengar.

My work in Hollywood felt empty to me now. Producing a movie or television show seemed thin compared to what I was learning about the realms of the mind and the body. I wasn't enjoying much success either. I knew from the Feldenkrais workshops and my experience with Seth that I had a wonderful touch. Many people suggested that I consider a career as a bodyworker. There was a period of time before our daughter was born when I seriously considered changing my career to bodywork. I began asking myself whether Seth's circumstances were a sign that I should reexamine the purpose of my life. The opportunity to write about my experience with Seth and the Feldenkrais method resulted in an article for *Family Circle* magazine. I finally concluded that my mission is to communicate information to the world with words and to my son with my hands. I would devote myself to writing.

I know and believe in the power of the mind, the unique and unparalleled capacity of the brain and the human spirit. While I had yet to discover the worlds of Cranial Osteopathy, Homeopathy, and the physical therapist and researcher Glenn Doman's neurosensory therapy, I intuited there was more. I saw that there were many options beyond the mainstream medical establishment. I already understood the innumerable opportunities alternative therapy offered. I knew I was no longer comfortable with the conventional approach to Seth's physical growth. I had crossed over into another sphere. There was no turning back.

◦—

The winter before our daughter Haya's birth was calm and routine. Seth went to Charles Bonner twice a week, and I asked nothing except how the sessions were going. Seth was standing alone and unsupported for longer periods of time. He still "walked" on his knees, but he also experimented by taking a step or two independently. Although he was shaky, we were excited and optimistic.

Seth was attending the Studio Elementary School in the mornings, but we hoped to make a change the following autumn. We were committed to sending him to a Jewish day school. The Abraham Joshua Heschel School was a few years old and was in our neighborhood. We visited and liked what we saw. They agreed to enroll Seth in their preschool program for the following September. They accepted his limitations, his not walking, believing, as we did, that the next six months would bring new developments.

Many factors influenced our decision about the Heschel School, not the least of which was that the building had elevators. There were other primary considerations, though. Heschel's academic philosophy and the school's willingness to accept Seth attracted us enormously. The questions we didn't ask would come back to haunt us later. Some of these concerns had to do with class size and groupings, academic objectives, and the phonetic versus the whole-language approach to teaching reading.

In early March I noted in my journal that Seth had gotten himself onto the toilet, cleaned himself afterward, and was able to steady himself while he pulled up his pants. Around this time he also began to pull his sweatshirts and T-shirts on himself. We were overflowing with hope and anticipation.

Haya was born on April 29, 1987, not without incident, but without the same trauma we experienced with Seth. I watched in a mirror as my 9 pound, 10 ounce baby girl came through the birth canal (Carola was so right!). The episiotomy was routine, and I held Haya in my arms, with her sucking at my breast, moments after her arrival. Just my luck, I experienced another go-around with the Neonatal Intensive Care Unit (NICU). The birth was smooth, but there was a scare about an infection from vaginal herpes.

For five weeks before my due date, I had been monitored at the infectious diseases unit of the hospital to see whether I was developing any vaginal herpes, an infection I had contracted years earlier and manifested once before. Vaginal herpes is very dangerous for a newborn. For five weeks the tests were negative. They were administered on Tuesday mornings, and we'd get the results by noon on Wednesday. I went to the hospital at midnight on a Tuesday, and Haya was born at 5:30 on Wednesday morning. The labor was difficult, and I asked for an epidural, but my spinal fusion rendered the epidural ineffective.

A few hours after Haya was born, the doctor came to tell me that Tuesday morning's test for herpes had been positive. Haya was at risk for infection and would have to be quarantined. I was frantic, on the verge of hysteria. I couldn't believe it. Not again! My babies were so hard to bring into this world. The hospital wanted me separated from her entirely. I made a huge fuss, and they eventually capitulated to my demand that I at least be allowed to nurse her inside the NICU. She only had to spend a short time there in the end, but this was a different hospital, a different doctor. This doctor was by my side all through labor and delivery and supported me through the ordeal of nursing in the NICU. All in all, Haya's birth was a healing experience.

The irony is that had the doctors known at the time of the delivery that the herpes test was positive, I would have had to have a cesarean section. Because they didn't know, and because the epidural was ineffective, I had a completely natural childbirth with Haya. The experience I had so hoped for with Seth finally was mine.

CHAPTER EIGHT

shifting currents

THE PLEASURE I TOOK IN HAYA'S BIRTH was immense. It suffused my universe with joy. I loved both my babies wholly, and now I had the perfect two, a boy and a girl. My children and family are the center of my life. They give my life meaning; they inspire me. Seth's circumstances have only emphasized this reality more fully.

Like Seth, Haya had a full head of hair and a beautiful face. She was big, just like Seth had been when he was born, with well-formed features and robust color. She was an easy baby, soon sleeping through the night and crying very little, and she sucked readily. I nursed her easily until she was more than a year old. When I stopped nursing, she adapted easily.

Seth was enthusiastic about his sister. While she was still in the NICU, he insisted on watching her from outside the observation window. He came to the hospital daily, and when it was time to take Haya home, he stayed close by, fascinated by her little hands and tiny feet, which he could now see up close. He was incessant with his questions—and advice!

Arriving home, Seth led the way to Haya's nursery. He remained vigilant through the entire settling-in process. He introduced his friends Kara and her sister, Lia, to his new baby sister. I noticed the proprietary way he had with his new sibling, especially when strangers came calling. This role is assumed under a different guise now that his sister has come into her adolescence and he is a young adult man.

The contrast between Seth's development and Haya's "normal development" was unsettling. That feeling was totally unexpected, not anticipated. Perhaps the books I didn't read contained warnings that this could occur, but I was unprepared. Haya's body felt different than Seth's. It was pliable and soft where his was stiff and brittle. Had she been my firstborn and had I touched her first, when he was born, I would have known instantly that something was wrong.

Haya never arched, and the little fists in her hands disappeared by the middle of the summer when she was four months old. Her rolling over, her hand-mouth coordination, her sitting, each milestone filled me with the joy of her achievements. Yet I was tormented by thoughts of Seth's situation. During the next year I finally allowed myself to touch the sorrow I had never given into after Seth's diagnosis.

We went to the Cape in June, Jay and I, both children, and Mayra. It was Mayra's last few months working for us. During the previous two years she had been studying to qualify as a candidate for nursing school. The time had come for her to spread her wings. I worried that summer about the effect her departure would have on Seth. And on me. She had been with us for four years. She had taken Seth swimming at the 92nd Street Y, sat through his therapy sessions, dressed, bathed, and carried him everywhere. She was my link to part of Seth's world, and I didn't want to let go.

All these changes were a lot to accept, particularly for a four-year-old who was still not walking but whose self-awareness was growing. Seth watched others, especially others his age, with new eyes. Although he never articulated his thoughts, I saw in his face the recognition that he was different, although he claims that he didn't recognize or become aware of his differences until later. My observation is that his awareness of his differences began that summer. Once when we were together we saw a man with lots of involuntary movement walking with two metal crutches. He was trying to maneuver himself onto a boat. Seth was visibly empathic.

That summer Seth attended the Woods Hole Child Center in the morning. It was a three-hour program for children with an emphasis on art, small science projects, and short field trips. There was substantial adult participation. Mayra took him in the morning and went on many of the field trips. Seth made nice friends there, and the program gave him a daily structure.

The Woods Hole Child Center was a "holding station" for the Children's School of Science. The Children's School of Science (CSS) in Woods Hole was a place where older children didn't just study science but did science for six weeks. To be eligible for enrollment, children had to have completed the first grade. Seth was already counting the years until he could go. Many of the children at the Woods Hole

Child Center were also waiting to be old enough. Seth's affinity for the ocean, his passion for the sea, the beach, and summer was apparent from the very first summers we spent on the Cape. The Children's School of Science eventually played a significant role in Seth's salvation. And still does.

Of course, the biggest change that summer was Haya, a new baby in the house. And I was nursing her. This took my time, but I tried to be cognizant of Seth and to set aside real time just for him every day. Having decided that I couldn't continue pursuing my career as an independent producer, I was writing my first magazine article that summer. I was reading extensively in the world of physics, anthropology, psychology, and bodywork. I felt compelled to know more, to educate myself more.

It was ironic that I was immersed in the works of Fritjof Capra, Gary Zukav, Alexander Lowen, Milton Erickson, Gregory Bateson, Margaret Mead, Karl Pribram, Ashley Montagu, and Moshe Feldenkrais but still had not read one book about cerebral palsy. Years later, when I finally did get around to perusing many of the conventional books on the subject that became available, I understood why they weren't of use to me. None of the ways I was thinking about Seth, about his potential or about the options for his rehabilitation, were represented in these books.

As I look over these books today, I am horrified by how irrelevant and how frightening they are. Completely absent from any book is discussion of even one of the alternative therapies and medical approaches that currently benefit Seth. There is no mention of the risks of immunization. Glenn Doman's groundbreaking studies, his twenty-five years of success working with brain-damaged children, receives no mention at all. Osteopathy, Homeopathy, Sensorimotor training, Feldenkrais work, Yoga, none of these disciplines is offered as an option. What is especially disturbing for me is the frequent implication that the life expectancy of a child like Seth might be curtailed because of his condition. No doctor has ever corroborated this claim.

Because of Haya's late April arrival I had missed the fourth segment of Mia's training, but I planned to resume in the fall. Brian photocopied his notes for me, and I read them. I went on practicing Carola's lessons daily. I remembered the work I had done with Seth

the previous summer and thought we should continue. If nothing
else, it would imbue his progress with that sense of well-being and
ease I had witnessed a year before. Of course, Haya's presence made
a difference. I had less time and less energy to devote to Seth. While
I tried to be diligent, I did less work with him than I had the prior
summer, especially at night, because I was tired.

I felt guilty. There were no perceptible developmental gains for
Seth. Everything was status quo, and I tended to let that be the fact.
I felt incapable of influencing his growth. The optimism and will-
fulness I had felt in the early years was replaced by languor.

Doubts and misgivings about Charles Bonner plagued me. It had
nothing to do with the efficacy of the Feldenkrais method. The difficulty was Bonner himself. He didn't have the extensive training of
other practitioners I had met, although I hadn't recognized this at
the start. Other practitioners never stop studying, taking and offering
courses, developing themselves to become more effective, with the
constant stimulation of information and exposure. Charles had not
pursued additional training beyond his initial course. Then, too, the
effectiveness of any direct-handling approach is dependent on the
individual treatment skills of the therapist. I was not enthusiastic
about Bonner's work. I questioned his effectiveness. Often I felt he
spoke to me without appreciating my own increasing knowledge, as
though we were strangers. At other times, I was complacent.

The Feldenkrais work appeared to be the best work for Seth, but
I wasn't exploring any other alternatives, and I had not done exhaus-
tive research. I believed in the efficacy of the learning, but deep down
I suspected that there were other possible routes to explore. And for
all my pride in being iconoclastic, the realization that the Feldenkrais
work didn't appear in any mainstream lexicon nagged at me. I continued to recommend the treatment to others, but my excitement
dwindled.

I did follow through on one intuition, however. Mia had shown
us videotapes of Feldenkrais. I saw Feldenkrais bounce children on
his knees as though they were riding horseback. The Fieldcrest Farm
Horse Stables was two miles from our summer house, so I explored
the possibility of putting Seth on a horse. Carolyn Weeks, the owner-
director of the stables, was amenable and open-minded. Seth was
only four years old, but she worked out an arrangement so he was

able to "ride" two or three times a week. While he was at it, I decided it would be good for me, too.

Seth loved being on horseback. Obviously he wasn't able to take lessons in the fullest sense, but his instructor demanded that he sit properly on the horse, keep himself erect, and push his heels down so that his hip flexors stretched. I could see his head and sacrum come into different alignment and his carriage on the horse improve. I experienced a change in my own body while riding. Later we pursued equestrian skills while I was also studying Yoga. The relationship between Yoga and riding was a revelation. In both disciplines, the heels are rooted while the torso remains erect, but at ease. The elbows are bent, but relaxed. The eyes are forward and concentrating. The pelvis and sacrum and head are in alignment.

Seth's relationship with the horses, such big animals, encouraged him to think of himself as more powerful. Riding was good for his self-esteem. He always rode Skippy or Midnight, two very large horses. His teacher kept them on lead lines but had them trot slowly so that Seth bounced up and down rhythmically. I was pleased by Seth's ease around the stables.

In the autumn Seth began at Heschel. We knew they wanted him. He satisfied their requirement to be inclusive without presenting them with the whole range of problems a child with cerebral palsy could have.

Seth's condition, for the most part, appeared relatively benign to the outside world. He was so handsome and intelligent and his movement seemed so regular that it was easy to think that his cerebral palsy was "mild" as Dr. Chutorian had suggested three years earlier. Dr. Chutorian was wrong; Dr. Bresnan had come closer to the truth when he described Seth's condition as "moderate." And we were wrong. His condition turned out to be much more complicated than we had thought, and, as Seth developed, we came to understand his challenges more clearly.

Knee-walking was his basic method of getting around, but he was experimenting with walking independently. He located props nearby to keep himself balanced and steady. He "walked" along the side of the big table in his schoolroom, leaving one hand on the table for balance. Or he stayed along the wall of the classroom. Either he found other supports or he fell back to knee-walking. Building with blocks, drawing, singing, manipulating shapes and forms were done sitting on the floor or at tables, so his clumsiness was a minor issue. The other children were for the most part unconcerned about Seth's differences. The roof playground presented a challenge, however.

When we had first toured Heschel, one of the school's most impressive features was the extraordinary playground on the roof of the building. It had been planned and built at great expense to be one of the most up-to-date versions of a child's playground. Seth went with the class every day to the roof. He didn't exactly run around like the other children, but he found ways to participate fully. There was a huge sandbox, a playhouse that was a duplex, and swings and slides. There were also some high elevations to which he could get himself, but he had limited options for getting down.

He got other children to help him do what he could not do by himself. That was the beginning of an enduring pattern. Seth has an uncanny ability to engage others to assist him. He chooses among the most agile, physically capable boys to be his best friends. He also picks the boys with the most compassionate hearts. His friends at Heschel helped him, and they adapted many of their own games to include him.

Jay worried about the safety of the playground. He was concerned about the extent of the supervision. He felt that there weren't enough adults in attendance during the time the children were playing. I thought he was being overprotective. I've always accused him of being overprotective, and still do.

My tendency is to be less heedful about safety issues. Why, I'm not sure. Even today I am surprised by my borderline nonchalance, as though there is something not real about it all for me. For instance, if Seth is sick and might need to get up in the night for water or to call for one of us, Jay immediately thinks about taking precautions: should there be a light on for Seth? How will his balance be affected by a fever? These things rarely occur to me. I'm focused on other aspects of Seth's care. I'm glad Jay is there to remind us.

Eventually one of the older boys suffered a serious injury on this playground, underscoring Jay's general and practical concerns. Seth, too, had some bad falls, although he was never hurt seriously. The parent body was galvanized, and we attended several safety meetings. Jay and I thought about a helmet for Seth once again. We both resisted the idea but considered it an option for playground time. We didn't want Seth to be different from the other children any more than was necessary, but we were worried.

We met with school personnel to discuss the issue of a helmet. I asked Dr. Lee what she thought. I looked at the pictures of the children in helmets in the brochures that came to the house. As with the earlier discussions about the inhibitory casts, we heard arguments on both sides. There were as many opinions as people. We put the decision on hold for the time being.

At home Seth was experimenting more and more with taking two or three independent steps. We were very optimistic. Heschel was six blocks from our house, and one of us strolled him to school every morning and strolled him home at the end of every day. The school day began at 8:30 in the morning and ended in the mid-afternoon. In the morning when he was fresh, we encouraged Seth to "walk" by pushing his stroller, but by the end of the day, he was much too exhausted physically. Seth was not different from the other children in this regard. Many of them also continued to need strollers. Outside the classroom there was a pile of folded strollers, particularly at the close of the school day. The children were still babies at four and five, easy as it is to forget, especially in the sophisticated world of New York. I can remember seeing many of Seth's classmates asleep in their strollers while their mothers shopped for dinner in the neighborhood after school.

Seth never slept in his stroller. His intellectual and emotional energy level was at an all-time high. School stimulated him. He was a star. The custodians and doormen, the other teachers, parents, everyone knew who Seth was. That remains true today. When I remember Seth at this time, all I see is the big smile he wore constantly. I remember his finesse in so many complex social situations, strength he still has. This is one of his strong points, and along with his intelligence it helped him through his adolescence and is assisting him as a young adult. My concern remains that he will rely too much on this magical trait and neglect to cultivate other parts of himself.

Seth's class was a mixed age group. Children ranged in ages from four to five years old, and some of the five-year-olds had their sixth birthday during the school year. So at times during that first year, there was a two-year age difference between Seth and some of the other children. For a child like Seth, the developmental differences between him and the older children were monumental. However, I noticed that he preferred the older children, was drawn to the more mature groups. They were more willing to help him and seemed less frustrated by his limitations.

We noticed no problems with Seth's speech. Nobody complained about having trouble understanding him. I never heard teachers or other children make any disparaging remarks. Not yet. What we did notice was that he wasn't learning his letters or numbers so well. We thought the other children recited the alphabet more easily and had grasped concepts Seth hadn't. He loved "Sesame Street" and sang along with the letter and number games. There was still no question of his innate aptitude. He was also intuitive and socially very skilled, more so than most children. So what was wrong?

I reminded myself that my son was learning to walk. His brain was consumed with processing information other children had mastered long ago. I convinced myself that what seemed like slight delays in letters and numbers were just that, slight delays. Not all the other children were proficient. And the girls seemed to be ahead of the boys. It was a mixed group, I told myself. But I remained watchful. I recalled Dr. Chutorian having said something about "learning problems," but it seemed like a long, long time ago.

What irked me was the complete indifference of the school administration to my concerns. The school was young and still in a formative stage. The current principal was leaving, and a new principal would be beginning the following fall. There was great expectation that with his arrival many of the glitches would be resolved. The early childhood director wanted us to wait until the following year before making any definitive assessments or interventions.

We did discuss which group Seth should be matched with for the next year, the kindergarten year. There were several options, and both of his preschool teachers met with us to explore the best situation. Their diligence was reassuring. Instinctively, I knew something was not quite right, but I set aside my concerns for the moment.

༄

Then, when we least expected it, when we were reconciled to the existing conditions, we were treated to a huge developmental leap.

Jay and I went away for an extended weekend in the late fall. At the time Seth was adjusting well to school, and Haya was an easy, cooperative baby just as Seth had been. Mayra's replacement was less capable than we had hoped she would be, but an old friend was willing to help with the children, so Jay and I managed to escape. I couldn't remember having been away and alone with my husband since Seth was born. We spent the entire weekend sharing our deepest worries, fantasies, dreams for our children. We vowed to face the future with a balance of hope and realism.

We returned home early on Monday evening. The house had a long corridor that extended from the front door to the rear of the first floor. As we opened the door, there was an eerie silence. Then we heard "Shhh. Wait. Stand still." We stood quietly. We saw Seth standing at the very far end of the hallway, at the very back of the house. He began walking toward us alone. He was a little unsteady, but one step at a time he came closer and closer. It was a good distance. Jay was quiet. I fell to my knees with my arms outstretched waiting for him. I was crying as he came toward me. He never stumbled once. He was four and a half years old. He was finally walking.

Why? My mind entertains several answers. He was plumb ready. The information the Feldenkrais teachers, Anat, and Charles had given him was finally integrated. We had been away. He was less inhibited when we weren't around, not needing our approval. He had the space to experiment without our hovering, watching and hoping for every move. Seth and our friend wanted to surprise us. They conspired, so to speak.

Later our friend described the hours Seth had spent practicing, the trial runs. He had been persistent and determined, she said. There was no turning him back. He would get up, take a tentative step or two, "fall" down, and get up again. He had done nothing but practice for days, preparing his ultimate victory. Our joy could not be contained. I think we must have called everyone we knew to tell them.

Seth still tired very easily and still needed the stroller for a long time, of course. I see that I noted in my journal what a great accomplishment it was when, a few months after those first steps, Seth walked from Eighty-sixth Street to Ninety-first Street. Seth expended enormous energy in this effort to do something the rest of us take for granted.

◦◦

In September, before we went away for that long weekend, I had rejoined Mia's group, having only missed a segment the prior spring. Haya came to the training often during that first year of her life because I was nursing. Our mother's helper brought her at the appointed times. Mia occasionally asked if the group could observe her developmentally. It was fun. When Haya visited one morning, the group sat at a distance and watched her nurse. She was our demonstration.

That September the group was studying various stages of evolution in the human organism. We considered eye-ear organization; how it was connected to the stomach and abdomen. We played with sucking, forming our lips to suck, observing what else was involved, especially the jaws, cheeks, and the space between the upper lip and the nose. (These are all places where Seth makes involuntary movements, but I hadn't made the connection then.) We observed relationships between the ears and sucking by listening and hearing. We asked, What does our tongue do? After lunch one day we each worked with a partner, feeling each other's necks, clavicles, and sternums, the base of our partner's skull, as our partner simulated sucking. Haya was my partner.

Because of this work with the training group, I had many thoughts and insights about Seth. I was swept up in the recollection of his initial nursing difficulties and his eventual rejection of my breast. I realized that had I been exposed to these exercises, I would have known there was something wrong with him long before the diagnosis was made.

One fundamental I wish I had understood earlier was how trauma, especially the trauma of being born, is the commonest cause of structural problems in babies. Because so little of a baby's structure is available to assess at birth, sucking and how the baby sucks and swallows is an excellent barometer of problems. These two symptoms of sucking and swallowing indicate how the area at the back of the head, the occipital artery, is affected by the stress or degree of compression it sustains as the baby is pushed through the birth canal during the birth process.

Issues of timing and comfort continually occupied us during the trainings. I realized that an unpleasant learning experience can hamper the learning process. Feldenkrais said, "Learning involves an improvement of the brain function itself. To facilitate such learning it is necessary to divorce the aim to be achieved from the learning process itself. The process is the important thing and should be aimless to the adult learner just as is learning to the baby. The baby is not held to any timetable, nor is there any need to rely on force." These were very important concepts for me to keep in mind as I thought about Seth's progress.

Mia was using Feldenkrais's Awareness through Movement (ATM) technique because it resembles the learning that occurs with human development. We saw that the human infant has everything necessary to maintain life and growth, and that these elements are already connected into the nervous and glandular systems at birth, but that the specific human functions are not wired in at all. As Feldenkrais said, "No baby was ever born who could speak, sing, whistle, crawl, walk upright, make music, count, think mathematically or tell the hour of the day or night. As far as these specifically human functions or activities go, the connections, or the wiring-in, of the neural structures are nonexistent at birth." We are very complex systems interacting with numerous "feedbacks and feedforwards." At birth the organism-environmental link is largely passive.

By and by, passivity is replaced by more and more intentional activity. All the mechanisms concerned with movement are incompletely developed in the infant, whereas most other mammals are quite advanced in this respect. On the other hand, behavior in other mammals is primarily reflexive and fixed. Learning new or different responses is slow. However, in humans the brain grows and forms while we adjust to life. The parts of the nervous system that develop after birth are connected with the actual patterns of the cortex. The human motor cortex is unique. The stages in the programming of the brain are of major neurological significance. Missing stages along this road of development means that a child will not progress normally.

As my studies progressed over the years, I began to recognize that the insights of others matched and enhanced what I had learned during the training with Mia that year. That this information is not more readily available to parents of special needs children astounds me. The relevance and relationship between Feldenkrais's observations and the results of other studies of development is enormous.

At this time I made a memorable discovery about the big toe. Mia insisted that we look at the action of our feet (we were always bare-foot) when we rolled over or began to sit up. We played with using the big toe to paw the ground, rubbing it along the carpet in the studio where we were studying. We saw that we could not roll our-selves over from our backs and propel ourselves up to sitting without the action of the big toe.

As luck would have it, during the September training Haya was beginning to sit up. She was almost six months old. I was on our bed at home with her one rainy weekend afternoon when she began stroking her big toe over and over again along the bed's coverlet. The repetition was unceasing. As Feldenkrais wrote and demon-strated: "The tendency to repetition leads, in the end, to repetitive constancy and order." All of a sudden Haya sat up.

Haya's accomplishment flooded me with joy. I was seeing the normal developmental process for the first time. With every one of Haya's milestones, I realized more clearly how Seth was different. I would never see Seth sit up like that. Haya's development telescoped Seth's limitations. The work with Mia underscored time and again the resounding subtleties of the differences of my two children.

Seth had never sat without assistance. He always needed to be set into position or to be propped up. To this day, getting up from a sitting position, especially from the ground, is very difficult for him. I never saw him simulate any action with his big toe. For eighteen months after his diagnosis, his big toes never even felt the ground because he was wearing the inhibitory casts.

Although Seth didn't use his big toe to progress along the normal path of development, other professionals used his big toe in years to come to stimulate him. And I still use his big toe to help him. I learned that through his big toe I could influence Seth when he was tense, or even spastic, in his movements. During the times he "cocks" or "arches" his big toe, I have a clue to his discomfort. I acquired tools from the Feldenkrais work and other bodywork that helps me put him more at ease, helps him with body tension by relaxing his big toe. When we go to the dentist and Seth has to hold his mouth open, it causes him to gag. He gets very uncomfortable. I sit nearby and say, "Relax the big toe, Seth. Just keep your toes soft." It works. We have to keep at it. I keep reminding him, keep him focusing, recapturing, and the effect is dramatic.

I wouldn't have believed the connection until I discovered it for myself. In all the other bodywork I've studied, especially Iyengar Yoga, which I began studying in earnest many years ago, the importance of the big toe has come into focus time and again. At the beginning of almost every Yoga class I've been in, "join the big toes" is the first direction. One of my senior Yoga teachers describes the big toe as the conduit to the inner groin, and, therefore, the entire basis of action of the spine. The tongue is the other medium that signals the body. Just as Anat emphasized: bare feet and a limber tongue!

I am involved today in Iyengar Yoga because of its emphasis on alignment and focus. Like many of the other philosophers, researchers, and bodyworkers I have studied, Iyengar saw the body as a frontier and explored its capacity to achieve balance. In the Iyengar system, postures are explored to penetrate remote anatomical layers of the body. The intelligence of the body and the dignity of the spine are the focus of the work. Active postures in Iyengar Yoga are performed with eyes open, muscles firmly engaged to the bones, and the body lifting, expanding, and stretching with strong internal action. Eventually what I learned in my own Yoga practice enhanced my insights into Seth. Since beginning Iyengar Yoga, I've taken Seth to several senior teachers. I hope Seth will return to this discipline one day, and so I continue to encourage him to work with two of my teachers.

The links between all the body parts and the body and mind were real for me because I myself was immersed in work where their reality was certain. If someone had come and told me these things, I would have doubted them. But actually experiencing the insights myself, and, in the case of the Feldenkrais work, witnessing them in Haya simultaneously, was astonishing. It changed the way I look at everyone, but mostly it opened my eyes to the magnitude and consequences of Seth's differences. And it gave me ways to help him. I was too busy absorbing the new information to ask why the medical professionals and the physical therapists did not have this information or did not impart it to me if they did know about it.

What the Feldenkrais work showed me was that Seth was learning differently than most of us do. He was learning to sit, stand, walk, and speak using different parts of his brain. His patterns were at variance with ours, but he still had the resources he needed to learn. What these divergences in learning meant in terms of his schooling were only beginning to come into focus.

~

Seth had completed the first year of preschool, and we were giving a great deal of consideration to his grouping for the second year. I was haunted by all of his academic delays at this point, wary that I lacked the energy to make changes. By late fall of his second year at Heschel, I saw clearly that he was not progressing "academically." He was five and didn't know his alphabet, didn't write or read any letters or numbers. There was no question about his innate ability. I wasn't convinced that his delays were caused solely by the cerebral palsy. I felt that the school should be more attentive and foster a better learning environment for him. My sense was that the school was failing him, not that he was failing. It hadn't yet occurred to me that "special education" might be the answer.

The school was still in the throes of its own growing pains. A new principal had arrived, but he wasn't all they had hoped for. (In fact, one year later he was gone too. His replacement was an extraordinary choice, a visionary woman, whose prior accomplishment had been the founding and building of a nursery school, where we eventually sent Haya. Had I known that she was coming aboard at Heschel, we would have a different story to tell.) The director of the lower school remained aloof and unresponsive to my concerns. It was impossible for me to be focused on Seth because I was distracted by the frustrations of dealing with the school administration. I began to feel hysterical and persuaded Jay that we needed to investigate another school. It never occurred to me that it should be anything but mainstream. Learning differences were not part of my vernacular.

We applied to an elementary school, Rodeph Sholom, which was part of the synagogue where we were currently affiliated. Despite the fact that their nursery school was where we had first heard the suggestion about a wheelchair for Seth, we were still looking for a Jewish day-school education, and I was ready to forget the past. The nursery school was administered and housed in a separate building from the elementary school.

The subject of Jewish education and the disabled is very much in the center of any discussion of Jewish life and education today. Many people, educators and laypeople, believe that Jewish education does little to address the needs of children with learning differences; that Jewish people would rather ignore or hide special needs children who cannot achieve the pinnacles of academic success associated with Jewish achievement. In the case of Rodeph Sholom, we didn't realize that there was such a debate until much later, when it was too late.

We approached the school directly, communicating openly the problems we were having and what our concerns and goals were, to the degree that they were clear to us at the time. The admissions people at Rodeph Sholom wanted outside testing for Seth to assess his abilities and disabilities accurately. We arranged for testing at the Education Review Board (ERB); they administer standardized tests to the independent schools. Because of Seth's cerebral palsy diagnosis, we were able to arrange an untimed setting for the examination.

The testing was conducted over two sessions. We were not shown the test results. Instead, we went to a formal session where they were described to us. As we expected, Seth tested in the above-average to superior range. Manual tasks brought his test-score averages down. We were not surprised by this. His verbal ability was extraordinary, as was his ability to make inferences. We were pleased. The test results were compatible with those of Dr. Kessler's two years earlier. Every indication of Seth's intelligence put us at ease.

Based on the ERB results, our interview and Seth's interview, as well as our long, active association with the synagogue, Rodeph agreed to take Seth for their first-grade class in the fall of 1989. There was one requirement. The administration wanted us to commit to a tutor for Seth for the fall. Based on Seth's interview and the report from Heschel, they believed that Seth would need support in academic efforts. They didn't want him to lag behind. We agreed. They suggested that we consult Dr. Betsy Horowitz, an educator and neighborhood resident who tutored other children from the school. We took Seth to see Dr. Horowitz in May for a preliminary evaluation.

Dr. Horowitz also administered a battery of tests over three sessions. Her findings corresponded with those of Dr. Kessler and the Educational Review Board. At the conclusion of the first interview,

Dr. Horowitz recommended two or three sessions before we went away for the summer. That way Seth would have an opportunity to get to know her and get used to the routine. I liked the plan, too. Seth was not anxious to prolong the school year, though, and offered some resistance to being tutored at the beginning of his summer vacation. Because I saw myself as being very diligent and responsible, I insisted that Seth attend these sessions.

Like Anat, Dr. Horowitz had a very specific arrangement regarding money. She designated two sessions every week for Seth, and we were to pay for her time whether he came or not. Except for a death in the family, or a serious illness, she expected him to appear for those two sessions every week. If we had to reschedule an appointment in the week, we could count it toward our committed weekly bill. If she didn't have any other time available, we were still billed.

That spring we were also granted an interview with Seth's teachers for the fall. The two teachers met Seth and us in what would be his classroom the following September. We hiked up the six flights of stairs necessary to reach the classroom, not realizing that this would be Seth's trek every day. At the time we believed that the room we were meeting in had been chosen at random. Later we asked ourselves why Rodeph, knowing Seth's situation, had chosen to house the first grade on the top floor. What were they thinking about? Why hadn't I asked them?

One of the teachers was sweet and somewhat interested in Seth. The other, the more senior teacher, was clearly unimpressed. I would go so far as to say that she was put off by Seth. They were discussing Ninja Turtles, all the rage those days. She could have cared less about Seth's interest in them. Seth's speech difficulties came to the fore during the interview. Many times the senior teacher asked me to repeat what Seth said. She was clearly not expending any effort to understand him and was not interested in what he was talking about. She made no attempts to engage him in any other discussion. While Jay and I sat there beaming at our pride and joy, she was glum. The other teacher was only slightly warmer.

Seth always made a wonderful impression. I cannot remember one person who wasn't swept up by the joy he emanated. He was growing even more handsome, and, with his head of blond hair and his twinkling blue eyes, he was striking. While his speech wasn't always perfectly clear and he did drool some, the enthusiasm he exuded more than compensated. The older teacher's lack of verve and her lack of rapport with Seth were signals I wish I had reacted to.

Jay and I left the interview on that spring day, 1989, believing we had made the right decision, hoping that the senior teacher was just having an off day. As I strolled Seth home through Central Park, I silently assessed the situation. For almost three years Seth had been a student of the Feldenkrais method. There were no other rehabilitators or therapists in his life. The only conventional medical care he received was from Dr. Lee, the pediatrician. Seth was walking independently, and after two years of preschool and kindergarten, he would be beginning first grade at a reputable mainstream Jewish day school in September. He was six years old, and his sister was two. I was finishing the second year of the Feldenkrais training and keeping up my work with Carola, but I was doubtful about pursuing Mia's training to its conclusion.

What I didn't know was that I was about to instigate a monumental change. Our lives would shift so radically in the next three months that outsiders considered the change a mutation. By the end of the summer, nothing was the same.

CHAPTER NINE

gyrations

IN THE EARLY WINTER OF 1989, I had a fungal infection in my right index finger. Though one of several nagging health issues for me, it was especially nasty. It had persisted since Haya was born. I'd consulted every medical professional I knew including a renowned and expensive dermatologist. Nothing they recommended worked. Finally I went to see Dr. Domenick Masiello, a Homeopath who was also an Osteopath. His practice was in Queens, an hour ride by subway from home.

A close friend who knew me very well had recommended Dr. Masiello. A serious recurring illness had originally led her to another Homeopath, Dr. Masiello's mentor, and eventually to him. Admittedly, I was skeptical. Homeopathy? I had only vaguely heard of it. But I was at my wit's end, as I'd been earlier with my back problems. I was game for trying anything. After I scheduled the consultation, a packet arrived in the mail describing what to expect during the intake. There was a detailed pamphlet on how to report symptoms, as well as directions for getting to the doctor's office. I paid attention only to the directions.

The first interview lasted over two hours. The doctor asked me questions no one had ever asked me. Was I thirsty? Did I like hot or cold drinks? Did I object to being hot or cold? Did I like the water? Did I prefer sugar or salt? Did I wake in the night? How often did I urinate? He wanted to know about the onset of my puberty. My family's history was subject to scrutiny, but not just their health. My parent's work, education, their relationship, and my relationship to my siblings was examined.

He probed more areas than had ever been considered by a doctor. He provoked recollections of whole parts of my history and my life that were lost to me. I thought about things I hadn't thought about ever before or for a very long time. We discussed Seth and my pregnancy and delivery. He was interested in our course of rehabilitation for Seth.

The doctor gave me a "remedy" to take and asked me to come back in three weeks. He also recommended that I read two books about Homeopathy and buy a home health-care guide about Homeopathy. When I left his office, I felt genuinely connected to a health-care professional for the first time ever. Dr. Masiello was actually trying to get to know me.

"Doctor" is the appropriate sobriquet because Masiello is, in addition to being a Homeopath, an Osteopath. At this point I knew nothing about Osteopathy, had never heard of it. I knew as little about Homeopathy. The only part of the equation I keyed into was that the insurance company would reimburse me because an Osteopath is a "doctor." In the months and years to come I learned that Osteopathy is the oldest bona fide medical healing art; that Osteopaths are primary-care physicians, licensed to practice medicine, perform surgery, and dispense drugs.

While M.D.s (allopathic physicians) think of the body as a number of discrete systems, doctors of Osteopathy (D.O.s) view the body as an interrelated whole, with each system and organ in constant contact. They believe that the body's structure plays a critical role in its ability to function. Osteopaths use their eyes and a battery of manual techniques to identify structural problems. They focus on the neuromusculoskeletal system (the bones, muscles, tendons, tissues, nerves, spinal column, and brain) and work to support the body's natural tendency toward health and self-healing.

Osteopaths believe that the manipulation of bones, the palpation of tissue, and the use of Osteopathic Manipulative Therapy (OMT) reestablish the structural integrity of the body, leading to the free flow of blood. But this is only the beginning of what Osteopathy is. It is the belief of the Osteopathic physician that once the underlying causes have been diagnosed and treated, the body is then free to repair itself or to respond to other appropriate therapies. For the moment, I had come in search of Dr. Masiello because he was a Homeopath.

As explained in the *Family Guide to Natural Medicine,* Homeopathy dates formally from the year 1810 and the publication of Samuel Hahnemann's *Organon of Medicine.* Hahnemann, a Germany physician and chemist deplored most popular medical procedures as "heroic," preferring to treat the whole patient instead of the disease. Homeopaths believe that illness is not localized in one organ, but instead involves the entire person, both body and mind. Homeopathy is based on two major principles, the Law of Similars and the Law of Infinitesimals.

Simply put, the Law of Similars states, "Like cures like." A substance that produces a certain set of symptoms in a healthy person has the power to cure a sick person manifesting those same symptoms. The Law of Infinitesimals states that the smaller the dose of a remedy, when properly diluted, the more effective it will be in stimulating the body's vital forces to react against disease. A third principle, the Law of Chronic Disease, states that when disease persists despite treatment, it is the result of one or more conditions that affect many people and have been driven deep inside the body by earlier allopathic therapy.

Three weeks after the visit, my fungal infection had not improved, and I returned to Dr. Masiello. He asked me more questions, but many less than before, and he concentrated on the details of the most recent weeks. He gave me another remedy and asked me to return in two weeks. Two weeks later my fungal infection was the same, but there were new symptoms to report. There were other changes in my body. My digestion was different. My energy level was higher. Some of the other small health problems were being transformed.

During our interviews we discussed my back fusion. Dr. Masiello was interested in the history of my back and interested in getting a perspective on my back problems based on my work and my attitudes toward myself and those close to me. He wanted me to describe my daily routine. I was impatient with him. I had come to him for a cure for my finger, and everything else seemed secondary and irrelevant.

Beginning with the third or fourth appointment, the doctor began suggesting that I step into the adjacent room for an osteopathic treatment. I resisted. I still knew nothing about Osteopathy. I wanted him to treat the fungus, which I thought was worsening, actually. At this point I wasn't even sure why I was sticking it out with him. It took many years for the finger to heal, but as it did, other fingers mani-

fested the same fungus. The doctor always said that I would heal
from the top down, the inside out, and last things first, first things
last. His vision has been proven correct.

In February Dr. Masiello finally convinced me to walk next door
to his osteopathic treatment room. I can't remember how he finally
prevailed upon me. Maybe I was tired of listening to him extol the
benefits he kept insisting I was missing. I lay down on the treatment
table, a table exactly like the countless others I knew from my previous physical therapy sessions, from Seth's days with Anat, from
both of our sessions with Charles Bonner. After manipulating my
whole body, lifting each one of my legs, rotating them in the hip
sockets, rocking my pelvis, standing behind me to feel my shoulders,
sitting me up and touching my back and neck, the doctor lay me
down and stood behind me, placing his hands gently around my
head.

How long I "slept" I cannot say for sure. When I awoke I possessed a sense of well being and openness that I had never known
before. The lightness and ease I experienced was empowering, intoxicating. It was a completely unique sense of myself, and the feeling
lasted well into the next day and for days afterward. "I have to get
this for Seth," was my first thought, my first words. What had this
doctor done? I learned that Dr. Masiello was a "Cranial Osteopath."
When I asked him about treating my son, he said, "If you want this
for Seth, there is only one place to go, and that's California. Call Dr.
Viola Frymann in La Jolla."

Cranial Osteopathy is a specialized form of osteopathic medicine
that follows the teachings of Dr. William Sutherland. Dr. Sutherland
discovered that the bones of the skull are not fixed, but move slightly.
Changes in their normal arrangement and motion will affect the
brain. Osteopaths who have studied and specialized in this system
maintain that because of the linkage in the system of fascial tissue
and the vertebral column through the sacrum, palpation of the skull
and sacrum can pick up rhythmic pulsation distinct from the respiratory rhythm or the heartbeat and pulse of the blood. This pulsation is the reverberation of the cerebrospinal fluid, which bathes both
the brain and the spinal column.

Restrictions that result from injury or inflexibility in the spine and
cranium can cause abnormal motion in the craniosacral system. This

abnormal motion leads to stresses that can contribute to poor health, especially in the brain and spinal cord. The purpose of craniosacral therapy is to enhance the functioning of this system. The relationship of one cranial bone to the other is normalized, and the cerebrospinal fluid pressure is adjusted. As a result, the whole physiology of the central nervous system functions more efficiently. Nerve tissue is generally healthier. Common conditions such as earaches, sinus congestion, vomiting, irritability, and hyperactivity have been successfully treated using only craniosacral therapy.

Osteopathic physicians who are trained in craniosacral therapy use their techniques to identify all kinds of disturbed patterns of movement, to diagnose and treat many disorders in a gentle, non-invasive way, and the effects of this treatment can be very far reaching. Children in particular respond well to the gentle approach of this treatment. It is especially helpful in assisting children to attain full recovery after common childhood illnesses, but also after such episodes as falls or traumatic births. Seth was definitely a candidate for this treatment.

The next afternoon I contacted Dr. Frymann's office. They told me that there was a one-year wait to be seen as a new patient. I asked to be put on a waiting list. We were planning to be in Los Angeles for business and to attend a wedding in June. I thought La Jolla was close enough to incorporate a visit into our plans. I couldn't see missing an opportunity like that while we were on the West Coast, and I wouldn't take no for an answer.

After the initial phone call, I called every few days. I was very persistent and very pushy. Ultimately, I succeeded in securing an appointment for the first week in June, so the whole family drove from L.A. to La Jolla on June 5th. When I arrived, I think the staff in Dr. Frymann's office was expecting the wicked witch of the East.

The Osteopathic Center for Children was in a small, bright yellow clapboard house that sat above the staggeringly beautiful La Jolla Cove. Nestled among the glitzy high-rises and condominiums of downtown La Jolla, the building was an oddity. The blazing yellow color was a symbol of the center's "promise." In that house we discovered everything we needed to know and do for Seth from that day to this.

True to form, as I came to realize and accept, Dr. Frymann was always late. We had a 4:00 appointment, and we were seen at 6:30. By then we were all cranky, hungry, and tired. Except Dr. Frymann. At that time she was a woman in her late sixties with a head full of white hair secured in a chignon, and she was without an iota of hesitancy. She personified forthrightness and frankness then as she continues to do today.

Dr. Frymann interviewed Jay and me while the children played in an adjacent room. She wanted to know about the pregnancy and birth history. Next Dr. Frymann went out to watch Seth. She observed him momentarily and then asked him to crawl to her. She wanted him to stand. She asked him to walk. She shook his hand hello as he approached her. She asked him some friendly questions. After having him weighed and measured, the doctor took Seth to the examination room. Jay and I were not invited. Three quarters of an hour later the doctor met with us again in her office.

Dr. Frymann presented the most succinct assessment of Seth we had ever heard. Although she used medical terms, what she said was totally understandable to us as lay people. She comprehended his movement patterns, identified his speech anomalies, and described him personally. She summarized his crawling and standing, his relationship to gravity, his teeth and the shape of his head, the movement of his eyes, his general muscular coordination, and his lack of balance. She also told us that she was concerned about an early scoliosis.

The doctor recommended that Seth be treated for one month, twice weekly, in La Jolla. She wanted us to arrange this as soon as possible and to plan to repeat the one-month treatment three times in the course of the next nine months. She wanted Seth to get a CAT scan and an electroencephalogram (EEG) and be evaluated by a neurologist, Eugene Spitz, M.D., at his clinic in Philadelphia. She asked us to read *What to Do about Your Brain-Injured Child* by Glenn Doman and to enroll Seth in a neurological evaluation program. She suggested that we call Dr. Peter Springall, also in La Jolla, and coordinate a program to coincide with her treatments. Without arrogance, she presumed that we were planning to heed her advice and resituate ourselves, our whole life, to fulfill her prescription.

Dr. Frymann told me that the best thing I had ever done was to put Seth on a horse, and that the Feldenkrais work was good too.

While acknowledging the worth of his previous treatments, she was unequivocal about what Seth would gain from her. His potential was great. Her program was going to help him realize that potential. I was stunned.

Maybe it was the impact of the staggering visual surroundings. Perhaps it was the immediate trust I felt watching the doctor with Seth or the straightforward way she talked to us, but I knew that we had to return to La Jolla for the first month of treatment as soon as possible. We'd come for a wedding in Los Angeles and for an evaluation in La Jolla. We left Dr. Frymann's office and the yellow clapboard house that overlooked the most awesome scenery I'd ever seen with plans to alter the course of our lives.

When we returned to New York, I contacted Rodeph and told them about our plans. Serendipity intervened yet again. The school had a sister school in San Diego, the Beth Israel Day School (BIDS). I called the school in San Diego and succeeded in securing a spot for Seth in the first grade for one month for the coming fall.

Finding the Beth Israel Day School was one of the luckiest occurrences in our lives. We have them to thank for much more than providing a school for Seth, and eventually Haya. In the final analysis, the only positive result of Seth's enrollment in Rodeph was the relationship Rodeph had with the school in San Diego. The first-grade experience at Rodeph turned out to be the worst nightmare we could have imagined for Seth, whereas the Beth Israel Day School in San Diego became a safe haven for years to come.

School personnel at BIDS recommended a place to contact for a preschool setting in La Jolla for Haya. Real estate agents in New York helped us locate agents in La Jolla to find a house. By the time we left for the Cape in June, I knew I was on the verge of a fantastic and risky voyage. Once again I was setting a new course.

Not everyone can afford to seize the opportunities we did for that year, and not everyone would have leaped the way I did. I had looked into the eyes of the medical establishment and said to myself, "they are not helping Seth." I was taking a risk, thumbing my nose at the conventional, both personally and medically. But Dr. Frymann's competence and her skills were irrefutable. She had been practicing in La Jolla for forty-five years and had been affiliated with the Osteopathic College of the Pacific since 1980. She held the promise of something new, and, in its own way, something very conventional. I knew how I myself felt after a cranial treatment. I saw the doctor with Seth and heard what she said to us. I felt that that was enough to justify my decision.

Maybe I should have been more afraid, less daring, considered all the ramifications. Instead I plunged; diving in as I had years ago, going on gut instinct, raw feeling. I was uprooting the family, just at the beginning of Seth and Haya's first year in new schools. I was leaving my husband alone at home for a month and going to live in a new city. With what guarantee?

I called the Spitz clinic in Morton, Pennsylvania, and scheduled a visit two weeks later. Usually the evaluations at the Spitz clinic require an overnight stay in a nearby motel. I didn't want to have to do that because it would mean leaving Haya behind in New York. It would also mean being away overnight only two weeks before we were leaving for the Cape for the summer. I pushed hard to arrange all the testing in one day. I crossed my fingers and got on a train with Seth and Jay early in the morning of June 20th.

The experience of visiting Dr. Spitz's clinic was unsettling. The facility was busy with severely disabled people, most of them young. It shook the three of us to our cores. Later I tried to get Seth to talk about his feelings about what he had witnessed in the clinic, but he resisted.

The tests Dr. Frymann requested probably should have been done a long time ago at the time of Seth's initial diagnosis. Dr. Chutorian had not wanted to order them, suggesting that we didn't need them for such a "mild" case. By the time we had seen Dr. Bresnan, who did want to order the tests, we didn't want to pursue anything more.

After Seth completed all the tests at the Spitz clinic, the doctor concluded that Seth had a minimal static encephalopathy. Along with his auditory skills, his intellect was preserved. There was no reason to believe that he was at risk for seizures. There were no bony abnormalities, no atrophy, and no growths. Dr. Spitz made me feel better about Seth than any doctor, especially any neurologist, we had ever seen before or any we have seen since.

Based on his investigations, Dr. Spitz located precisely all the deviations in Seth's brain and communicated them to Dr. Frymann. Seth would be in the hands—literally—of someone with the most complete medical picture of him ever. We were ecstatic. Dr. Spitz thought that Seth was an ideal candidate for the remediation the Osteopathic Center for Children offered and for an intense sensorimotor-stimulation program. He, too, wanted us to get in touch with Dr. Springall in La Jolla.

I was acquiring a new lexicon. "Osteopathy," "Doman," "Sensorimotor"—all of this was new and very exciting. I was also acquiring a number of new responsibilities, not the least of which was explaining to everyone what we intended to do. My parents and Jay's parents were more than doubtful. There was disapproval. We were incurring further financial burdens. I was separating the family from Jay, who couldn't leave his law practice for a month, but was planning to visit for less than a week in the middle of our stay. And who was this Dr. Frymann? What was Osteopathy? Cranial Osteopathy? My parents remembered that Osteopaths were doctors who had treated them in the 1930s and 1940s. If we needed an Osteopath, why not find someone who did this in New York, or in the Midwest? Endless questions. I was jittery, but I kept warding off their scrutiny and tried listening to my quiet inner voice that was saying, "It's okay to try."

Rodeph was cooperative, but they were skeptical. I was planning to relocate us for the month of October in La Jolla, judging that the best course was to have the month of September for Seth to get acclimated to his new first-grade class in New York. In the meantime, the tutor, Dr. Horowitz, informed us that we would be financially responsible for the eight sessions Seth was going to miss during October. Of course, the school in San Diego expected a portion of tuition. The irony was that the most minuscule aspect of the cost of our expedition was Dr. Frymann's fee. At the time, it was fifty-five dollars a session. (Twenty-five percent of her patients are seen free of charge.) Airline tickets, renting a house, leasing a car, tuitions, tutor's fees for absences: these were the costly items.

✧

The entire summer was devoted to arranging our move to La Jolla for late September. I was immersed in a maze of details about living in the new city. My emphasis was on creating a smooth transition for the children. To that end, I wrote letters of introduction to teachers, to friends of friends, and to distant relatives. I made lists. I consulted museums and libraries, guidebooks and maps. Seth spent the summer at the Woods Hole Child Center again and participated in a few other activities. Haya spent the summer near me. I had a new helper, and she was the best since Mayra. She would be going with us to La Jolla. By the end of August we had finally secured a house in La Jolla, which I would see for the first time when we got there.

That summer resonates with special significance, aside from the responsibilities for arranging our trip. Several events are particularly memorable. During these months I recognized with new clarity and with a new acceptance that Seth had cerebral palsy. One day I was sitting on the floor of my bedroom with Haya in my lap. Seth walked away from me and stood in the frame of the doorway, his back to me. The distortion of his alignment, the abnormality of his spine's shape was unmistakable. It was typical of every cliché about cerebral palsy. The truth of his condition glared at me with new intensity. Denying his circumstances was not possible anymore. I had to be realistic about who he was.

That same summer I became reacquainted with two women I'd known in high school. One of the women had a son, Michael, with a severe behavior problem. His birth had been traumatic, and the consequences were apparent even though Michael was seven years old. My friend and her husband had consulted many neurologists and tried various forms of rehabilitation, medication, therapy, and schooling. There was a question of his being institutionalized. I wanted us to be friends, his mother and I, believing we shared some of the same disappointments and frustrations in our mothering experiences. I was also eager to share some of the information I had picked up over the years. I invited Michael and her for dinner.

After dinner we decided to go for a walk to the beach. Until then the children had played well together, needing minimal intervention or supervision. Seth demonstrated compassion and willingness. Haya went along, observant, following Seth's lead. When we got to the beach, Michael began throwing Seth and Haya's collection of small horses and animals into the woods and shrubs. There was no retrieving them.

My children got very excited, crying and asking him to stop. I tried to mediate and downplay the significance of the toys, while remaining sympathetic. We returned to the house, and, as Michael and his mother were leaving, I tried to put my arms around her in a gesture of comfort and reassurance. She spurned me thoroughly. While I have never understood why, from that day to this, she barely acknowledges me when we encounter one another anywhere. She looks right past me as if I don't exist.

From that experience and other later ones, I learned that my developing instinct to open myself, to share my feelings, to embrace the circumstances of Seth's cerebral palsy and my fate as his mother, would not necessarily be welcomed by everyone. Later in my experience I was accused of exploiting Seth. I reassess my emotional stake in his destiny every day, but at the same time I also realize that there is no rest from being attentive, involved, responsible, self-aware.

What is my emotional stake in Seth's circumstances and in his progress? I ask myself this question frequently. My fate as Seth's mother has given me an identity. But I want my selfhood to encompass more than this definition. I do have a high personal stake in outcomes for Seth. While all parents struggle to keep their hopes and expectations for their children distinct from their children's dreams for themselves, the battle for me feels more difficult.

Do I gain more importance when good things happen for Seth? Honestly, I believe Seth is special, and his feats are more significant than others because of what he has to overcome. I try to maintain autonomy, but I know when he shines, some of the light falls on me too. I do bask in it. All parents feel enlarged by their children's accomplishments. However, I have to constantly remind myself to be especially aware of who I am and who Seth is.

On the last weekend of that summer, Jay and I took the children to Provincetown for the day, where we intended to spend an afternoon at Race Point Beach and an evening strolling along Commercial Street. We rented a motel room for the day so that we'd have a place to shower and change after the beach. The desk clerk persuaded us to skip Race Point and cross the jetty that extended from the hotel to a very private, pristine beach. He said it would take about fifteen minutes to walk across. It took us over an hour.

The jetty started out smooth, and we walked along normally. Then it developed into a craggy congregation of dangerous rocks that had to be navigated very carefully. We were too far out to turn back by the time we realized our situation. For Jay and me it would have been a walk of minimal difficulty, requiring only some caution. But Haya was only two, and for Seth it was an almost impossible challenge.

Ultimately we reached the beach. True, we could see the whales in the distance, but the beauty of our surroundings was mitigated by the terror I felt when I thought about returning across the jetty. My anxiety spoiled the picnic lunch for me. When it was time to start back, I took a deep breath and told the children, "We'll take it slow."

Haya responded, "We'll go one step at a time." She was learning the lessons of life quickly, I thought.

With Jay supporting Seth every minute, we traversed those rocks at a snail's pace. Anxiously, Seth never flagging, Haya constantly looking behind to watch and encourage him, we made our way across. "One step at a time," Haya repeated over and over. My baby girl demonstrated the wisdom and insight of an adult. Her concern and her attitude struck me.

Seth smiled a smile of accomplishment and pride when we finally got back. The return walk had taken more than an hour and a half. He seemed undaunted by the ordeal and wanted a dip in the motel pool while Haya and I showered. His energy was high. He knew how great his achievement was. The trip across the jetty felt like a passage to me. It was the symbol of what and how we do together as a family in the face of unforeseen challenges.

During this same summer I was angry with Seth one morning in a primal way, and my reaction was not wholly warranted given the infraction. I yelled forcibly, so he retreated quickly, but not too far. Almost immediately he tripped and fell, cutting himself badly on the edge of a piece of furniture. I had to take him to the hospital for stitches. Being out of control was not an option for me, but it was less of an option for him. It was too risky. Danger lurked wherever he wasn't on guard. Vigilance was required at every turn.

My adulthood was fully upon me, and there was no escaping my responsibilities to my son. This meant taking charge of my emotional life and learning to respond differently. My anger, which at times feels demonlike, aberrational, would have to be held in check. Self-examination revealed my weaknesses and where emotional growth was necessary. I was committed to behaving as a model for my children to help them in their emotional growth. This realization came none too soon.

⌒

School began in September, and so began a nightmare I thought I would never wake from. One week after Seth started in the first grade, he stopped sleeping through the night. He got up and came to me. "When is it going to be morning?" he asked. This was only the beginning. For the entire month of September, until we left for La Jolla, Seth came to me every night and woke me. Sleep deprived, I was a wreck. Night after night I returned him to his bed, firmly, but often I couldn't get back to sleep myself. When I asked him about sleeping, he gave me evasive, nonsensical answers. I didn't recognize that something serious was troubling him.

Was I blind? I thought he was torturing me, but also I felt that I was failing him. I was caught up entirely in how to respond to him without killing him. At one point I considered staying in a hotel for a few nights to get some sleep. At times I believed I was in a power struggle with Seth. Then I thought that the problem was the anxiety of going away, Seth's anticipation about the new school. The children were asking me so many questions about where we were going. I had to give answers but be truthful to some extent about my own ignorance. We were going on an adventure together, and there were unknowns.

That September was very demanding for me. I was settling both children and myself into routines that were going to be disrupted soon. In addition to his new school and his tutoring regime, Seth was taking swimming lessons. Haya was in a part-time program and also had some additional activities. I was trying to make time to write, prepare for La Jolla, spend time with the children, and still be available in the evenings to go to the theater and attend business functions with Jay. The days were long, beginning for me before six and sometimes not ending until late in the evening. My patience with Seth was limited because of my fatigue.

The month passed quickly, however, and suddenly it was time to set off for California. Seth was strangely happy when we got ready to leave. I still didn't recognize the clues to his discomfort. The children and I boarded the flight to San Diego with tons of luggage and with hearts brimming, full of excitement. My sense of adventure took over as I summoned all resources. We were risking, trying, hoping. Our departure coincided with the Jewish New Year. It would be a New Year with definite new beginnings.

new directions

ON THE EVE OF THE JEWISH NEW YEAR, we landed at Lindbergh Field in San Diego. I had the two children, ages six and two, and the housekeeper in tow, as I followed directions to a house I had never seen and where we would live for the next five weeks. Accompanying us on a board packed in ice was a whole fish for Rosh Hoshana. The fish is part of the ritual of the holiday, representing the full circle of life.

As a result of meticulous and obsessive planning on my part, just hours after we arrived in La Jolla we sat down in our new home to a holiday dinner, catered by a local Jewish delicatessen. We had an invitation to spend the second night of Rosh Hoshana with a family whose daughter was also in the first grade at the Beth Israel Day School (BIDS). Another invitation to "break the fast" ten days hence was in hand. By the end of the first weekend, I had located the supermarket, the library, and the best place to get fresh-squeezed carrot juice in La Jolla. Sunday afternoon we knew where Seth's new school was. Less than a week later Seth was in a car pool, and I had secured a preschool for Haya within walking distance of the house.

The qualms, doubts, and jitters I harbored evaporated instantly when I saw Seth after his first treatment with Dr. Frymann. He was a changed person. His eyes were set in his head differently. His gait was unencumbered. The next day, when I picked him up at school, he was swinging on a gate outside the school courtyard with freedom and an absence of inhibition I had never thought possible. The change was almost too good to be true.

Seth loved California. We all loved our home there, the setting, the change of pace from New York. We missed Jay, but we were absorbed and distracted with our new surroundings. The astonishing beauty never failed to leave me breathless. To this day the sheer drama of the mountains, La Jolla Cove, and the bend of the seascape captivate me.

The Beth Israel Day School was everything we ever hoped for in a school. Friendly, small classes, housed in a two-story building constructed around a large open courtyard, it combined academic excellence, Jewish learning, and California casual. The first-grade teacher, Ellen Solomon, welcomed Seth into her world. Everyone loved him. He had instant friends. He was a star.

Dr. Frymann's sessions with Seth, as with all her patients, took place behind closed doors. The only other person present in the room with the doctor and her patient is someone playing the piano. The doctor believes in the importance of music. She indicates to the therapist what she wants played depending on her assessment of her little patient. As the session progresses, the music changes. Bach is always played at the close of the session, "the perfect blend of science and art," the doctor insists. Sitting outside in her waiting room, parents always know what the doctor thinks of the condition of their child by the music that they hear emanating from behind the closed door. Currently art and music therapy enjoy true status as part of rehabilitation, but Dr. Frymann perceived their worth long before.

We had four weeks of relative bliss. Beautiful October weather contributed to our pleasure. Seth was extremely happy at school. Each session with Dr. Frymann brought him new ease. There was only one unsettling episode, and it took place during Jay's time with us in La Jolla. Jay's visit coincided with the Jewish Day of Atonement, a day of fasting and prayer. We arranged for Seth and Haya to take part in the children's activities at Seth's school while Jay and I and the other parents attended the prayer services at synagogue.

At the end of our prayer service, as we came up the hill to the school, we saw an ambulance and paramedics parked outside. My first thought was that this couldn't be about Seth. Jay's first thought was that this was about Seth. He was right. Seth had fallen in the playground during one of the games. He had banged his head hard, and there was lots of blood, as is always the case with head injuries. The paramedics concluded that there was no serious injury just as we arrived. Haya, only two years old, was very disturbed by the incident. It was one more reminder of the reality of Seth's condition.

The coincidence of this event falling on the Day of Atonement, a day of fasting, renewal, and forgiveness, felt significant, too. It made me think even more about my emotional life, about Seth, about my daughter, and about my husband. It challenged and renewed my faith. I had to tell myself once again how much worse it could have been. In my personal journal I wrote that when Seth was born, I had no idea that being his mother would take me on this kind of journey. More than anything, the spiritual phase was emerging strongly, clearly as it continues to do so today.

Jay and I met with Dr. Frymann during Jay's visit. The doctor told us that Seth was struggling for control in his life and struggling with her, too. She wanted us to clearly establish the lines of acceptable behavior for him. (This was familiar from our days with Anat.) She told us that we should constantly orient him to solutions rather than problems. Dr. Frymann also said that it was a mistake for us to discuss Seth's circumstances in his presence.

The doctor believes that children do not need to be involved in every decision, nor do they need to be privy to every insight. Providing any child with information influences his or her self-perception. If adults discuss the possibility that the child may or may not learn to do something within earshot of the child, the child may doubt his or her ability, and the prophecy will be self-fulfilling. "Interpretation follows the mouth," is a well known Talmudic saying.

She told us that she was interested in hearing from Dr. Springall after he evaluated Seth. (Dr. Springall is part of the team in the new Center today.) Toward the latter part of our stay I was finally able to arrange for an appointment with Dr. Springall and a visit to the Springall Academy.

Dr. Springall is a sensorimotor developmentalist. Here was more jargon, another mouthful. Eventually I discovered that his work was based on the findings of Glenn Doman, the founder and head of the Institute for Human Potential, that were outlined in Dr. Doman's book, *What to Do about Your Brain-Injured Child*. Doman's work emphasizes the brain rather than the body. As I began to study his theories, the philosophy of Moshe Feldenkrais became relevant and pertinent again.

The evolutionary stages of a child's development were in the forefront of Doman's research and conclusions, too. In Glenn Doman's world, parents fix their children better than professional people do.

This view reinforced something I already knew intuitively, something I had known from the summers when I had worked with Seth myself.

After first working mainly with stroke patients as a physical therapist, Doman realized that the answers to why some people's muscles didn't work properly could be found in the nervous system, and the more complex the individual's system, the more evolved the tasks of learning would be. These insights matched Feldenkrais's exactly.

After years of research and observation Doman was convinced that there were stages on the road to growth. As he explains so wonderfully in his book, the old saying that you have to creep before you can crawl was verified and extended by him and his team of researchers, doctors, and therapists. You have to creep on your belly before you can crawl on your hands and knees; you have to learn to move your arms and legs in the air before you can crawl. Doman explains that crawling and creeping are essential stages in the programming of the brain, stages during which the two hemispheres of the brain learn to work together. If any of the basic stages are slighted, not even wholly skipped, there will be adverse consequences such as poor coordination, failure to develop proper speech, even failures in reading and spelling.

There are five functions that only humans have. They are the ability to walk upright, the ability to oppose thumb and forefinger, the ability to speak and write, the ability to understand speech, and the ability to read. These are all functions of the cortex of the brain. When the cortex is damaged, there is a loss of one or all these functions, the Doman study claimed. Doman and his colleagues set out to "dig a tunnel," or "build a bridge" across an injury to the cortex and/or midbrain. As he describes in his book, they experimented with teaching the hurt brain the function it would have been able to perform had it not been hurt, to awaken its inherited instincts.

They developed different ways of putting brain-injured children through motions called "patterning." The motion the therapist performs mimics the activity the child would have performed if his brain had not been injured. I hesitate to use this term, especially in such a curtailed explanation of sensorimotor work. Patterning has gotten a bad rap and is often misunderstood. Dr. Springall never called the work Seth did "patterning," but many understand it in this narrow way.

When Doman's work first came into the public consciousness, there was tremendous excitement about its possibilities. Many saw it as a panacea. The common misperception of the work was that a room of adults in round-the-clock rotations constantly worked on a child in an effort to stimulate the child's brain. In fact, three to five people manipulate the child's head, arms, and legs. However, that is one small aspect of a whole sensory-stimulation program. "Patterning" refers only to one aspect of the whole therapy program.

What is commonly overlooked is how unique patterning is in and of itself. No one had ever employed these techniques with brain-injured children until Doman and his team did. What was unique was that they were targeting a beginning level of development and function. They were stimulating the sequence of developmental steps as the brain would, providing an opportunity for the brain to program itself. Unfortunately, Doman himself has a very big ego (like Feldenkrais). Because of his larger-than-life persona, it is often difficult for other professionals to listen to his ideas.

Doman understood that no privilege is more important to people than the ability to speak. The same brain injury that stops a child from walking also affects, or stops, his or her talking. Seth was drooling, and his speech was not terribly clear. With Dr. Springall's intervention there was the promise of a treatment that would help Seth in that important sphere, as well as an orientation that would take into account all of Seth's challenges.

Dr. Springall assessed Seth in two respects. He evaluated Seth's functional strengths and used our input to gauge Seth's other capacities. Dr. Springall's lens focused specifically on the academic, educational, and learning aspects of Seth's life, and the doctor related these areas to Seth's sensory and motor functions. He looked at Seth the way I wanted an educator to look at him. He assessed Seth's telebinocular vision, his auditory and visual strengths, his perceptual strengths and deficits. He noted that the weakest links in Seth's abilities arose when cortical resources were needed.

This observation corresponded to the deficits that Dr. Spitz had identified in the neurological tests and also to what Doman described in his book. It also harkened back to everything I had learned from the Feldenkrais training. In the Feldenkrais training I learned that high brain development and complexity of life go together. The complexities of our nervous system and of our life are one. To understand human behavior we must look at differences as well as similarities. We must look at the origin of the individual response in order to find a "cure."

Dr. Springall concluded that Seth needed a program of developmental sensorimotor training as a means to overcome his motor dysfunctions and to create strategies so that he would learn more easily. For instance, we learned that when Seth was presented written words in the "word-sight" or "whole language" method, or that when words were written very large or supported with auditory reinforcement, that Seth was able to read well. This was my initiation into the debate between phonetics and whole-language approaches to reading. The path to wisdom was endless.

By engaging in a program of exercises designed especially for Seth, Dr. Springall believed that Seth could stimulate and reorganize his central nervous system and achieve more. Seth could practice on his own at home for a few minutes twice a day. The exercises simulated crawling and cross patterns of creeping. The doctor also believed that Seth's reading would develop more quickly once he began doing these exercises. And many of the objectives involved the big toe. Dr. Springall wanted Seth's big toes to drag on the floor during one part of the simulated crawling exercise.

The doctor's evaluation reassured me I was in the right hands. There was nothing cursory about his analysis. It was thorough and detailed. I was at ease with him and knew I was working with another knowledgeable, caring professional.

In the last week of our residence in La Jolla I visited Ellen Solomon, the first-grade teacher, to discuss Seth's progress. She praised Seth's social skills, his ability to integrate himself into the classroom, the pleasure she had in his presence. She thought that the other children benefited from having Seth in their class, that his courage and fortitude set great examples for them. Seth was still having difficulty reading, but he was creating little games for himself as a way to remember his letters. She thought this was very clever of him. She also said that there were other children in class who weren't reading yet. She was confident that Seth's reading and writing skills would develop nicely as the year progressed.

Mrs. Solomon believed in the "whole-language" approach to reading; whereas in New York the approach to teaching reading was based on phonetics. She viewed the phonetic approach as outdated, a "dinosaur," she called it. She supported Dr. Springall's view that Seth needed auditory support and large print. (Dr. Horowitz had also said that Seth would do better if words were written large or in upper case.) Later Dr. Springall explained to me the physiological and developmental steps that are needed in order for a child to progress academically. Phonetics, in his view, did not make sense until a child was seven. Seth's struggles academically still seemed out of step with his tested intelligence, and we had yet to figure out how to turn this trend around.

We left La Jolla at the end of October, in time to be home for Halloween. Before we left, I went to talk with Dr. Frymann. She reiterated many of the same things she had told Jay and me when we had met with her earlier in the month. The doctor wanted Seth to have a break from treatment, but she also made a point of noting his progress. She said, "He's much more serene." That was true. There was a new composure about his demeanor. He was a much more tranquil person.

His schoolteachers in New York had no reaction, but everyone else who came into contact with Seth when we returned home perceived the change in him. It was irrefutable. His aura was different. His gait was more steady, open, balanced. There was less spasticity or tension in his body. Even Jay's parents and my parents were quick to acknowledge the improvements.

Seth returned to his class at Rodeph and renewed his friendships immediately. He also remained in touch with many children from the Heschel school. I thought that his social skills were excellent, and I was full of pride about the ways in which he and Haya had integrated themselves into first one routine and then the other. They were flexible and adventurous. I was more focused on Seth and his needs, his schooling and doctors. I hadn't yet read any books about the siblings of special needs children. I bragged about Haya's inclination to go along, fit in, and adapt. A year later, when Haya was four years old, I had a rude awakening, however. I wasn't prepared when Haya demonstrated feelings and fears about her brother that had been brewing and festering all along.

༄

By the middle of December, I was constantly battling with Seth. Every time I asked him to do something, he resisted or gave me an argument. I attributed his behavior to my own failures. My patience was at a low. I was busy house-hunting in New York in contemplation of a move. I was frustrated by the lack of progress we were making and how time consuming finding a new home was. I had been home from La Jolla only a few weeks, and already I needed to think about getting ready to return there in January. I was also busy visiting and applying to nursery schools for Haya. Time for writing and doing things for myself simply slipped away in the face of my other responsibilities. Everything seemed overwhelming. I was sure that my level of tolerance was lower than usual.

Jay and I scheduled a meeting with Seth's teachers. We wanted to get a sense of his progress, especially before our departure for La Jolla in January. They had had no contact with us, nor had we had contact with them since our return at the end of October. When I think about this now, it seems as though my unconscious was telling me to stay away.

The first thing the teachers told us was that Seth was a discipline problem. I was floored. I had never heard Seth described that way in school. I knew that I was battling with him, but I had been quick to tell myself that the gains he was making from Dr. Frymann's work were probably opening other channels. Maybe it's not so bad that he's finally acting out, I thought. I would have preferred, however, that he not act out in school.

His teachers went on to describe him as aggressive during transitions, full of anxiety and frustration not just in school but in social situations. They said that his academic subjects frustrated him, that concentration was a major issue. They claimed that he did not recognize sight words used in class from ten to fifteen times a day. He didn't know his addition facts and was not good with materials that required manipulation (hardly a surprise). I had difficulty believing their assertions, but I did verify that Seth was behaving poorly in the classroom.

A wave of panic washed over me, and then I let it recede. I just didn't believe all of it. Ellen Solomon in La Jolla had given me such a different picture of Seth. Despite all my struggles with him, and my awareness of the battles Anat, Charles Bonner, and Dr. Frymann had had with him, I still thought of him as a reasonably well-adjusted youngster. What child in his circumstances wouldn't want to have control over some aspects of his life? We were leaving for La Jolla the first of January. Seth would be returning to Dr. Frymann and the Beth Israel Day School. I decided to wait until the end of January before pursuing things further.

Both children made a smooth transition to La Jolla in January. Seth returned to school and resumed his studies and his friendships with great ease. However, he continued to wake almost every night. I rescheduled a visit to the Springall Academy and looked forward to Seth's appointments with Dr. Frymann. I was so impressed by her and her results with Seth that I committed myself to attend her Tuesday evening lectures while we were in La Jolla. She offered the talks at the Bishop's School in La Jolla, and the room was always packed. I began taking notes and ended up taping the lectures. I was learning a lot about Osteopathy and a lot about the concept of healing. I knew what she was teaching were wise, sage insights, valuable beyond words.

Seth had excellent sessions with Dr. Frymann the entire month, cooperating without protest during each of his sessions. He instinctively knew that she was giving him exactly what he needed. He came out of every session looking great. He also had enormous energy and a big appetite. I was thrilled to see him at such a pitch and to see him eating so well.

In addition to being an Osteopath, Dr. Frymann is a Homeopath. She was born, raised, and educated in England. Homeopathy is widely accepted and practiced in England; the Royal family is one of its greatest advocates. Dr. Frymann has since been the guest of Prince Charles on more than one occasion. His Foundation supports Dr. Frymann's work in San Diego.

Homeopathy and nutrition are a major component of the doctor's treatment, though her practice of Homeopathy is secondary to her osteopathic practice. I believe that Dr. Frymann thinks that the organism has to be liberated and made ready for a remedy through osteopathic medicine first. Many Homeopaths, Dr. Masiello among them, believe that homeopathic remedies in and of themselves can liberate the organism.

During our first visit in October, Dr. Frymann had given me a remedy for Seth, his first homeopathic treatment. I was already familiar with the little white pellets from my ongoing care by Dr. Masiello. I had had enough experience myself to trust taking Seth in this direction. Dr. Masiello almost always had told me what he was administering homeopathically, which is not common among most Homeopaths. Dr. Frymann did not tell me what the pellets were, but simply instructed me to give them to Seth at bedtime and to use "no other medication."

There are several reasons for this policy of silence among Homeopaths. Homeopathic remedies are readily available, usually without a prescription. Even the most potent doses of the most powerful remedies can almost always be bought over the counter. Knowing the name of a remedy could prompt a patient to buy the remedies and take them, and self-medication could prove dangerous. It is not advisable for patients to manage their own case, in other words.

Many of the homeopathic remedies are made from poisons or from pathogenic material, and knowing what he or she was taking could create in a patient's mind a repulsive or worrisome image. The patient might resist taking such a remedy. Or the patient might think about the remedy in a negative way, which would color the patient's response to the remedy. Homeopaths prefer not to influence a patient's case in such a way. They believe that reading information about a remedy and its possible content or purpose could influence the patient's response or the way in which the patient reports symptoms.

After our arrival in La Jolla in January, Dr. Frymann gave me another remedy to give Seth at bedtime. The first night he reacted very violently, waking in a cold sweat two hours after falling asleep, screaming for me. I calmed him down eventually, but he was up later during the night, calling for me as though delirious. He woke again the next evening, but he was easier to put back to sleep.

When we went for our next appointment with the doctor two days later, I told her about Seth's reaction to the remedy and the pattern of waking in the night. I wanted to know about the remedy that she had given him. "Let's just say it was directed at the trauma of his birth," she answered.

Soon Seth began sleeping through the night. Throughout the month Seth's energy level remained enormously high. Many months later, when we knew each other much better, Dr. Frymann began telling me which remedies she was administering.

We returned to Dr. Springall for a reevaluation. He was very pleased with Seth's progress and modified Seth's exercise program so that Seth would be "digging in more with the big toe." (I laughed to myself.) The doctor wanted us to get a special keyboard for Seth's computer, a device that he thought would help to further enhance the cooperation between the two hemispheres of Seth's brain.

He also wanted us to emphasize skills that did not rely totally on the visual process. He put me in touch with a place that had books on tape. I also got in touch with a library for the blind. The doctor wanted Seth to read large print, but to do his paperwork with an audiotape as additional support. He said that Seth's crawling had become a cross pattern even though the exercises were homolateral. Homolateral exercises used one side of Seth's body at a time, meaning the same arm and leg. Later Seth would do bilateral exercises where the opposite arm and leg were coordinated. He thought that from a developmental standpoint Seth's walking was improving. I was very happy about everything I heard. That month in La Jolla fulfilled all my expectations and then some.

My anxiety about the situation at school in New York continued however, festering throughout our month in La Jolla. I thought a powwow with the teachers, the tutor, Dr. Horowitz, the school psychologist, and the lower-school administrator was advisable. While still in California, I asked Jay to help me set up a meeting for when we returned. Because of the number of people involved, it wasn't until the end of February that we got everyone in a room together.

The meeting was devastating. I didn't write down exactly what was said. I didn't have to. I grasped instantly that the school had written Seth off, the teachers had written him off, and the tutor had no influence with the professionals or with Seth. We were at a dead end. Essentially what the school administration and the teachers implied was that they had a problem child with learning disabilities on their hands and, although they didn't come out and say so directly, they were completely unprepared to modify or adapt anything on his behalf.

I left the meeting reeling, completely at a loss. I had not been prepared for what I heard that morning. I was frantic. Where should I begin? What was the next step? I thought that the next logical step was special education. Where would I start looking and exploring? Four years earlier the only way I was able to cope was through action. Four years later my response was the same. This time I called a friend who was a social worker. She suggested that I call someone I vaguely knew who worked in the special education programs at the 92nd Street Y. I didn't really have the tools or information to formulate any questions, but I called immediately.

The acquaintance at the Y gave me the names of several schools for special education in New York and advised me to contact the Board of Education's Committee on Special Education (CSE). She insisted that we contact private education evaluators to secure our own assessment of Seth's education and learning status. I was surprised by the limited options for private special education and nervous about getting involved in the public sector. This was New York City after all, and I was not going to let Seth get lost in the labyrinth of public education, special or otherwise. My own education and initiation into a new world began instantly. The instinct toward advocacy began to brew.

Desperation engulfed me, and the feeling was fueled by our time frame. It was almost March. We would be returning to La Jolla for the month of May. Time was running out. We needed a school setting for Seth for the following September. There was no way we were going to continue at Rodeph. My contact at the Y recommended several people who could conduct the private evaluations. Purely on the basis of location, I chose people in our neighborhood, on our block: the Oldbergs. I wanted as little added inconvenience as possible.

We met with the Oldbergs immediately. They were a husband and wife team. Phyllis Oldberg, Ph.D., would be doing Seth's educational evaluation. Her husband, Julian Oldberg, Ph.D., was a psychologist and would evaluate Seth from an intellectual and psychological standpoint. They both thought that we should hire a special-education advocate to help us navigate the maze we were about to enter at the Board of Education.

It was almost April. As T.S. Eliot said, April is the cruelest month. I knew we were embarking on still another voyage. This time I was much less confident than before. The circumstances felt more pessimistic for some reason. I was entering a land where my instinct for survival would be tested differently. With the physiological issues, I had found a niche, a way to relate, a system for integrating and adapting. And I had been lucky that my own body beamed light on paths helpful to Seth.

The realm of special education was more complex. And my picture of Seth was always colored by my sense of his phenomenal intelligence. I couldn't grasp the idea that he was not going to be an achiever in the intellectual sphere. Up until then I had comforted myself with the idea that although he wouldn't be captain of the basketball team or compete in the Olympics, his intellectual capacity was superior and would develop even further because of his circumstances. I had hypothesized that the Feldenkrais training and the work with Dr. Frymann were enhancing his inherent abilities and providing him with opportunities others didn't have. Whether my idea was true or not would have been hard to measure or ascertain of course, since there was no "control" in the experiment.

Our resistance to accepting the probability of a special education setting for Seth complicated the process. We were desperate for a school that would address Seth's special needs, but at the same time we were struggling with our disappointment after learning that our son was not a star pupil. Our reconciliation would evolve slowly.

On our expedition to assess Seth and place him in the best education setting we could find, Jay and I were, however, about to encounter denial anew. It had been difficult enough to encounter Seth's diagnosis of cerebral palsy and to cope with many of the consequences. Each time we learned something new about Seth it meant adapting to a new set of circumstances and reassessing our attitudes, being honest with ourselves about our deepest prejudices. We would change our view many times. Facing Seth's educational challenges meant confronting the core of our own value system. What we discovered ultimately had more to do with us than with Seth.

a whole new world

TOWARD THE END OF THAT WINTER, we scheduled the tests with the Oldbergs and the appointments at the Committee for Special Education. There were eight appointments all together. Our watershed meeting at Rodeph had occurred in late February. Seth's first evaluation with the Oldbergs was March 3. I had wasted no time. Two more appointments were scheduled with Dr. Phyllis Oldberg toward the end of March, because we were going away on vacation with the children. We also had additional appointments with Dr. Julian Oldberg.

The costs were prohibitive (and that was years ago). The first round of tests with the Oldbergs cost $1,900. I don't know how other people meet these financial requirements. I thought that we were very comfortably off, but every time we turned around there was more financial pressure. The first evaluation at the Board of Education was scheduled for April 21. The cost of this meeting would be purely emotional.

On March 26, less than a month after our meeting at Rodeph Sholom, we met with lawyer Marion Katzive, a special-education advocate. Her fee at the time was $2,500. She advised Jay and me about what to expect at the Board of Education and how to prepare. She suggested what our goals should be. Lawyer Katzive informed us that our goal was that Seth be certified by the Board of Education as learning disabled, but that we should also have his intellectual superiority recognized. They—the Board of Education—would be saying "mainstream," she told us, but we would have to say, "no mainstream."

The purpose of the proceedings was to prove to the Board that there was no suitable setting for Seth in the public schools. If the Board sided with us, the city and state would have to provide funding for a private setting. Jay was very conflicted about this. He did not think that we should take money from a city where there were so many in need. We both knew that we could afford private education for Seth if we gave up other things. Ultimately, the conflict was resolved because we chose a school (or they chose Seth) where there was no public funding.

Suddenly I was thrown into the world of Individual Education Plans (IEPs), Public Law 94 (free, appropriate education to handicapped children), mainstreaming, least-restrictive environments, the Parents' Advocacy Network, and so on. New books with new titles were added to my growing library of special-needs literature. It was all very confusing. Marion Katzive was important to us, providing us with ongoing education and an overview. For others who don't have our resources and who are compelled to navigate within the bureaucratic world of New York City's Board of Education, having someone like Marion is especially important. The panoply of information regarding special education is as wide and complex as the issues of special needs. Being an advocate for your child, or having one, is of the utmost importance.

Unfortunately, most people cannot afford the services of Marion Katzive or anyone like her. In New York the nonprofit organization Resources for Children with Special Needs fills this gap. They provide advocacy and education services and training. Their staff counsels and/or accompanies families through all the public mazes: special education and entitlements to other public services.

The Oldbergs tested Seth five times, three visits with Dr. Phyllis and two with Dr. Julian. The contrasts between their results and the results of the tests that followed at the Board of Education were substantial. Dr. Julian Oldberg reported that Seth separated from us without hesitation and was well motivated. Six weeks later the tester at the Board of Education reported that Seth "had difficulty separating from his father. His anxieties regarding the evaluation were suggested, and somewhat eased by the reassurance of his father's proximity."

The Special Education Committee went on to write about Seth's "avoidance of material whose anxiety may hamper his adapting to external demands...that he appears easily stressed and pressured, quickly overwhelmed." Dr. Julian Oldberg described Seth as "friendly and talkative and easy to engage in the testing situation...that he generally did not become frustrated too quickly and tried his best to solve the task. His interest and motivation remained quite high throughout the evaluation. Seth's intellectual potential is, at least, superior."

At the Committee for Special Education the tester described Seth as "feeling isolated from others, concerned with winning approval, with frustration and an ultimate sense that he cannot meet perceived expectations...quickly stressed by emotional impact." As with the debate about the inhibitory casts, there was little consensus between the testers, and the disparities worsened when we compared the educational results.

The New York City Board of Education submitted to us their IEP, which described Seth as orthopedically handicapped/impaired and learning disabled. They recommended a special class at a public school with related services like occupational therapy and modified instruction. They recommended two sessions per week of speech and language. In all academic areas they indicated that he was lagging well behind. The only positive result of their testing was a certification that Seth never needs to take timed tests. Timing on standardized tests will always be waived for him. As you will see in later chapters, this was very important for Seth.

Dr. Phyllis Oldberg described Seth as tending to drool when he tried to express his thoughts rapidly and as having to struggle to reproduce his internal language. She wrote in her report that he was "deficient in math; a nonreader with few merging phonic skills although the difficulty was strengthened [sic] on the Woodcock Auditory Visual Learning Tests which simulates the whole-word approach to beginning reading."

She went on to report that Seth had "excellent listening comprehension with strong verbal and reasoning skills and an underlying desire to succeed, [but] he has a specific learning disability in the area of decoding written language. Deficits in reading will also affect his ability to spell and produce written language. In addition, his performance places him as a nonreader." (Pretty amazing for a kid who is going to an Ivy League college.)

Fortunately for us, I sent these reports to Ellen Solomon, who called me immediately to disagree with all the findings. She said that Seth was NOT a nonreader, and that she objected strongly to the label. In fact, soon afterward, when we returned for our next four weeks in La Jolla in May, she helped Seth learn to read and provided us with a resource for "whole language" books so that Seth could practice reading all summer.

From then on Seth was one of the best readers among his peers, reading at a grade level way above his current year. He was also tops in spelling in his school, a subject he loves and excels in. Mathematics can be one of his strongest subjects; he remained tops in his class in this subject. Years ago, when the Educational Records Bureau administered the standardized tests for independent schools, Seth tested in the ninety-second percentile in mathematics. Many of these accomplishments were realized with the help and support of the Stephen Gaynor School, the school Seth was to attend for the next five years.

However, if he had been at the mercy of the Board of Education's Committee for Special Education or the independent evaluators, if we hadn't had the insights of Ellen Solomon and eventually the Stephen Gaynor School, where would Seth be today? What happens to other people who do not have the opportunities and backup we have been so lucky to have?

At the same time that we were testing Seth at the Committee for Special Education and with the Oldbergs, we were assembling a list of private special-education schools to visit and decide about applying to. The list was surprisingly short. There were five schools, and one of them, the Stephen Gaynor School, did not accept public funds. Another was in New Jersey, and a third was in Brooklyn.

The need to find a special education setting for Seth was more daunting than anything that had come before. My anxiety level was at an all-time high. I finally realized why Seth had not been sleeping through the night. His self-esteem had been dwindling because he couldn't keep up in school. He felt he was being left behind. He felt he was failing. I faulted myself for being so slow on the uptake.

My journals from this time are overflowing with information on special education and learning disabilities. There is new terminology, new issues of self-esteem, cognitive and verbal aptitudes, social-emotional adaptations, as well as attention or organization topics. Internal language, auditory blending, adaptive physical therapy, decoding, inferential versus listening comprehension, reversals, and so forth, became part of my lexicon. Each school has a different approach, but I heard this terminology everywhere.

The Gateway School was a place for bright, gifted children with learning disabilities. It felt very "precious" but appealing. It was the first special-education school we visited, and I felt it could solve many problems for us. It was an oasis in the midst of my turmoil and anxiety. Surrounded by experts and specialists and other children who were challenged in their learning, but considered very bright, I was relieved. There was a place in the world for children like my son.

They didn't accept Seth into their program. Although I took reams of notes about our visit, I never wrote down why they didn't take him. However, their presentation, the information they provided, helped me immensely in organizing my thoughts and forming impressions of the schools we later visited. I started to learn which questions to ask.

The Churchill School, which was the best known and which accepted public funds, told us, "We're not interested in children with cerebral palsy."

I was flabbergasted. "What are children with cerebral palsy like?" I asked. Seth was not in a wheelchair, while other children with cerebral palsy were. Seth had no intellectual deficit, but others with this label might. There was no physical reason why Seth should not be a candidate for the Churchill setting. We were searching for a place to minister to his learning challenges. As far as we knew, Churchill had no guidelines that excluded Seth.

Lawyer Katzive, who was a board member at Churchill, was upset that anyone at Churchill had made such a statement to us. Public money means no discrimination. It was a legitimate concern on her part and, had I been inclined, I would have pursued this issue. For the moment, I cared only about what the label "cerebral palsy" meant to others, and what this label would mean to Seth. The Churchill people had never met Seth, yet they ostracized him because of his diagnosis. What would that mean in the future? I was devastated, appalled. This was the all-time low for me.

The McDowell Learning Center was in Brooklyn. We were disappointed in the facility and would not send Seth such a long distance to such a depressing environment. The school's intentions and philosophy were admirable, but the physical surroundings were deplorable. At the time, there were only two remaining options. One was the Community School in New Jersey; the other was the Stephen Gaynor School on Seventy-fourth Street in Manhattan.

We made several treks out to New Jersey to the Community School. Seth went for two interviews. It was an appealing place, although its location worked against it. In addition to his education, I worried about Seth's socialization. How would we organize play dates and birthday parties with his schoolmates? How many of them lived in the City? A friendly place in a suburban setting—their program went through grade twelve—the Community School assigned students into small academic groupings. All of the staff were special-education people. The school accepted Seth the week before we left for La Jolla, but because it was located out of the City and a substantial bus ride away, we stalled.

Our interview at the Gaynor School was scheduled to take place after our return from La Jolla. We were stalling about the Community School but were anxious not to miss out on the best opportunity and only option we had come upon thus far. We also wanted to investigate the Stephen Gaynor School. We knew nothing about it, and neither did the Oldbergs. That was why it wasn't one of our first scheduled visits. We knew that everyone spoke against it because it was a small school and the tuition costs were prohibitive.

⌒

In the late winter, early spring, we had taken the children to a remote and primitive fishing village on the Pacific coast of Costa Rica. It was a wonderful vacation, very different from any of the traveling we had done before with the children. There were no distractions: no television, no hotels, nothing but beach and dirt roads. Walking, swimming, playing on the beach day after day, Seth soon began to open up and share some of his feelings of inadequacy with me. I was very touched and dismayed.

"I'm such a klutz," he told me as we arrived on the beach one day with all our paraphernalia. He was having difficulty maneuvering himself and his buckets.

"Whatever makes you say that?" I inquired, my antennae on alert.

"Well, you know that's what the kids tell me in school. The teachers agree."

"The children tease you about your difficulties? Don't the teachers stop them?"

"The teachers don't like me. They never help me. Mostly they're mad because I'm always the last one. You know, making everyone late."

"What do you mean, Seth?" I asked with a pounding heart.

"There are so many steps. Up six flights in the morning just to get to class. Then right away to the basement for gym or something like art. Down six flights, then up six flights again. I'm slow. That makes me tired too, all day."

As he revealed many of the details about his experiences, his ordeal at Rodeph came into sharp focus. My heart bled. Again I blamed myself for not being wiser, more vigilant.

During our stay, the children met the one other North American family visiting the area. Their daughter, Ingrid, was two years older than Haya and two years younger than Seth. The children played marvelously together. Ingrid's and Haya's abilities in the water and navigating the shoreline increasingly challenged Seth, though.

One day he was left behind during their antics. He sat himself down next to me on the beach. The girls were swimming out over their heads and frolicking in the water. One of the village boys had canoed out to them. The girls were hanging off the small boat, laughing and playing. Seth began to cry, excluded by his limitations in the water. Even though Ingrid was closer in age to Seth, she and Haya were becoming bosom buddies. For Seth, the inclusion of his little sister and his own exclusion was devastating.

He said to me, "I hate my problem. It sticks to me like my skin. I wish I could go far out into that ocean and bury it."

What could I say? I was mute. Here was my beautiful son spilling his tears, letting me in on his grief. I wanted to do the right thing, but I was unsure what that was. I couldn't deny the truth of his circumstances. I couldn't tell him it wasn't so. I summoned all I knew about respecting him and the integrity of his challenge and responded, "It must be very difficult for you. I think you're brave and trying hard. Daddy and I are giving you everything we can to help you. Use it as well as you can."

Alone later, I grieved deeply. Sad for Seth, but while I was sharing with Jay what had happened, I realized the complexity of parenting

a special child. I didn't want to deny him his feelings, but I wanted
him to know that there was hope. Allowing him to feel that he could
talk to me was paramount. I wanted him to know that we, Jay and
I, were there for him. At the same time, I had to let him know that
I expected him to make good use of his strengths as well as the available therapies.

When we returned from this trip, Seth completed the testing with
the Oldbergs and with the Board of Education, and we pursued the
school interviews. In the meantime, we were through with the tutors,
the Committee for Special Education, the special-education advocate, and testing. One person remained: Dr. Julian Oldberg. In the
Oldbergs's reports, and for that matter in the written information
from the Board of Education, Seth's psychological state appeared to
be delicate. Both of the Oldberg reports recommended that Seth have
ongoing "play therapy."

The recurrence of the words "low self-esteem," "isolation," "manipulation," "avoidance," made Jay and me think it would probably be
a good idea to engage some outside support for Seth. He continued
to exhibit difficult behavior at home: he was challenging, defiant,
always negotiating. We signed on with Dr. Julian Oldberg for two
sessions a week for Seth, which meant that we signed on for another
expense, too.

I was not entirely comfortable with Dr. Oldberg. I like making eye
contact with people, especially people involved in my psychological
and emotional life or those I love. Dr. Oldberg had an odd anomaly,
making it very difficult for me to establish eye contact with him, to
feel that I was actually looking into his eyes. I also think that somewhere deep down I didn't really trust that Dr. Oldberg liked Seth or
me. He was challenged by us, impressed with Seth's innate intelligence, but not appreciative of Seth's joie de vivre or my forceful personality.

Why did I start with him? Why did I stick it out with him for years
to come, despite the fact that I felt completely alienated by him and
avoided most contact with him? The truth is I started with him
because his office was across the street from where we lived. I was
exhausted. I could not face one more demand in our lives. But I also
realized that Seth, and Jay and I for that matter, needed some guide-

lines. At our initial meeting with him, Dr. Oldberg had offered some helpful suggestions.

He helped us sort out how to wake Seth in the morning, especially after a night of many wakings, and given the obvious fact of Seth's not wanting to go to school at Rodeph. Seth was late for school every day. Dr. Oldberg made suggestions to the school, and we asked them to cooperate in the strategies to deal with Seth's lateness. The doctor's involvement legitimized our requests at Rodeph. He helped us with strategies for being consistent. We initiated systems for rule making, which included getting Seth's agreement. We began to see how much Seth was used to having his own way. So in addition to seeing Charles Bonner, Seth began going to Dr. Oldberg twice a week. Finally, in early May, we left for La Jolla.

The trip to La Jolla was very important for me. I went with specific questions for Dr. Frymann and Dr. Springall. I also went with information, and I wanted to talk to the doctors and to Ellen Solomon about the various evaluations Seth had recently undergone. The issues of self-esteem and expressive language were paramount. Dr. Frymann thought the solution to Seth's speech difficulties was improved breathing. Work on his breathing, she told me repeatedly. For all my prior work with Carola Speads, my actual response was to find a speech therapist in New York who would do this, and I scheduled an evaluation for our return.

Dr. Springall thought that Seth was beginning to crawl in a cross pattern, although the movement was not as well organized, as he would have hoped. But Seth's creeping had improved, and there was less pronation in Seth's feet. The doctor added new and more challenging exercises including bilateral forms, insisting once again that Seth needed to dig in with his big toe.

Dr. Springall suggested that we purchase a machine called the Exer-Cor. You could stand or lie on it, and it simulated patterns of cross crawling and walking. Athletes use it to strengthen their movement patterns. He also suggested that Seth use a trampoline and monkey bars. I wasn't sure how to make this happen over the summer, but an innovative solution would soon present itself.

The doctor was very patient in describing to me once again the physiological and developmental steps that need to occur in order for a child to progress. He showed me how learning occurs developmentally. Discipline problems, he said, arise when a child is passed by in academics. Again I felt comfortable with all of his assessments.

It was true that Seth was much less challenging in La Jolla than he was at home in New York, but he still had some difficulties sleeping through the night. Dr. Frymann suggested that Seth needed time to unwind and to fantasize, time every day just to be at peace.

Ellen Solomon, Seth's teacher at Beth Israel Day School, said that Seth's writing was improving dramatically and that he was a nonreader only in phonetics. In the whole-language environment Seth was working at grade level. She got me a slew of whole-language books from a special catalog. Seth began to read all the time.

The other observation Ellen made was about how social Seth was, how much of a potential leader he was. Her upbeat assessment of Seth contrasted sharply with the negative observations offered by his teachers in New York as well as Dr. Oldberg. Dr. Oldberg had said that Seth was always expecting things, especially new things, new toys, all the time. He claimed that Seth acted bored during the sessions, pushing and testing and reluctant to talk about some themes, especially his disability.

Dr. Oldberg had also remarked that Seth was living in a fantasy that he was exactly like other children. Dr. Frymann did not seem to think that such a fantasy was so bad. I always felt that Dr. Oldberg was judging Seth, whereas Dr. Frymann was simply stating the facts. Seth was six years old, about to turn seven in June, and finishing the first grade. Haya was three years old. Our lives were much more complex than the lives of other families we knew.

Our lives were split. We split our home between New York and La Jolla. The evaluators and the school in New York saw Seth's nature as oppositional. They were pessimistic about him academically. In La Jolla the view of our child was completely different. The doctors and the school noted his progress, academically and socially. The school went so far as to predict his capacities as a leader and guide. In La Jolla his health was ministered osteopathically and homeopathically. In New York we were still using Dr. Lee.

⌒

We returned from La Jolla at the end of May and prepared for our visit to the Stephen Gaynor School. Everywhere we had gone for interviews we had been asked to send ahead Seth's test results and school reports. Not at the Stephen Gaynor School. Yvette Siegel, the admissions director, wanted to spend two hours alone with Seth and then meet with us. The entire intake was done on the basis of a written application and her personal evaluation of the child, as well as a meeting with the parents. The interview was one of the high points of our experience.

After two hours Yvette Siegel, much like Dr. Frymann when she did her evaluation of Seth, presented us with the most comprehensive, accurate, and thorough understanding and appreciation of our son we had heard since we had begun the special-education process. Her insights into his learning abilities were awe inspiring and in sync with the results of the most positive testing. When it came to expressive language, inferential and abstract reasoning, she said he was terrific. She thought he was wonderful with sequential picture stories and with size concepts. Her analysis was very different from what we had heard from the Board of Education and from the Oldberg testing. Her appreciation for his humor and life force matched our reactions to him. Her prescription for his success was grounded in the values we aspired to at home.

Yvette Siegel saw Seth's limitations primarily in terms of dwindling self-esteem, but she also placed his diminishing confidence in himself in the context of the enormous effort required of him. It was the first time that anyone besides Jay and Dr. Frymann and I had recognized this aspect of Seth's life. She perceived Seth's rough cover, his difficulty letting his deficits show.

Once we saw that Seth's psychological, emotional, and academic states were perceived clearly and that Gaynor wanted him, there was no question about enrolling him for the fall. Finally we had a home for Seth in September. I breathed a sigh of relief. Seth did too. Our plan was to enroll Seth at Gaynor and have a month in New York in September before going to La Jolla in October to resume Seth's treatments with Dr. Frymann. Yvette Siegel was concerned about our ongoing commitment to La Jolla, but she said she would reserve judgment until after our first visit in October.

I scheduled a speech evaluation and had Seth's hearing checked once again just to be certain that there were no major changes. Everything about his hearing was fine, which meant that the speech issues were not being influenced by auditory challenges. The speech evaluator described Seth's general lack of precision, his tendency to posture with a tense jaw and stiff upper lip. He said that Seth's tongue was restricted in movement and that breathing was a factor, especially when Seth needed to sustain his voice over a lengthy amount of time. He suggested that we should be working for sound production and recommended that Seth work with a speech therapist at least twice a week. Among those he mentioned was Jackie Morisco. I contacted her about a possible fall slot.

After we settled on the Stephen Gaynor School, there was a marked change in Seth. Our commitment to a new setting, his knowledge that it was going to happen, put us all at ease. I began to prepare for our summer on Cape Cod. Seth was finally enrolled at the Children's School of Science (CSS) in Woods Hole. This was the summer he had been waiting for. After Science School he was going to spend afternoons in the older children's program at the Woods Hole Child Center. I planned for Haya to spend her mornings there, too.

The Children's School of Science was Seth's ultimate salvation. At the CSS children come to *do* science projects, not just think about science. The school occupies a historic house in Woods Hole, overlooking Eel Pond. All morning the children from the Science School populate the environs of Woods Hole, wandering about in supervised groups with their nets and buckets, budding scientists, all of them. Seth enrolled in "Seashore Life," the only course for which he was eligible that first summer. He found his niche. He was already investigating which classes he could take the next summer. When he wasn't in class or at the Child Center, he was at the beach with his nose and his net in the ocean.

After the first three weeks, there was parents' night at the Science School. I approached the evening gingerly and alone. Jay was back in the City and not expected until the weekend. I anticipated the evening with some anxiety. The years at Heschel and Rodeph, the ordeal of the previous spring, made me slightly reticent, never sure now about what I would encounter. A minute after introducing myself I heard, "Shoot the moon with this kid," from Seth's teacher and one of the curriculum advisors. "You have a real scientist on your hands."

The teacher, Marion, and the teaching assistant, the son of a prominent local scientist, described Seth as plunging in, raising his hand with answers and questions, fearless and undaunted by challenges. The course demanded several field trips, and although Seth lagged behind slightly, they said that he never lost his sense of humor, his positive outlook and purpose. Seth was an inspiration to them and to the other children, to everyone who came into contact with him.

I saw that evening that everyone in the school knew Seth. All the people who spoke with me that evening mentioned his good nature and natural social grace. Later, after returning to the house, and in the exquisite pleasure of my solitude, I cried quietly for a long time. My son was finally out of the darkness.

Seth's exercise program was essential to his ongoing progress, so we purchased the Exer-Cor on Dr. Springall's recommendation. We also planned to bring a small trampoline to the Cape with us. Monkey bars and other paraphernalia were available at local playgrounds, but I knew I would have limited time and inclination to involve myself in these efforts. Jay would be away during the week, so he could devote himself to such activities only on the weekends. Seth needed a regime to engage him in the program that Dr. Springall had outlined.

Serendipity intervened magnificently. The Falmouth Commodores are part of the Cape Cod Baseball League, a serious college league that recruits baseball players from colleges all over the country to compete in a summer-long series. The players are often contenders for the major leagues, whose representatives scout and recruit the players throughout the summer. One of our greatest summer pleasures has been attending Commodore games. A picnic, a blanket, and a folding chair accompany us to Fuller Field in the early evening at least twice a week to cheer our team.

We were very aware of the Commodores because our neighbors, Worthington and Dorothy Campbell, served as a host family every summer, providing housing for at least two boys. The community also takes responsibility for finding employment for the players. Because the boys are only available in the mornings, having practice and games in the afternoons and early evenings, it can be difficult to find them jobs. Some of them work painting local houses or doing odd jobs for residents.

Aware of all this and knowing that two Commodores would occupy the lower half of the Campbell's house, I called Worth two weeks before we left for the Cape. I asked him to explore whether there was a player among that summer's crop who would be interested, available, and suitable to work with Seth for three hours every morning before Science School. Worth said that he would investigate. A few days later he called to inform me that one of the boys living with him seemed a likely candidate.He was the catcher for the Commodores.

A native of Avon, Indiana, Stoney Burke was a physical education major at Indiana State University. I interviewed him a day or two after we arrived at the Cape. Stoney became not only Seth's "trainer," but his friend and our family friend.

Together, Stoney and I created a program for Seth that included the monkey bars, the trampoline, and stretching exercises. Working on the monkey bars was very challenging for Seth. Dr. Springall had encouraged it because the exercise involved accomplishing a cross pattern overhead. I wanted Seth running along the beach in the water, doing things to encourage his hand-eye coordination such as hitting a baseball and playing Ping-Pong.

I made one other request. It was intuitive. I asked Stoney to keep a journal of his summer with Seth. I wanted him to make an entry every day describing what he and Seth had done together. My asking Stoney to keep the journal was motivated by a desire to keep track of what actually happened every day, but there was another aspect to it. Stoney was nineteen and focused on college and baseball. I didn't want this job to be just passing the time, the two of them riding around in Stoney's car from the baseball field to the ocean, listening to rock-and-roll, although I saw that that part of it would be good for Seth, too. I wanted it to be a two-way street. I knew from being a writer that committing things to paper in a journal would benefit their relationship. Both Stoney and Seth needed to grow together.

As a surprise for my birthday at the end of July, Stoney presented me with the journal. It remains one of my treasures. In it Stoney wrote about how he took Seth to Woodneck Beach to run on the sand or to the baseball field to run on the track or practice hitting.

Gradually he began writing not only about the things they had done, but also about Seth's progress and what had happened to Seth during their workouts. In one entry he noted, "Seth worked up a good sweat, and I told him a good sweat was a really good thing to have."

As the journal progressed, Stoney included his own feelings about watching Seth's struggle. His record of Seth's progress had other dimensions. Reading these entries gave me insight into their relationship and provided me with a record and a lasting memento for Seth. Jay says that to this day Seth has one of the best batting stances of any kid he knows. Stoney went on to play professionally and to complete his college education. We stay in touch by exchanging cards over the holidays, by informing each other of significant events in our lives.

Recently I read over the last entry in Stoney's diary from that summer. It says,

> Dear Laura and Jay,
>   I really appreciate all you have done for me. You made my summer worthwhile. I hope that the time I spent with Seth helped. I wish the best for him to succeed in all that he does. I know he will. It makes me feel good to see the expressions on your faces when Seth accomplishes something. The joy I see in you makes me feel like I have accomplished something too. Seth has really taught me a lot about myself, and life in general. He is a great kid. The experiences and moments we shared will last forever.

After spending the summer jumping on the trampoline, working on the monkey bars, running on the beach, playing baseball, Ping-Pong, and soccer, Seth's progress was significant. We were ecstatic. In addition to the mornings with Stoney and the Science School, Seth went horseback riding two or three times a week. When I called Dr. Frymann at the end of July, it was to report how happy and cooperative Seth was, how energetic and independent, how self-reliant. At the same time, I thought that Seth was not walking particularly well and that his speech was not improving, although his expressive language was. His progress was always a mixture.

Another significant experience for Seth that summer was that he would go from Science School to the Woods Hole Child Center accom-

panied only by a twelve-year-old girl from Science School. I paid her
ten dollars a week to walk with Seth each afternoon after Science
School up the hill to the Child Center. This meant that Seth was not
collected by his mother or a babysitter. He was more independent
than ever before in his life. Seth and Jennifer Gifford walked the half
mile up School Street every afternoon. At the end of the summer,
Jennifer wrote Seth a letter about how he had inspired her, and how
spending the time with him every day had made her grow in ways
she had never imagined. We were incredibly impressed by her feelings about Seth.

Our son's "karma" was touching everyone who had close contact
with him. Out of the darkness of the previous year we drew great
light during those beautiful summer months. The treasure of Seth
was reinforced. It was becoming increasingly clear how special circumstances create special people, and how through recognizing our
limitations we strive to know our potential. I redirected my thoughts
to how lucky we were. I was fortified for the coming year.

When we returned to New York in September, Seth began at the
Stephen Gaynor School. It felt like a safe haven after the experience
of the prior year. A small school, founded in 1962 and located in a
large, white townhouse on the West Side of Manhattan, the Stephen
Gaynor School (SGS) is staffed by special-education teachers and
learning specialists and has a devoted administrative staff. Classes
are small, at the most six to eight children. The children are grouped
on the basis of their social, chronological, and academic compatibil-
ities. Children attend Gaynor from as early as preschool up through
the sixth grade or until they are thirteen years old. So we would
have to find another school for Seth sometime in the future.

The guiding principle of the Stephen Gaynor School is to create
an environment in which children can grow academically, socially,
and emotionally. Gaynor's primary goal is to have children return
to a mainstream classroom as rapidly as possible. Their success rate
is dramatic. Ninety-five percent of Stephen Gaynor students go on
to complete their studies at mainstream schools and colleges. For us
that was the most significant aspect of the program. We were sure
that Seth would eventually be a candidate for the mainstream. We

wanted to think of him as a child who was making a temporary stopover to get better prepared.

What we didn't foresee was what it would mean emotionally for us to move into this world of special education, especially since we started out with the attitude that Seth was only at Gaynor temporarily. It took time for Seth and for us to become reconciled to his new school situation.

At first we were so relieved that Seth had a place at Gaynor, we "dumped" him there and had little involvement in the school. I paid little attention to anything I heard that fall at school. I was blotting out all the problems of the previous year, especially the ordeal of the past spring. Of course we attended the parent orientation and other school meetings, but deep down I was in a stupor, totally fatigued. I needed for someone else to deal with Seth. I know now how wonderful the Stephen Gaynor School was for Seth. We could jettison Seth at the Gaynor School, and they took care of him just fine.

We had another child too, and I wanted to turn some attention toward Haya. She always seemed easy and adaptable, going along with all our moves, our sudden changes. Just like the rest of us, she lived in the orbit around Seth. Seth was always the center and the star. I hadn't yet recognized how she was affected by being Seth's sister.

My stupor had its limits, however. I called Jackie Morisco, the speech therapist, and scheduled appointments. There were also other changes on the horizon. Seth developed an ear infection the first week we were home from the Cape, and I took him to see Dr. Lee. She prescribed amoxycillin, an antibiotic. Seth had not had any allopathic medicine since we began with Dr. Frymann a year earlier.

Like other children, Seth had his share of ear infections early on. My diary documents several routine visits to Dr. Lee for ear infections and follow-up visits. Antibiotics were administered repeatedly, sometimes to no avail. When we adopted a different route to health by pursuing osteopathic and homeopathic care, I concluded that antibiotics were often useless, especially for viral infections. Osteopaths have known for a hundred years that small children are more susceptible to ear infections because their Eustachian tubes are shorter. This means that infections reach the middle ear more easily. By the time Haya was born I knew much more about routine ear infections and how viral infections run their course with or without antibiotics. So I decided to ignore Dr. Lee's prescription this time and treat Seth myself with a homeopathic remedy.

While overall self-management is not advisable when a condition is acute, Dr. Masiello always encouraged his patients, to become competent at deciphering symptoms and choosing remedies to administer for ourselves when there are minor ailments. That is very much a part of practicing homeopathic medicine, learning to analyze, respond to, and report symptoms. The doctor doesn't have to be called for every little ache and pain.

Because of my obsessive journal entries, I knew that Seth had had exactly the same kind of cold a year earlier, the same week we left the Cape. I used that information as part of my analysis. I gave the homeopathic remedy a try with Seth, and it worked. I never had to give him the antibiotic. Within a day, he got better. We returned to Dr. Lee ten days later, and there was no infection in his middle ear. I knew it was time to start thinking seriously about a change in our overall medical approach.

In early September, I attended a "Back to School Night for Parents" at Gaynor. There was information about the weekly structure of the children's academic life at Gaynor, classroom instruction, after-school activities, teaching structures, evaluations, and reports. Outwardly I was attentive. Inside I was absent. Gaynor was a salvation, but in my mind it was also just a stopover.

Two weeks into the school year I met with Seth's teachers, and they said he was doing well. I was glad to hear that Seth was participating fully in everything and that he was first in his class in math. As I review my notes, I see that I attended these first two meetings alone. Even more than I, Jay was distancing himself around this time. I remember that later that fall, or perhaps early that winter, I went alone to a forum on "Life after Gaynor." I was already looking beyond, but Jay was too tired to be involved. Although it took some time and many other developments, eventually our attitude would change.

Seth was very proud of himself and brought home one of his tests. He was keeping up in reading and didn't need any outside tutoring. We decided to cut back the sessions with Dr. Oldberg to once a week. The doctor did not support this move, but I was determined not to make my son a full-time patient. The big question in everyone's mind was how La Jolla would figure into everything. I was still committed to returning for more treatments for Seth.

⌒

In La Jolla that October, when Seth had his first appointment with Dr. Frymann, she said that he had more control over his body and much more energy. Dr. Springall evaluated him and said that Seth was reading 99 percent of all the sight words presented to him, doing more with his left hand, and integrating his creeping and crawling. Seth's speech was definitely inconsistent, but there was more volume in the phrasing. He had more breath. I didn't really know what Seth and Jackie Morisco were doing together during their sessions, but whatever they were doing was obviously working. Before we left for La Jolla she had begun coming to the house twice a week.

I was still completely tuned out. I was exhausted from the traveling back and forth to California, adjusting the kids to their September programs just after returning from the Cape, and then hauling us all to California. Drs. Frymann and Springall would be in charge while we were in La Jolla. That was enough for me. I couldn't think of another thing. Seth did though, and his ability to advocate for himself was about to come into sharp focus.

When Seth went back to the Beth Israel Day School in San Diego, the school recommended that he remain in the first grade with Ellen Solomon. Three days into our first school week, Seth came home and asked to talk to me immediately.

He said, "I've been to see Jill Green." Jill was the principal of the school. "And I've talked to Cindy. She's the second-grade teacher. I want to be with my friends from last year. I told them I can do it."

"Have they decided? Do you want me to call them?" I asked, surprised by his initiative.

"No. I told them I want three days to prove I can be in class with Evan and everyone. I know I can keep up. No problem. I just have to show them."

"What do you want me to do? I can call Jill and talk to her." I kept on the same track, not fully realizing how well he had thought everything through.

"I just want you to back me up."

I was astonished. Seth had come up with his objectives and decided on a course of action without discussing the details of his plan with me. Then he had proceeded to find the people who could help him realize his goal. Over the years Seth's ability to advocate for himself has continued to serve him. I want to think that he learned some of this from us, his parents, but I also think that his circumstances offered him two directions. One option was to become a victim, someone not entitled to or not capable of getting what he wanted. The other was to become motivated to get what he needed, knowing that he would have to do extraordinary things to overcome his situation.

At BIDS he knew that he had to act for himself, so he did. He succeeded, too. At the end of the first week of school the teacher and principal called and said that Seth was right. He belonged in the second grade. He had a wonderful month in school, reaching new academic heights. Sometime in the middle of the month, Cindy, the second-grade teacher, called me. For half an hour I listened to her sing Seth's praises, the joy she had in teaching him. It helped me forget the painful meetings with the teachers at Rodeph a year earlier.

Seth continues to elicit immense satisfaction from his teachers. He loves to learn. He approaches the classroom with excitement and curiosity. Time and again, we listen to his teachers say what a wonderful student he is. Now in his teenage years, hormones dominate, and there are more inconsistencies, but one thing remains constant, and that is his sense of responsibility, his eagerness to know more. The key is a friendly environment.

During my last visit with Dr. Frymann before we left La Jolla that fall, she said something very disturbing to me. She thought that something of a psychic nature, some very negative sway, had influenced Seth for a time. I was appalled at the suggestion. It sounded as though she meant that some kind of voodoo had been visited on him. I was shocked and worried.

In retrospect I think what Dr. Frymann was describing was something Seth himself identified years later. So many pairs of hands had touched him. There had been three physical therapists before Seth was eighteen months old. A multitude of other professionals had handled and examined Seth: neurologists, podiatrists, Feldenkrais practitioners, orthopedists. There is enormous power and influence in touch—something you have to experience to know. The sense of touch is the great sense. The whole skin sees and listens, and not only the skin, but the entire body, bones and muscles, heart, and mind. Whoever Seth is is a product of a lot of input, the result of the sway of many hands.

CHAPTER TWELVE

anchoring

WHEN WE RETURNED FROM LA JOLLA, the teachers and staff at Gaynor immediately recognized and acknowledged the differences in Seth. However, they remained wary of our ongoing commitment to working with Dr. Frymann because of the interruptions in Seth's schooling. For the time being, I didn't listen to them, only to my own inner voice that told me we had to return to La Jolla in January. I wasn't listening to anything they said anyway, because I had yet to accept that Seth really needed special education. Gaynor was a way station in my mind. It was only a matter of time and my getting organized before Seth returned to the mainstream. So we thought.

Before we left La Jolla, Dr. Frymann prescribed "time out" from treatment. She also wanted me to "stay calm." We were becoming better acquainted, the doctor and I. She was less of a deity to me, which made her more approachable. She respected my seriousness, my strong sense of purpose. At the same time she had insights into me. I always "took something away" from our encounters (and I still do today).

Months before our October trip to La Jolla though, I began thinking about access to treatments in New York, or at least in the local environs. Relying on a doctor three thousand miles away unsettled me. At the time Dr. Masiello didn't seem like an option because his practice was not exclusively pediatric. So I began searching for a New York–area Cranial Osteopath who was also a pediatrician.

Dr. Michael Burrano fit this description. From what I remember, he also practiced Homeopathy, although he was not a Homeopath. He practiced in Brewster, New York, two hours by train from the City. We went to see him once. I liked him, and I liked his insights into Seth, but Dr. Frymann's admonition in October persuaded me that I shouldn't be in such a hurry to put Seth into any more hands. And Brewster was still quite a commute from Manhattan.

We spent the autumn nesting Seth into Gaynor, Haya into nursery school at the 92nd Street Y. Haya spent two weeks in the classroom before we left for La Jolla, and she adapted splendidly when we returned. "She never misses a beat," I said to her teachers. We were all astonished by the apparent ease with which she slipped into the regime. Everyone was suitably impressed. Little did we know.

⌒

In the early winter we settled the lawsuit against the doctor and the hospital out of court. At the eleventh hour, just as a court date for the trial was scheduled, the insurance companies for the doctor and hospital made us an offer. At the time, Jay was preparing me to testify at the scheduled trial right after our January trip to La Jolla.

The lawsuit had been a thorny issue, creating terrible disquiet for me. I had given my deposition years earlier in the winter of 1987, while I was pregnant with Haya. The experience had been extremely difficult. The defendants' lawyers were understandably adversarial and made me recount the night of Seth's birth in painstaking detail. They constantly goaded me on, couching their questions with the implication that I should have done more to protect my unborn child. "Didn't the nurse tell you that the baby wasn't getting enough oxygen?" asked the woman interrogator. Such questions only underscored my own sense of guilt and responsibility, which I was already wrestling with constantly.

Another aspect of their inquiry focused on Seth's actual circumstances. The defense lawyers wanted to establish that in fact Seth was highly functional and suffered from little impairment as a result of his birth trauma. I needed to stress the extent and ramifications of Seth's limitations, a task that was painful and arduous for me. Because my entire life is devoted to helping Seth realize his full potential, nothing caused me as much grief as those days I spent giving my deposition, claiming and insisting on the darkest aspects of Seth's challenges.

During the winter of 1990, the defense required us to take Seth to one of their doctors for an examination. I was outraged. With all the medical information, all the reports and diagnoses already available, the idea that still another person was going to examine Seth incensed me. Then our lawyers also wanted someone of their choosing to examine Seth. I felt sick about all of it, offended by the continual probing and the ongoing scrutiny of my son. I raged and ranted. Jay had to calm me down before taking Seth to each of these examinations. I will never forget them. By this time Seth was more aware of his circumstances, so the examinations were difficult for him, too.

The settlement of the case in 1991 meant an end to a nasty legal episode. Although the court set severe restrictions on how Seth's money could be handled until he came of legal age, limiting its growth potential by circumscribing investments, they did grant us an allowance to help meet many of the financial demands we were facing. An appearance before the judge later that spring ultimately closed the door on the legal aspect, although many of the emotional scars remain even today. But we had scored a victory. Because of Jay's hard work with our lawyers, Seth will have resources to help him meet the ongoing challenges and health-care needs throughout his life.

∽

In November and December our life felt stable. Both children were settled in the schools where they would remain for at least another year. Both children had after-school activities. Seth's consisted of one visit with Dr. Oldberg every week and two thirty-minute speech sessions at home every week.

We had one meeting with Dr. Oldberg during this time. He was disappointed that he wasn't seeing more of us. He wanted more input. He felt that Seth had returned in good shape from La Jolla and then had begun to regress. Seth had stopped being creative and had become increasingly secretive, he insisted. I couldn't muster the energy to see Dr. Oldberg again. I had all I could do to contain the relative equilibrium and semblance of a normal life before preparing for our return to La Jolla. I was content that Seth saw Dr. Oldberg once a week, and that there was someone to take him. The doctor's proximity meant that the current babysitter could simply drop Seth off across the street then pick him up at the end of the session.

After twenty-two speech sessions Jackie Morisco wrote in her report that, "Seth's vocal production was complicated by inadequate loudness owing to the limited neuromuscular control of his respiratory function." Although I was aware that inadequate control of

breathing was the obvious impediment, I was still not employing
any of Carola's techniques with Seth. Dr. Frymann also had told me
to work on Seth's breathing as a way of improving his speech, but I
simply turned Seth's speech issues over to the speech therapist. My
own energy was directed elsewhere.

⁓

I decided to inform myself as well as I could about Osteopathy. Unlike
with the other disciplines I was pursuing, I couldn't become an actual
practitioner or do a training unless I was prepared to go to medical
school. I considered this option, but I quickly realized it was not for
me. I knew I could know more though, so I set myself to the task of
learning as much as I could as a layperson. The prior spring I had
attended all of Dr. Frymann's lectures in La Jolla. In November I
asked Dr. Masiello for a bibliography and for some time to study with
him. I settled down to work.

Osteopaths use the muscular-skeletal system as a basic approach
to treating their patients. They include all body systems, treating
tops, bottoms, sides, and fronts. Doctors of Osteopathy believe that
the body's structure plays a critical role in its ability to function. They
use their eyes and hands to identify structural problems and to support the body's natural tendency toward health and self-healing.

Osteopaths are licensed physicians. Fully trained, they can prescribe medication and perform surgery. Doctors of Osteopathy (D.O.s)
and M.D.s (allopathic physicians) are the only two types of complete
physicians. Doctors of Osteopathy practice in all branches of medicine
and surgery, from psychiatry to obstetrics, from geriatrics to emergency medicine. However, D.O.s are trained to be doctors first, and
specialists second. Osteopaths use their hands diagnostically, per-
ceptually, and therapeutically. The founder of Osteopathy was an
M.D. surgeon who trained physicians to use their hands for healing
along with simple and natural remedies—diet, rest, meditation,
prayer.

The osteopathic approach accounts for the entire function of the
body, bones being considered the foundation for the body's structure and therefore its function. This is not to say that an orthopedist
is not appropriate in other situations, be it cerebral palsy or many
other problems as, for instance, in the case of a broken bone. But

we think about Seth in terms of his whole body, including his sensory experiences.

Osteopathy's insistence on treating the whole person and not just a disease entity coincided with my growing awareness of somatics. Somatics says that bodies are not different structures, but that through structure we can look at the different ways different bodies function. The first time I read about somatics was in the work of Thomas Hanna, who wrote extensively about how humans function best. Mr. Hanna was the editor of the magazine *Somatics* and the author of several books. He was director of the Novato Institute for Somatic Research and Training in California.

The somatic view pays homage to the evolution of the physical life of humans. It sees the Homo sapiens as a genetically ancient animal whose physical characteristics are the result of a long series of functional adaptations that have enhanced its survival. The ideas of Carola, of Feldenkrais, of Doman are in perfect sync with this evolutionary concept. Osteopathy is also attuned to this historical view of human function.

Osteopathy recognizes that there is a systematic integrity in each individual, that there is a self-balancing and self-adjusting ability in the human species. But we must be allowed to be self-healing. Osteopathy fosters change in a preventative way, helping us become less susceptible to toxic stimulants in the environment. The manipulative techniques Osteopaths use are designed to improve circulation and stimulate the immune system. The theory is that all bodies are in process; they are not static. This view of process is also essential to the somatic vision.

The Osteopath's view centers on the patient's constitution and not on one episode of acute illness. Dr. Frymann had said early on that you can not touch someone without influencing his or her whole body. I had seen this for myself in Carola's classes and in the Feldenkrais work. I liked the fact that Osteopaths were involved with the structure of the body, not only in their heads but also in their hands, because they "listen" with their hands. Osteopathic Manipulative Therapy (OMT) is nonjudgmental; it is a compassionate approach to healing, to resonating, to establishing a link with our structural being.

Osteopaths are not chiropractors. Chiropractors are not physicians and have not had the training of an Osteopath. Their objectives are limited to alignment and symmetry. For Osteopaths, function and integration are the goal. The intention in Osteopathy is to help life come into balance in the way it intends.

In his book, *Osteopathy: The Illustrated Guide,* Stephen Sandler, D.O., describes the cranial Osteopath as a highly trained physician who uses refined hands-on techniques to detect and treat subtle disturbances in motion patterns of the skull, which are often symptomatic of certain disorders. Sandler describes how Osteopaths who have studied and specialized in cranial work maintain that palpation on the skull and sacrum picks up a rhythmic pulsation distinct from the respiratory rhythm or the heartbeat and pulse of the blood. This pulsation is the reverberation of the cerebrospinal fluid, which bathes both the brain and the spinal column.

Cranial Osteopaths explain that the brain is suspended inside the skull by sheets of tissue known as the meninges. These meninges extend all the way down the vertebral column to the sacrum. This linkage connects the movement of the skull bones and the movement of the pelvis. Cranial work tries to balance the rhythmical forces at work in the body by gently guiding and releasing the tensions within the reciprocal tension of these tissues.

Osteopathy can be especially valuable in helping to diagnose and treat developmental problems in children. Dr. Frymann claimed that only ten percent of children have normal body structure. Ten percent of children have distortion that is visible to the naked eye. Eighty percent of children's structural distortions are not visible. Eighty percent of children with learning problems had suffered difficult births. Dr. Frymann thought that all children should have an osteopathic evaluation at three months.

As I wrote earlier, the brains of very young children have a greater capacity to repair themselves than do adult brains. A young child's nervous system is still forming, still in flux. There is a plasticity in a child's central nervous system, an ability to recover completely or partially after an insult to the brain. A child's central nervous system produces many more brain cells and connections than are eventually used for complex motor tasks. As long as a child's nervous system has not yet matured, there is still a chance that the child can make at least a partial recovery from early movement problems.

An Osteopath would have known immediately what Seth's circumstances were. When I think back to all the routine physical examinations Seth had with our pediatrician, I realize that an Osteopath,
trained to know what the "norm" *feels* like, would have recognized
Seth's anomalies immediately. If only I had known to take him to
one. There is no doubt that earlier intervention for Seth would have
made an enormous difference. Cranial work at an early stage would
certainly have been significant for Seth and for his future. My hope
is that I can use what I know to persuade others to act and intervene early.

◦～

Settling in at home during those eleven weeks felt good, but then
we were off again, back to La Jolla in January for almost five weeks.
Seth's adjustment was immediate. He loved our life in La Jolla, his
school in San Diego. And everyone at Beth Israel Day School loved
him. California was his milieu. Haya's adjustment to La Jolla was
not as easy. She didn't like her school program as much as Seth liked
his. She missed her nursery school at the 92nd Street Y, a superb
program without peer. La Jolla offered a day-care environment, but
it would be another year before she would be able to participate fully
in the principal school at Beth Israel Day School. Nonetheless, she
adapted, rode to school in the car pool, and made a few friends.

Dr. Frymann thought that Seth was in better shape in January
than he had been in October. She maintained, however, that he had
a deep conflict about taking control of his body. Dr. Springall thought
that there had been an improvement in the clarity of Seth's speech
and in his writing. Seth's reading was excellent, including the phonics,
the approach that was emphasized at Gaynor. The drooling had subsided, the walking had improved, and Seth's creeping and crawling
were better organized, but he still needed to dig in more with the
big toe during his exercises.

During Jay's visit to La Jolla in January, we went together to see
Dr. Frymann. The doctor described Seth as having a violent, opposing
nature. We were both surprised to hear her say this. And sad. This
was a departure from her usual positive outlook. I knew she had
been disappointed when he was not cooperative, but I had never
detected this strong criticism before. She emphasized that this char-

acteristic was a result of the rage Seth feels deep down, a rage he does not often express.

When I questioned Seth about his rage, he avoided the discussion. Except in the few instances I've described, it was rare for Seth to be forthcoming about his deepest feelings. Mostly I had to divine what was happening beneath the surface. Sometimes his behavior did betray anger at his situation, but he was not frustrated easily or often. What had occurred occasionally was anguish, demonstrated by his breaking down into tears and expressing profound sadness about his circumstances. These days the sadness is more intense and complex. He contains it for long periods of time, but it eventually overflows.

The doctor went on to say that Seth could and would eventually do better. He was motivated and sometimes very cooperative, but he still offered a lot of resistance. (This all changed later.) His aggressive attitude toward issues with his body persisted and was making him disrespectful of the work. She wondered whether we should elicit his input about the treatments. She suggested that Seth needed to mix in a more casual way with other children with disabilities. We had never sought out such opportunities.

Dr. Frymann still believed that Seth required discipline and limits, but she also thought that many of his problems had to do with his possessiveness about me and not having me all to himself. This observation echoed some of the insights Dr. Oldberg had passed along earlier in the year. Dr. Oldberg had made me aware of the heightened competition Seth felt with Haya concerning me. My reaction was that it was typical for siblings to compete for attention. Then I began to wonder, why me? Why not Jay? I chalked it up to being the mother, and I always believed that meant being a "container." There were always so many responsibilities, so many distractions, that I neglected to explore how better to handle this tension between the children. Later I examined how I contributed to their stress. As I dealt with my own anxiety and my feelings of inadequacy, the darker disagreements faded between Seth and Haya.

During our visit to La Jolla, Dr. Springall and Dr. Frymann together presented a lecture entitled "The Developmental Process of Children with Special Needs" in which they pointed out the strong correlation between how much a child progresses in individual stages and a child's intellectual development. They emphasized what happens to children who do not pass through normal developmental processes. These children do not function as well as other children who do pass through normal stages of development.

Sensation and motor ability are vital to the programming of function. Each stage in children's development is essential to the development of the next stage. Each stage in the human individual, even on the cellular level, recapitulates the prior stage. Development can be viewed as an ever-expanding spiral. As the child moves along the widening turns of the spiral, there occurs a return to various developmental themes, but each time they are experienced, it is with a broader perspective, with new knowledge, new skills, and greater independence.

They also stressed the importance of leaving the future wide open, of removing obstacles, especially by not listening to the typical prognoses. They said that providing a child with the opportunities to evolve was the most important job of parents. That encouraged me enormously. I was ready to be open-minded and assess things as we progressed without any prescription for the future. As Carola had suggested years earlier, I wanted to remain open-minded about the developmental possibilities. I intended to continue pursuing new possibilities to enhance Seth's potential.

⌒

We returned to New York in February, knowing that in May we would go back to La Jolla for the last time that year. My focus was on two things: seeing whether I could find a setting or an opportunity for Seth to mix casually with other children with some disabilities and getting Seth's eyes fully examined. I never succeeded in finding the casual setting Dr. Frymann had recommended—an opportunity for Seth to encounter other children with disabilities. Everything I investigated was extreme. I only accomplished the eye examination.

Seth had complained about headaches. I was aware that visual acuity and visual constancy are paramount for learning, and that any visual impairment interferes with development. In *Children with Cerebral Palsy: A Parents' Guide,* I read there were very common vision problems among children with cerebral palsy. The symptoms can be indicative of underlying disorders including sensory delays that affect balance and body awareness, trouble discerning background from foreground, and so on.

Seth's auditory skills had always tested better than his visual ones. However, I had never taken him for anything more than a routine eye examination. I consulted Dr. Richard Kavner, a vision specialist and behavioral optometrist. His specialty is "vision training." Dr. Kavner believes that vision skills can be improved through exercise and nutrition geared to the eyes.

In his book, *Total Vision,* Dr. Kavner defines behavioral optometry as the combined knowledge of psychology, neurology, biology, child development, and other related fields. He writes that our eyes are receptors of the brain. The eye is not just a camera, but a part of the entire visual apparatus, which begins and ends at the back of the brain. The eyes take in the data and channel it along neural impulses to the cortex, where the central control makes sense out of the information.

Case studies demonstrate that enhancing or expanding vision changes personality and behavior. That theory melded perfectly with the information I had gleaned from working with Feldenkrais's teachings, studying Doman, and with my increasing interest in and understanding of somatics. As vision changes, so can personality and behavior. As Dr. Kavner explains, our eyes are active seekers of the essence of life. They are constantly searching, scanning, and selecting from the environment. The eye is a living organ that is always in communication with other vital centers of the body. What we think and how we feel are constant companions of the images we pay attention to.

The basic premise of vision therapy is that vision is not a passive occurrence but a learned process. Vision therapy teaches a person to use his nerve and muscle systems better and put them at the command of the mind. Good vision involves a whole spectrum of skills. How do you use both eyes together? How quickly can you judge left from right? How well do you see objects in space? Can you shift focus from near to far quickly and easily? How good is your visual memory?

Dr. Frymann and Dr. Springall explain development based on the stages of growth. Similarly, Dr. Kavner understands vision. If certain behavioral patterns are not acquired in the usual sequence, more advanced patterns may be damaged. To repair them, therapy may have to begin at the base level. Then that level opens a path to the next level. In vision therapy, body balancing skills which are learned in the first few years of life, often must be rehearsed and perfected as a way of reaching the specific problem that is interfering with eye-body coordination. The actual therapy a person receives depends on age and the exact nature of the problem. This is a highly individualized program of assessment and treatment. Dr. Kavner says the ability to use the eyes and actively examine the environment is so intimately connected to growth and development that without it, normal development could actually cease to occur.

Dr. Kavner discovered that Seth had some focusing difficulties, that Seth was not always able to hold focus. He identified premigraine symptoms and the possibility that Seth would develop vascular headaches, a symptom of a problem with the reactive nervous system. Otherwise, he thought that Seth had the best visual ability of any child with cerebral palsy he had ever seen. We all agreed that the Feldenkrais training and the cranial work were the reason. The doctor recommended some vision training, exercises Seth could do at home (along with the Springall exercises). We also planned a course of biofeedback for the near future.

Biofeedback is not a medical treatment, but a learning process that helps patients develop their own ability to achieve relief from symptoms. In this kind of biofeedback, sensors measure muscle tension, skin temperature, or other bodily processes. The sensor readings are then amplified and translated into signals that you can see or hear—or both. As you become accustomed to sensing certain of your body's processes, you can gradually gain some control over them.

Eventually Seth participated in a program of biofeedback with Dr. Kavner. Seth reported how good he felt after each session. I was pleased with the results and with Seth's reaction to the sessions. At the same time, I felt the gnawing of the warning "too much therapy, too many hands, too much being a child with cerebral palsy" for Seth. I wanted to de-emphasize the therapeutic in his life.

At the moment, Seth participates in another form of biofeedback (I write about this in Chapter Fifteen), but for a while he went to

Dr. Kavner's office for biofeedback. I also took him for regular eye examinations with Dr. Kavner. During one visit Dr. Kavner suggested that Seth could benefit from more biofeedback sessions. Seth resisted ardently, already overwhelmed with his academic responsibilities and some of the other rehabilitation work we insisted on. He always said how good the sessions of biofeedback made him feel, but he just didn't want to do anymore. There is no denying that ultimately I surrendered to Seth about how much therapy. I knew that one day he would return to this work and benefit from it enormously, and I turned out to be right.

◯

The most significant recollection I have of our return to La Jolla in May was the welcome Seth received from his classmates and from the school, especially from the teacher, the very teacher who had been cautious about admitting him into her second-grade class. Cindy Cohen called me shortly after we arrived to say, "Thank you for bringing your beautiful son back to me." No wonder Seth loved California.

Seth made an incredible transition, slipping right into the routine without a misstep. He was sleeping through the night and was generally cooperative. There were continuing instances of manipulation and deception, but nothing extreme or out of the ordinary—the regular testing of limits. Bedtimes, how much television or junk food: these were the issues (and still are).

Things had been going just as well in New York. Before we left for La Jolla his teacher at the Stephen Gaynor School reported that Seth was doing well academically, reading with good comprehension and progressing in math. I was happy to hear the reports, but anyway I lacked energy, so I doubt I would have done anything if the reports hadn't been encouraging. I also knew that Seth was happier in California, and at the time I was more comfortable with the Beth Israel Day School, the children, and their parents. The difference, of course, was that the Beth Israel Day School was a mainstream school. The Stephen Gaynor School was a place for children with special needs.

This contrast was especially noticeable among Seth's classmates at the two schools. At Gaynor some of the children had severe

behavior problems, a facet of learning disabilities we hadn't anticipated when we first applied to the school.

Seth told me, "I'm more comfortable in my chair in San Diego.
At the Gaynor School I feel like throwing my chair out the window.
My ideas are always accepted at BIDS, even just part of them. Every-
thing at Gaynor is black and white."

I encouraged him to tell me more, even though my heart was
sinking. What kind of a place was Gaynor? I knew many of the children had to be kept in check, that their difficulties were being treated
with medications such as Ritalin.

Seth told me, "We are a group in San Diego. We're together.
Nobody puts anybody else down. There is more acceptance of my
ideas. I like the cooperation in San Diego. All of us share answers
and information. At Gaynor the kids taunt each other when someone
is wrong."

"But why is that? Why doesn't everyone cooperate in New York?"
I wanted to know specifically.

"Because the whole class can be punished at Gaynor for one kid's
misbehavior. They're all too out of control."

Seth went on to say, "If I tell someone at BIDS to stop, it's like
having a key to open a door. At Gaynor I can shout 'stop' forever,
and it's like a key that doesn't fit."

He described a sense of feeling welcome in San Diego by teachers
who didn't even have him for a student. This was not true at Gaynor,
with its strict discipline.

"But we live in New York, sweetie," I had to tell him. "This is
where your daddy works and Haya goes to school. It's here that we
have family."

"Everyone else in my family has more of a life in New York than
I do," he replied. "My life is here in San Diego, where I want to stay,
where I intend to return to study, where I have real friends with
whom I really feel safe."

When I recounted to Jay my conversation with Seth, he became
very uncomfortable. Neither of us knew exactly how to respond.

Suddenly I realized that we had a monkey on our backs. There
were problems with returning time and again to La Jolla. It was true
that at Gaynor there were many rules and regulations. Some of these
were responses to the behavior of the students; some were part of

an overall philosophical approach. On the other hand, Seth was not a full-time student at BIDS, but a "star," somone who came and went, enjoying a certain status and occupying a unique position. It was easy to romanticize his San Diego school life, a transient, temporal existence, set in the mesmerizing grandeur of the scenery.

I was aware of this phenomenon. At the same time I wondered whether Gaynor was the right alternative, given that so many of Seth's fellow students were battling emotional and behavioral problems. In my mind, Seth didn't have those types of issues, not, at least, to that extent. I suggested to Jay that in the autumn we should explore some other schools, mainstream settings that could support some of Seth's special needs. Seth's San Diego experience had been so good, I easily forgot that other educational settings had not been as successful.

Once Seth got wind of our doubts and some of our dissatisfaction, he adopted our attitude. The message Seth got was that Gaynor was a temporary situation, that he didn't belong there and didn't have to give it his all. It did not help him in the classroom or in other school activities. He felt that he had one foot out the door, and he even went so far as to tell the administration that he would be leaving anyway.

In retrospect, it was a major mistake for Seth to have so much access to our opinions about his school. As Dr. Frymann had so astutely pointed out two years earlier, it wasn't a good idea to allow Seth to be privy to the decision-making process. It was better not to discuss his circumstances within his earshot. Now that we've learned our lesson, Jay and I thrash things out between us first, then we invite Seth to participate in selected aspects of decision making.

We almost let ourselves be flung out of Gaynor, and at one point, Gaynor was willing to let us go. It took more than a year for us to repair our mistakes. Once we took hold and hauled ourselves up onto sure footing, we sent a different message to Seth. Afterward, his experience at Gaynor metamorphosed him and us, and, as a result, a mainstream setting became a real possibility.

Meanwhile, I began getting us ready for the summer. Seth was to spend his second year at the Children's School of Science, this time taking three courses instead of one. He also hoped to learn to play tennis. I had to find someone to replace Stoney, who would not be returning to play with the Commodores. Eventually I found a great college student who was spending his summer in Falmouth.

Haya was going to the Woods Hole Child Center in the mornings, and I planned to use the free time to do some writing. Everything "fell" into place. (I was exhausted from all the careful planning. I wrote in one of my journals that once I had managed touring theatrical shows, and now I felt that I was one.)

That summer I became acquainted with a woman who was an associate professor and director for learning-disabled students at a small college on Long Island. I talked with her over several cups of tea and began thinking about learning disabilities and other kinds of disabilities in a new light. She encouraged me to consider whether there is a valid way to measure innate potential, and what it means. In the core of my being, my values were challenged.

She and I talked about what we mean when we speak of a brain injury and a disability. At the instant of conception we were all intended to have a good brain. At some time after that instant, if something happened that hurt the good brain—something that may have occurred a minute, an hour, a day, a week, a month or a year or more after conception—a good quality brain is hurt. It may be severely hurt or it may be mildly hurt. It may be hurt in a way that limits walking or talking or hearing or seeing or feeling, but it is a good quality brain nonetheless, and not an inferior brain. We talked about what terms and labels mean. Too often she felt that the trouble with all the names and labels is that it mistakes the symptoms for the disease.

I was forced to confront my deepest prejudices. I had grown up in a home where intellectual, athletic, and social achievements had an objective standard. My brother and sister had both gone to Ivy League colleges. We had all been encouraged to be competitive, especially intellectually. When I thought of my children's future, I wanted nothing less than the best for them, the pinnacle.

It was dawning on me that these gifts of nature, bequests of intellect, of grace, these favors, abilities we so easily take for granted, are simply that, gifts. People with disabilities are not really essentially different from the rest of us. We are all "temporarily able-bodied."

We are each of us only seconds, only a fall or an accident away, from disability, from incapacity. All types of disabilities reside in us. Seth already knew what he needed to confront in himself in his life. Some of us wait an eternity to find out, and then we must start over. Who among us doesn't have special needs?

Another enlightening incident occurred at the annual summer picnic for the Children's School of Science. Seth and Haya and I went with much anticipation, knowing that it was quite a shindig. Everyone brings their own supper, and CSS supplies the drinks and the watermelon and, more important, the volleyball game. Seth was very much part of the community of CSS now and committed to being a student for as long as he could be. The picnic was emotional, since it signaled that three weeks of classes were all that remained of the summer.

That evening, we were happily sharing our picnic dinner with a New York family we had gotten to know over that summer. Their daughter, Anna, asked her mother why Seth talked like he did, why he was so difficult to understand. Immediately I began to give Anna an explanation.

"Everyone has things that challenge them, Anna," I began. "Seth has some differences that make it hard for him to do many things you and Haya and I do very easily. Talking is one of them."

Seth put his hand on my arm to stop me. He turned to Anna and said, as clearly as he has ever spoken anything, "I have a friend in San Diego named Evan. He listens to me even in the noisiest room. He understands everything I say. When he isn't sure, he asks me to say it again."

That was the last time I felt I needed to answer for Seth. The implications of his answer, that it was the responsibility of others to make the effort to understand him, were enough to silence my crude attempts at a response.

᷍

Returning to Gaynor in the fall was not easy for Seth. It was made more difficult because he began the year in La Jolla, arriving directly from the Cape. Dr. Frymann's schedule demanded that we be there in early September if Seth was to get all ten treatments. I scheduled private testing in New York for our return. Jay and I wanted objective advice about applying to mainstream schools for Seth. It would be a busy year of school visits since Haya was "graduating" from nursery school and needed a kindergarten for the following September.

We were also buying a house in New York and would be moving in November. Given the mammoth responsibility of the move and the financial demands, we could no longer maintain long sojourns in another house in San Diego. The constant instability was taking a toll on Haya, too, because I was so tense, so torn by the demands of our commuting life.

Jay and I rethought our plans and decided that I would take Seth alone to San Diego in January and March for shorter but more frequent visits and stay in an apartment-hotel. I didn't love the idea of being separated from Haya, but the new plan seemed like a good compromise. We agreed that in June, after the school year was finished, I would take both children to La Jolla for a more extended stay before going on to the Cape for the summer. I was beginning to think that I would never get out of a suitcase.

We had an excellent visit in La Jolla that fall, although I was busy packing up both the house in La Jolla and the house in New York for the move to our new residence in New York. Dr. Springall reported that Seth had made a two-year leap forward in reading. He said that Seth's focus was significantly better and always improved when he was interested, engaged. Seth was demonstrating persistence in tasks and greater strength and accuracy. His hand-eye coordination had improved also. His sessions with Dr. Frymann proceeded without major incident.

Both Seth and Haya were given standardized tests during the autumn when we returned. When I scheduled the appointments for Seth's testing in New York in early October, the psychologist-evaluator reassured me that she would make recommendations about schools once the test results were known. The tester for Seth didn't want Seth to be too tired, since the tests were taking place after school, so Seth's testing sessions were short and the tests untimed. Haya also needed to take standardized tests, which were routinely administered to children her age at the 92nd Street Y Nursery School. These tests were

necessary for application to kindergarten. I was sanguine about Haya.
Her self-possession, her lovely presence, prompted others, strangers
and intimates, to comment constantly about her intelligence and her
demeanor.

Our research persuaded us that girls succeed more easily in an
all-girls school. In Haya's case, since she was so tall and so beautiful,
I wanted to emphasize academic subjects. I believed that in an all-
girls school we would encounter fewer social distractions. She would
wear a uniform. With an older brother at home and with other social
settings like our synagogue, I wasn't worried that Haya would want
for a social life. I scheduled visits and the necessary interviews for
five girls' schools in the City. October and November were about
evaluations, visits, interviews, and applications. It was also about my
fantasies and expectations for my children.

In early December we met with Seth's teacher at the Gaynor
School. She reported that he was happy in the class; his group was
made up of boys he knew, and there were only two new students
in the group. Seth loved the social aspect of his school day, she
observed. Of course the speech issues remained. But Seth was reading
beyond his grade level and had good comprehension and decoding
skills. In math there were some memory problems when it came to
facts. In receptive language he needed simple directions because he
jumped in before all the directions were completed, going off on a
stream of consciousness, or going off on a tangent. Because of his
impulsive nature, he would blurt out answers, jumping in, feeling
pressure to get it out. Her strategy was to give him information in
parts.

His teacher said that Seth demonstrated a tremendous love of
learning, a love of being taught. That is something we hear often,
and it acts as a flag for me. If I don't hear this from Seth's teachers,
then I know something is wrong. We all agreed that Seth's behavior
indicated how much he was constantly comparing himself to others
and finding himself inadequate.

An occupational therapist routinely saw Seth as part of the Gaynor
curriculum. She said that he hated working with her. Their sessions
challenged him on the most fundamental levels of motor skills, so
he avoided the work, resisting and struggling. The old patterns of
manipulation were at play in a big way. This information reinforced

my belief that Seth needed one place where he could be absolutely comfortable, even if it was in front of the television.

There were accomplishments and progress, but the gains seemed to be accompanied by immense anxiety on his part. I wanted him to relax more and put some emphasis on pleasure. While I felt committed to finding occasions for him to unwind, I recognized that he was busy with speech therapy, Dr. Oldberg, and more testing. Summer is Seth's balm. In the summer Seth recharges and rejuvenates. Fortunately, there is no television in our summer house. Seth reads voraciously every summer and relaxes with his books, fishing, sailing, and the beach.

The test results repeated what we heard from the beginning. Seth is very bright, with a superior intelligence and excellent reasoning skills. He was ahead of his second-grade standing in reading. In math and spelling he scored in the high third-grade range. He worked hard but needed tricks to remember things, especially facts. The psychologist who administered the tests recommended three possible mainstream schools to consider moving Seth into the following year, when he would be in the fourth grade. I sent for the applications and scheduled visits.

The entire first six months of that school year were spent looking at mainstream schools for Haya and planning which ones we would investigate for Seth. Again, I was challenged to meet my inner expectations head-on. In terms of finding appropriate school placements for the children, my hopes were hanging in the balance. There were some ironic and enlightening twists.

Because Seth and I were away in La Jolla when Haya's test results were delivered, I didn't learn about Haya's surprise performance on the standardized tests for almost two weeks. The expectations I had of her matriculating at one of the two girls' schools I had my heart set on were dashed. I was devastated and confused. My child who was without a flaw suddenly had only a marginal chance of going on to one of the other schools I preferred. The daughter I thought was untouched by the demons that haunted my parenting experience with Seth suddenly presented the biggest challenge of all in my agenda.

New York parents are nuts on the subject of the best schools. I was a New York parent, and I discovered that I was just as batty as everyone else. I had thought I was immune to the concerns that plagued the other parents, but I was far from it. Questioning everyone and every possible reason for Haya's weak performance, I even wondered about her intelligence. How I could doubt her abilities is ludicrous to me now, but I was ignorant about what was really troubling her.

Over the following few weeks and well into the next eighteen months, I learned much more about Haya and even more about myself—what kind of mother I was, what values motivated and informed me. I got a new grasp of "special needs" and who had them. I was embarking on another voyage. Except this time the path wound solely into my very visceral self.

CHAPTER THIRTEEN

haya

"IS THIS GOING TO HAPPEN TO ME? Why did it happen to Seth and not to me? Will Seth die from cerebral palsy?" These were the questions Haya asked when she was four. The questions that came later were asked silently—with her eyes, her body language. And the later questions were different. The questions today are different still.

When Haya asked those first questions, I was shocked. Was I blind to what had to be her deepest, unspoken fears? What was I thinking about? I was thinking about many things—about Seth, Haya, and my husband, about schools in New York, getting to California, Dr. Frymann; sometimes I was thinking of nothing but getting dinner on the table. I had been reading more of the special needs literature, but there was nothing written about siblings and special needs until later. Research on the siblings of special needs children had only begun in earnest in the 1970s.

Haya was a big, beautiful, and poised baby and little girl. She is a tall, beautiful, poised young woman. She has always demonstrated wisdom beyond her years. Because of her physical maturity, everyone always forgets how old she is.

She was never babyish, not even when she was an infant. First she was a big baby (over nine pounds at birth.) As a little girl, she was always very mature, and her presence was matched only by her height. As a young woman, she gives the impression of being strong and wise. I count on her to let me know "to get over it" when I'm going off the deep end. But her size and maturity meant I neglected to treat her like a baby or a little girl. It has always been difficult for me to remember how young she is. Mea culpa.

Haya's early years were peripatetic, to say the least. We spent one Halloween when she was two in California and the next Halloween when she was three in New York. We would leave New York in the midst of a snowstorm and arrive in San Diego where it was eighty degrees and sunny. Our apartment in New York had a small terrace, but in La Jolla the Pacific Ocean was our backyard.

We traveled back and forth to California, with Haya switching schools, switching homes, spending long periods of time apart from her father who remained in New York except for short visits. We trekked around New York in strollers and on buses, and then in California we lived in our automobile. Our summers were spent on Cape Cod, which meant Haya was sleeping in three different bedrooms during the year. She never complained. She went along cheerfully, anticipating each move with nonstop questions:

"When we get to La Jolla, will it be sunny?"

"In January when we get home, will Helen be there?"

"Will I go with you when Seth goes to Dr. Frymann?"

Haya is affectionate and sweet and has been since birth, but she also has a stubborn streak. I am often surprised by her strong mindedness. I can always trust her to hold her own with Seth and with us too. Now in her teenage years, I believe it is a quality that distinguishes her from her peers and protects her from the cultural onslaught our children endure. She is very independent minded.

When Seth and Haya were children, they shared a secret language. It was extraordinary. Can I say I felt jealous? Their closeness continues today. It constantly takes new forms. I see how their eyes meet and lock when they are united in agreement against another adult alien, or me—or the way they exchange glances in conversations with others. When either of them comes home from a day at school, they ask for the other right away. There is intense competition, rivalry about who has more work or is studying more or which movies are appropriate for the other. And there is great intimacy.

As Haya and Seth grow, their relationship changes and develops. The closeness they had as children is mixed now with the individuality they express as young adults. They both have very strong personalities. Seth demands a lot. Haya does not permit him to be the constant center of attention. Seth's going off to college in the fall is a mixed blessing for her. She will enjoy only child status and be free of the "torture" her brother inflicts. On the other hand, she will have no one to torture.

At the time Haya was getting ready for kindergarten, I received a wake up call. It seemed that the kind of elementary school I had dreamed about for her, those places were interested only in standardized test results and not whole people. In kindergarten no less!

Haya was not a good test taker. Her scores made it appear as if she was below average intelligence. The teachers and the head of the nursery school were shocked, as were we. Haya, while quiet, still set a standard for the class in behavior and participation. Everyone remarked about her exceptional memory and keen intelligence. In fact, we took it for granted. That she didn't perform well on this kind of standardized test was no reflection on her, but on the places that would evaluate her on this basis. I had yet, though, to take the leap to make the tests useful to us.

Years earlier I had stood in the elevators of the 92nd Street Y silently judging the mothers who were competing for places in the best schools for their children, one of which was the Y Nursery School itself. Here I was doing exactly the same thing. Later it got worse. I was blind to the syndrome I was caught in, though.

Obviously, standardized testing has come to mean something very different to us over the years. Seth's testing could never be standard but Haya's life has been affected by the anxieties standardized testing raised in her. And Seth had to work night and day for two years to achieve the standardized test results he needed to go to a top university. My own relationship to standardized testing has gone through many changes.

At the beginning, instead of asking what went on during the testing that made my very intelligent child perform below par, I worried about the status of Haya's future. Ridiculous as it may seem, Haya's scores made me also wonder about her intellectual abilities. Of course I have come to appreciate Haya's incredible, unique, and varied intellectual abilities. She has no peer in memory, wit, or insight. Her demeanor and charm allow the slightest criticisms to be delivered with love. None of that came through on the standardized tests.

I thought about the other children who performed better on the tests, children who still used a bottle, who were not as socially adept, or whose behavior made it hard to have them around. Yet these children, especially the girls, had performed better than Haya on these tests and would, therefore, go onto the preferred schools. Now, years later, many of these girls have had histories of learning disability. One girl, in particular, whose mother I know, has been medicated for years. The family agonizes and suffers with this child's special behavioral needs. The child's special needs are not being met in the highly competitive school environment either.

Haya, while easygoing, was no wilting wallflower. She spoke her mind at home and stood up for herself. She asserted her independence by tying her own shoes very early and selecting her own clothes (things that were very difficult for Seth to learn to do for himself). She asserted her individual preferences for food, for preferred activities. The assertiveness we witnessed at home, however, was hidden in public. She was quieter, shyer outside of the house, at least until she was more familiar with people and surroundings. But nothing felt out of proportion. I rather admire this trait in my daughter.

As soon as we received the test results, we consulted the school psychologists. What could the school psychologist tell us? What made our daughter tick? We expected the professional to tell us about our own daughter? However, we did need guidance. How could such a focused, well-adjusted child, always described as so smart, perform so poorly?

The psychologists described Haya as concerned about what "testers" wanted from her. Haya appeared uncomfortable when asked to perform or to assert herself. And the psychologist described her behavior as being "skewed." I realized that it was true: Haya either wore the clothes of or took on the attitudes of a teenager (playacting—and nothing like the real teenager she is), or she was sucking her thumb and talking like a two year old. There was no middle ground. Haya also felt—and still feels I think—that she had to pay special attention to Seth. Did she think he was our favorite child? Maybe not exactly, but she recognized early on that he had special needs. And she recognizes this in subtle ways today.

Our inquiry extended beyond the school psychologists. We also consulted the evaluator who was testing Seth for the mainstream school placement. That psychologist described Haya as extremely bright with an astonishing memory—still in evidence today—but not forthcoming during the testing period.

At that time the psychologist thought Haya was not using the skills she had and was very cautious and anxious. Haya still has bouts of self-doubt. In many situations, this caution is a virtue. However, it is also true that sometimes, she does not perform as well because of it. It is a fine balance.

Haya's reserve is a two edged sword. It gives her more time to be observant, to absorb the "lay of the land." She is not at all impulsive as I can often be. I respect and admire her cautious nature so different from my own. She will be a better judge of character and situations. On the other hand, it also betrays a slight reticence, a hesitation that may indicate a lack of self-esteem. I do not want her to fear mistakes. Deep down I do not believe there are any. And knowing when to take risks and trust yourself is one of the more important lessons of life.

The psychologist also thought Haya brought Seth into the conversation too often; she thought Haya compensated for him, worried about him. I witnessed Haya's obsessive concern for Seth at one stage but had not intervened. When the psychologist drew my attention to it, though, I became more alert. I realized I needed to pay special attention to Haya, to be more aware, give her extra caring. The intervention had to be thoughtful.

Although the children have had normal sibling rivalry at the appropriate stages, with typical name-calling and fights, Haya and Seth's situation was more complex. If there was anything amiss with Seth, Haya assumed responsibility for setting things right, even at the age of three and four. If Seth had a cold, she tended to him and administered all remedies. If he was hurt or disappointed, especially as a consequence of his disability, she was there to reassure him. Even then Haya sensed that Seth needed a lot of attention. Interestingly, she was also very aware of people's bodies, especially their feet, their bones.

Haya's compassion has evolved over the years. It has acquired many hues and shades, and has definitely been a defining force in her identity. I have never known her to participate in any of the vicious gossip and cliques that girls especially can generate. It is to her credit, but I believe it has a great deal to do with the sensitivity that she acquired because she is Seth's sister.

The need to tend, to be helpful, to be kind, is something required from everyone in a family when someone has a special need. Think of a family like a mobile. It does not matter how far away one piece of the mobile is from another piece. If a piece moves or is lost or off kilter, the entire mobile is skewed.

Issues I so obsessed about in Seth's case, I had not begun to examine in light of Haya's situation at that stage of her development. What emerged was that, as a result of her lack of confidence in herself at that time, her ability to take risks was being stifled. Her reticence was complicated by the concern that she would out perform her brother. Her natural reserve, her retiring instinct manifested themselves when she was tested. What we had failed to consider fully while we were working out the family equation was Haya's special needs as the sister of a special needs child.

Because of Haya's size and physical beauty, because of her seeming inner strength, our expectations were always that she could handle the demand we placed on her. She did and she does. What we overlooked was her fear of the unknown, her desire to please, to compensate. So we had to make sure she did not feel guilty about getting attention for her achievements. We wanted her to be confident to stake her claim for what she deserved. At the same time, we didn't want her to lose the sensitivity she had developed because she is Seth's sister. It balanced her apparent self-assuredness and lent her depth, dignity, and grace.

When a member of a family suffers from a disability or from an illness, the entire family experiences the stress. Each family member goes through a time when he or she feels left out, bereft of attention. At the time of Seth's diagnosis, I was concerned with Jay's feelings. My parents and my in-laws got "special handling." Later, it seemed normal for Haya to have intense feelings about her brother's disability. I knew everyone else did. I know I do. But I neglected to address those feelings with her then. I had a lot to learn.

When a child is young, he or she is less able to understand the conditions involved in a brother or sister's problems. We waited too long to provide Haya with explanations that were clear, honest, and age appropriate. She needed a forum for developing the language to express herself. We needed to start by bringing her into the equation in a conscious way. From that point on we talked to her differently.

～

My research shows that the majority of the studies of the effects of a special needs child on siblings were done in the late 1970s and 1980s, although there were also some studies in the late 1960s. As a result of those studies, there is now a Siblings Information Network that assists people and professionals interested in serving the needs of the families of individuals with disabilities. This network disseminates bibliographic material and directories, puts people in touch with each other, and publishes a newsletter written for and by siblings and parents. (You can find the information on how to get in touch in the Resource Guide in the back of the book.)

Debra J. Lobato's book *Brothers, Sisters, and Special Needs*, was published in 1990. Lobato's book provides concrete strategies for dealing with the sibling of a special needs child. It also has a companion packet for developing a workshop. I saw an advertisement for the book in *Exceptional Parent* magazine.

Each sibling of a child with a disability is unique. However, all of them have similar needs and concerns. Those needs change with age and circumstances, as we've seen with Haya. But most of our children need information about their sibling's disabilities, including how such problems can be treated. Knowing when to communicate this information is one of the great challenges. Lobato reports in *Brothers, Sisters, and Special Needs* that one of the most positive outcomes of sibling support groups is learning to identify when the non-disabled sibling is ready for conversation.

Studies confirm what we have seen in our own family, that a child with a disability has a positive influence on the lives of other children in the family. Children involved with a brother or sister with a disability often seem to have better relationships with one another and other people. They must know that they have to be especially agreeable and pleasing. But they also learn that difficulties can be surmounted. Haya has demonstrated this complex psychology. Many of her school chums at this age are very small and not nearly as developed as Haya. Haya never makes any of these girls feel smaller than she is. She has a way of lifting them up.

Since my sorrow about Seth is recurring, I imagine that Haya experiences this too. When I talk to Haya, I feel less isolated. Now she often gives me insight into Seth by offering her point of view. As she has grown up, I have watched her feelings change. I always maintain that it is fine to have strong emotions about Seth.

We try not to deny Seth his feelings about his cerebral palsy. We try to support the integrity of his experience by not confusing it with our own. The same holds true for Haya. We encourage Haya to express her negative feelings so that they will not fester or build up inside of her. We do not want to emphasize only strengths. Acknowledging differences is important. Her teenage years will bring change in her feelings about her brother I am sure.

∽

Resentment and bad feelings toward a brother or sister with a disability are highest I understand, when a sibling has a lot of childcare responsibility. Whenever Haya concerned herself greatly with Seth's well being, I thanked her and offered the reassurance that their father or I could be responsible for him. We deliberately tried to free her of responsibility. We did not want her to have any extra care-giving burden.

When Seth was small, he needed help tying his shoelaces. You can imagine what would happen at breakfast when everyone was rushing to get to school and to work. That used to mean that Haya would begin her day by helping Seth. Once I became more sensitive to Haya's needs, I made sure that no matter how busy I was—whether I was getting the breakfast on the table or into our stomachs, getting the children out the door or ready for the school bus—I made it a point to help Seth myself or to call on Jay or another adult (housekeeper, or house guest) to help him. I made sure it was not left to Haya.

Seth, too, has grown particular about Haya's help. I notice, however, that Seth often calls upon her for "fashion" help. I've known her to fix his hair—at his request—when he was about to have an important picture taken!

∽

Remind your children that failure is important in developing self-esteem—not in so many words, but by example and encouragement.

We encouraged both our children, but especially Haya, to risk more. We did this by asking her to express herself. Still, if she said she didn't want to go somewhere or try something, we supported her. For instance, one year she was not sure she wanted to participate in her ballet school's performance of *The Nutcracker.* I said, "Maybe you're right. You can be in it when you feel like it. Maybe next year." When it came time for her to participate in her first horse show and she was unsure, we did not force her. (She ultimately went on to win four first-place and second-place prize ribbons.)

Sometimes I left it to others, and still do. Her peers can do the encouraging if she needs it. Our emphasis is on our confidence in her. I keep the pressure to perform to a minimum, letting her find her own time.

If she complains about something, we do not contradict her. We try to do this with both our children and make it is a general rule. I express sympathy in what I hope is appropriate proportion, and I am always careful not to encourage self-pity. Sure things hurt, things are frustrating and difficult. We all struggle with issues of self worth. Learning that everyone is special and coming to terms with our own inner strengths and weaknesses are the keys to maturity.

The questions my husband and I were forced to ask about Haya's well being provided insight into our daughter and into ourselves. They also set us on a course of family conduct that serves us incredibly well today.

After contemplating the situation more deeply and consulting a family therapist, we began to have structured weekly, family meetings. The emphasis was on listening, on hearing one another. To begin each meeting we used to each take ten minutes to voice our anger, frustration, pleasure with each other or in life in general. There was no rebuttal or response, just an audience of three.

When do we give each other or ourselves this kind of time? How many of us sit together as a family most nights of the week to eat dinner? What time do we keep sacred? Researchers studying the freshmen class at Harvard found that Harvard freshmen were distinguished from freshmen at other Ivy League universities, because when they were in high school they ate dinner with their families more often during the week. I understand why. Our dinner hour is often a time of in depth discussions and lively talk.

Conflicts and feelings got ample ventilation during those sessions. When we first began our family meetings, nuances of the children's interaction were revealed, and this was helpful to me. I was able to grasp more of their struggles with themselves and with each other, as well as with Jay and me.

For the first time I was able to interpret their behavior more realistically. As soon as we had gone around once, then we would give each other a chance for a response. The rule was to preface each response with a repetition of what the other person had said, just to be sure that we all understood one another.

In one family meeting I recorded, Seth complained, "Haya helps me just to show off what she can do that I can not."

Haya claimed, "Seth only asks me for help when he is lazy about doing something himself. When he wants to be on the jungle gym alone, then he doesn't need me. And he never gives back."

"You only want to help when you can do it better than me. Like on the cross bars."

"That is not what I think," Haya responded. "And you want to sit at the table next to me on my birthday, but you don't want me to even come to your party. I had to come with Mommy." Then Haya got very quiet and wouldn't say anything for a long time. She only nodded or shook her head when Jay and I prodded her.

"Cluck. Cluck. Haya's in an egg," prompted Seth.

"What does that mean? Seth? Haya?" I asked.

"That I'm like an unborn chicken," Haya replied. That's why I'm not talking. You can't talk if you're not born," announced Haya.

I was amazed. How well these two understood one another! Obviously it was better for them to work things out without my interfering. They needed to engage one another in their differences. And they still need to do this. At that time, Haya said that her friends' questions about Seth, his speech, his gait, disconcerted her.

After school one day, Haya had friends visiting. They were sitting around the kitchen table when Seth arrived home from school. As soon as Seth came in and began talking to me, the girls began to stare and got very quiet. Then they began to giggle and be silly.

"Why does he talk like that?" one of the bravest girls whispered to Haya.

I waited to see how Haya would respond before I jumped in. Seth was listening too.

"He had trouble when he was born," Haya told her friend.

"Yes, but is he always going to be like that?" her friend kept on. "Is he retarded or something?"

These were difficult questions, and I felt compelled to rescue her. Seth demonstrated remarkable insight and resilience and self-identity in response.

"Are you having any difficulty understanding what I'm saying?" he gently asked the girls. Then I piped in.

"What are the differences that you observe in people? How are people different from you?" The conversation began here and went on for a few moments before Seth left the room with a goodbye grin.

"But is there something wrong with your brother?" her friend persisted more freely now that Seth was gone.

Together Haya and I explained to the girls that Seth has cerebral palsy and what it meant. But all of this took a toll on Haya and probably also defines her.

When Haya expressed embarrassment and hesitation about performing tasks of her own, Seth's reaction often reassured her. Those meetings were a source of revelation for me. I realized that both children had special needs in our family. I felt especially responsible for addressing these issues because Haya is not involved in a sibling support network. As she gets older, if it is something she wants, I will encourage her to join such a group.

Lobato also reports in her book that studies show one of the most powerful influences siblings have on one another is their ability to affect each other's relationships with other people. Many researchers and scholars believe that brothers and sisters actively shape one another's lives and prepare each other for the experiences they will have with their peers when they grow up.

Characteristic of the interactions between younger brothers and sisters are intense, uninhibited expressions of the full range of human emotion from love, affection, and loyalty to hatred, hostility, and resentment. Experiences of both positive and negative feelings and behaviors are a guaranteed reality of siblings' relationships, and an enduring bond.

Although the young siblings of disabled children share emotions and experience their disabled brothers and sisters in much the same ways that other children experience their "normal" siblings, there are stressful factors unique to the special needs family circumstances. Open communication within the family about the problems and sharing the negative and positive experiences of all family members, both seem important. Strategies for coping with stressful events, and especially peer and public reactions, as well as extra responsibilities at home, need to be developed.

The positive effects of growing up with a sibling with special needs are many. As we have seen with Haya, maturity, responsibility, tolerance, and compassion are fostered. Some of the potential negative effects siblings must deal with are embarrassment, resentment, and restrictions in social activity. (We are not a family that skis together or cycles together.) I saw how the questions about Seth changed as Haya and her friends grew older. I watched her friends observe Seth differently.

Haya's acceptance of Seth's disability is an ongoing process, just as it is for me. Naturally, when Haya was little, she wanted to do many of the things for Seth that we were doing. Her response to Seth is different now that she is older. I think she worried about how to tell friends that her brother was different when she was little. She obviously worried that the something "wrong" with Seth might mean there would be something "wrong" with her.

Appearance and body image are increasingly important to teens. So is the appearance of family members. Having a sibling like Seth may make Haya feel a little embarrassed as an adolescent. Sometimes she worries, I'm sure, that when she grows up and gets married and pregnant, she will have a child like Seth. She wonders if she will have to care for Seth in any way in the future. By providing her with clear and honest information, Haya will be able to deal with all these questions.

∼

In 1992, when Haya was in kindergarten, Seth and I began traveling alone to La Jolla for shorter times for his treatments. Haya was left behind with Jay, and I recognized the possibility that she might resent Seth's having special time with me that she did not have. I made it a point to carve out similar time with Haya. She and I went away for three days together soon after I returned from California with Seth on our first trip alone. It meant a lot to me and to Haya to have that time together.

Since the winter of 1993, we make the trip to La Jolla only once a year. We schedule it during the December holidays so the children are on a break from school, and we can go as a family. During the time we are together we savor every moment. When there are opportunities to spend time alone with each child, we savor those moments too. Awakening to Haya's needs changed us. It intensified our family bonds and helped to make us as close as we are today.

Haya's challenge provided the opportunity for my husband and me to change our behavior, not just in dealing with each other but in coping generally. Recognizing Haya's needs meant strengthening our love for each other, and it also propelled us toward an understanding of each other that may not otherwise have occurred. My own identity remains more intact. Listening to the children and Jay during our family meetings, and stepping back and just observing the children's interaction during dinner has enhanced my understanding and appreciation of my family while allowing me to keep myself separate.

CHAPTER FOURTEEN

ashore

IN NOVEMBER 1991, WE MOVED into our new home. We were busy with evaluations, school visits, applications, and interviews for both children. By the spring, we had happily accepted a place offered to Haya in a private girls' school that we thought was great. Seth's situation was different.

After considering the results of the private testing in the fall, Jay and I took the recommendations of the evaluator and went to visit several mainstream private schools. We determined that a co-educational school was the best setting for Seth. The emphasis on athletics in the all-boys schools would be too challenging. We wanted a setting where he could thrive. We needed Gaynor's cooperation in forwarding transcripts and school reports as requested. The staff seemed relatively indifferent to our requests.

Seth was received graciously everywhere, but ultimately we seriously considered only one school, and that was the only school that eventually offered Seth a place. The conundrum with this school was logistical. The school housed the fourth-grade class on the top floor, but all the "specials" including drama, music, physical education, and lunch, took place in the basement, six floors below. The stairways were narrow and steep and double height between some floors. As at Rodeph, Seth would always be the last to arrive everywhere, and he'd always be tired. Neither Jay, nor I, nor the staff at the school thought all that stair climbing was a good idea. Jay and I decided to wait. We went back to Gaynor for a meeting.

That was the turning point. It was obvious to the administration that up until now we had no great stake in Gaynor. In our minds Gaynor was only a stopgap. However, we were without options and wanted to explore Gaynor's view of Seth and to discuss the coming year and possible student groupings.

We met with the director of curriculum, the director of the school, and Seth's teacher. While the teacher was emphatic about Seth's progress, she also stressed the support and the work she thought Seth required. The director of the school was quiet, recognizing, I believe, that we were in an abyss. The director of curriculum, however, was tired of us and tired of our indecision. She was willing to let us go, and to send Seth packing. Even without serious alternatives, I was ready to capitulate and was on the verge of accepting this impasse.

Fortunately, Jay had the courage and foresight to jump in and say, "Wait a minute. We don't have an alternative for Seth next year. What can we do for the time being to realize a good year for him here?" Jay was not ready to write off the school so quickly. The discussion changed from that moment, and ultimately so did Seth's relationship to Gaynor and our relationship to Gaynor.

By the end of the meeting, we knew that Seth would return to Gaynor for the fourth grade and would probably remain for one or two more years after that. Recognizing Gaynor as Seth's best alternative, we became reconciled, committed, and ready to help Seth realize that Gaynor was his best chance to get ready for the mainstream. We already had decided that trips to La Jolla would take place only during vacation time or just after school let out in June of each year. We no longer had the energy or the money to keep enrolling Seth in school in San Diego. It was too much for everyone. The academic interruptions were another strain.

By the time we left for the Cape in June, we had the sense that both children had the right school waiting for them in September and that they understood we were not going to La Jolla until the winter recess. Seth was angry at first, but as the summer wore on, he forgot his frustration, absorbed as he was in Science School and fishing. We also let him know of our own satisfaction regarding the decision and were unwavering in our equanimity about Gaynor.

Fortune reigned. In the fall, after another spectacular summer when the children thrived, Seth's fourth-grade teacher, Mrs. Virginia Melnick, was a perfect match for Seth, an inspiration and a whiz. The class was an excellent mix of boys. Some of Seth's program was now departmentalized, meaning that he was grouped for reading, math, spelling, and computer with others at his level. That was very good for Seth.

Mrs. Melnick taught his homeroom, history, and social studies. She ran a tight ship but was a motivator. She focused on the students' writing and long-term projects as well as on behavior. Her own son was learning disabled, so she was extremely sensitive and astute about children with learning challenges. She was also highly perceptive about Seth, and she had enormous affection for him. At the end of the year she gave him the award for "Best Manipulator: May you use it in the service of humankind." It was a watershed year for Seth and for us. We knew we were lucky that fate had intervened, and Seth stayed put at Gaynor.

In June 1993 Mrs. Melnick suggested that Seth progress into "Team" the following fall. This was an enormous step for Seth and a reward for a year of hard, diligent work. "Team" was the one- or two-year program the children participated in before going on into the mainstream. It was a rigorous academic program that required another level of maturity and commitment. At Gaynor, it was the big time.

Our own promise to ourselves was to pledge to Gaynor some of our financial resources and the use of our new home. We became active in fundraising, the annual auction, and social activities. For three years we hosted the New Parents' Evening in September to welcome new families to Gaynor. Who understood better than we did the anxieties and disappointments that came with enrolling a child at Gaynor? Who knew better the possible rewards? We opened our home to the families, the staff, and the administration, always inviting Seth (who wouldn't have missed it for the world anyway) to welcome our guests. It made Seth feel he had access to people who had once seemed very distant. Once a year his teachers and the school directors came to eat cake and drink coffee in his home.

Seth understood we were committed to his school. It was a lesson for us with Haya, too. We immediately got involved at her school, recognizing that our children would take our lead and follow our example. If we cared, if we were committed, then they would be too. The other dividend was our increased intimacy with the staff, the other parents, and more often the parents of our children's friends.

Seth spent two years in Team, proudly graduating in June 1995 with an acceptance for the seventh grade at Friends Seminary, a Quaker school, and an excellent choice in our minds. Gaynor had prepared him exceptionally well in several areas. They coached him and readied him for the ERBs, the standardized tests. They taught him the subjects he needed, and made him confident about meeting his peers in a new surrounding upon graduation. They spent time helping him with school interviews. The Team members who were graduating met once a week to talk about their feelings and their anxieties about leaving Gaynor. Looking back, we couldn't have asked for anything more.

We were also lucky that we could afford Gaynor, a school with a hefty tuition; lucky, too, that circumstances prevented us from leaving Gaynor when we thought we should. Ours was purely an emotional reaction to having to face the fact that our son has special needs. Without Gaynor, Seth would not have the opportunities he has today. We were lucky that at the time of our indifference and fatigue, Gaynor was there for him anyway. I think they must fulfill this role for many parents, as we all struggle with the disappointments and denials we have to face.

⌒

In the fall of 1992, as we were beginning to commit ourselves to Gaynor in a substantial and conscious way and as Seth found himself so fortunately in the hands of Mrs. Melnick, we made another radical decision. We decided to eliminate Dr. Oldberg from the equation. Our weekly at home family meetings were consistent and extremely productive. By then we were living on the other side of the City, and the doctor's office was no longer convenient. Seth had complained that he had too much to do and didn't like going to Dr. Oldberg.

Seth also was in very good shape emotionally. He was happy. He performed his school work diligently. Except for routine issues, typical conflicts about television, bedtime, controls, and such, there were no problems of cooperation with Seth. For more than a year he had been sleeping through the night. At the same time, I was a little anxious, feeling many of the same fears and isolation I had experienced years earlier when Anat insisted that I cut off all the therapists.

Admittedly, Seth complained about the time-consuming demands of his various treatments. From time to time he would let us know his personal feelings about a practitioner. But Seth had never said,

"I don't need this treatment," except with Dr. Oldberg. Seth was adamant. He consistently voiced his displeasure about having to go to Dr. Oldberg each week. I could not see the point of his continuing. While I didn't want Seth calling all the shots, I also didn't want to make him a patient for life. But I didn't want to cut off Dr. Oldberg in such a way that Seth couldn't call him if something difficult came up, if he wanted to work something through with the doctor.

Jay and I discussed the situation and then talked with Seth about the best way to terminate the relationship. Seth didn't care if he ever spoke with or saw the doctor again, but I did not agree. I insisted that Seth visit with the doctor one more time after I called to say we would not be continuing. I asked Dr. Oldberg if he was willing to speak or meet with Seth from time to time if it proved necessary. While he was not enthusiastic about our decision, he agreed to be available on an ad hoc basis should it be needed. The truth is Seth has never seen or asked to speak with or see Dr. Oldberg again.

At this time Seth asked for a way to learn how to do some of the daily tasks that challenged him enormously, such as tying his shoes, buttoning his buttons, cutting up his meat, pouring from a pitcher. We found Kirsten DeBear, an occupational therapist, who took Seth on as a student for a limited number of sessions. Seth learned to tie his own shoes, cut his food with a knife alone, not easily, but successfully, and acquired a small tool to help him with buttons. Occasionally he asked for some extra lessons with Kirsten.

Once Dr. Oldberg was no longer part of our New York life, I realized that we had no real medical care in the City outside of the speech therapist and Dr. Lee. I was not happy depending solely on Dr. Frymann three thousand miles away. And I was not happy with Dr. Lee.

Each time I took Seth and Haya to see Dr. Lee—which by this time was only once a year for an annual checkup—she exclaimed loudly about how incredibly well Seth was doing. She remarked on how little I required her services for the children. They were never sick. (This wasn't exactly true. They had their share of colds, but I treated them with Osteopathy and Homeopathy.) She asked me what I was doing for them. When I started to tell her about the Cranial Osteopathy and the Homeopathy, she exclaimed that it was "witchcraft." I decided I'd heard that for the last time.

I wanted a pediatrician with an open mind. I am sure I did not accomplish this goal with the pediatrician we chose, but it felt better than what we had. And once again, things are changing. The children are older and Seth no longer wants a woman pediatrician. Earlier the fact that it had to be a woman narrowed the field dramatically, but Haya needed a woman doctor. She insisted on it, and, at the time, Seth did not raise any objections. So I am rethinking our situation once again.

∼

I thought both children needed osteopathic and cranial treatment on a consistent basis by then too. I phoned Dr. Masiello to discuss protocol with him. He made the most sense as our family doctor. And to this day he offers the best insights; I trust him the most, although sometimes I have to use allopathic doctors. Even then he helps me develop questions and consider the overview.

Dr. Masiello's role has changed over the years. Without him we would not be who we are today. We investigate and question doctors, ourselves, situations, in new ways because of Dr. Masiello. The relationship is always evolving. After many permutations, today Dr. Masiello is our Homeopath. Dr. Zinaida Pelkey is our Osteopath.

At that time, Dr. Masiello agreed to take Seth and Haya on as patients (he was already treating Jay and me.) He wanted to talk to Frymann about Seth, which was no problem for us. We welcomed it. And nothing suited me more than having a doctor who knew the whole family and knew us each individually and intimately. The fact that we are, after all, members of the same family accounts in great part for who we are.

Today we visit our allopathic physician only once a year for a checkup. The children need annual school forms filled out, and I also go to the gynecologist for a Pap smear. Since the time I turned forty, I get a mammogram once a year. We are only beginning to explore the anticipated changes for Seth now that he is moving away to live at college. What will Seth need in the future? How do we answer that? What are the questions that will lead us in the right direction?

Last summer Seth went to a fairly remote town in Mexico to live for two months with a Mexican family in a private program of Spanish immersion. Our pediatrician wanted him to be vaccinated for hepatitis

A. She was concerned about the food and water. Dr. Masiello and I
discussed the efficacy of this prescription. We knew that Homeopaths
have historically been effective with hepatitis A, whereas allopathic
physicians were only beginning to rely on this new "hybrid" vaccination. We decided to send Seth with two homeopathic remedies
known to be effective for "la tourista." In the entire eight weeks of
Seth's stay, he was sick for only three days. We spoke by phone and
recommended the remedy to take. He took it, and he got better
immediately.

Seth is receiving biofeedback neurotherapy at Stone Mountain
Counseling Center. Stone Mountain is licensed by Flexyx to do its
special form of neurotherapy. This treatment has shown itself to be
dramatically effective with a variety of problems involving "dysregulation" of the central nervous system. (I write more about Flexyx
in Chapter Fifteen.) Seth has benefited dramatically since he began
this work three years ago. The Flexyx neurotherapy work, along
with the visits to Frymann every winter, some Yoga, some swimming, some massage are his activities for now.

Can I say he does all that I want him to do? Perhaps not, but I do
not want to overload him. Anyway, he is at an age to resist all pressure. In Yoga I learned that the more you push, the more resistance
you meet. It is better to back off, let go, recede. Seth works hard,
and I respect his decisions.

For acute problems—I mean something "severe"—I call either Dr.
Masiello or Dr. Pelkey. Otherwise I try and let things run their course;
push the fluids, rest, and choose a remedy based on what I observe.
Colds, flu, cough, falls—we are in touch by phone if it is warranted.
This means we must be ready to report symptoms clearly to them.

It is not enough to know that one or the other of us has a sore
throat. We report which side of the throat hurts more, whether hot
or cold makes it feel better, when it began, if it is worse or better at
night or in the morning, if there is a change in appetite, and so on.
I administer the remedy the doctor recommends and keep an ongoing
watch on the symptoms. If they change, we often rethink the remedy.

In the case of sore throats, Dr. Masiello almost always requests a
simple test for strep and/or encourages us to get the pediatrician
to administer the test. Strep, tuberculosis, syphilis, can all cause

permanent damage. Years ago there were no treatments for these diseases. But now there is no need to put ourselves at risk when drugs to combat these potentially deadly bacteria are available.

Dr. Masiello and Dr. Pelkey are licensed to write prescriptions. If the children are sick, they usually make time that day to see them. Then they receive either osteopathic or cranial treatment if it is warranted. Dr. Masiello often prescribes a homeopathic remedy.

Dr. Masiello has been treating me for many years now, and Haya and Seth have been under his care since they were very young children. During this entire time I have not had to fill a prescription for an antibiotic more than five or six times. I administer Tylenol on occasion—to Haya mostly; to Seth almost never. Seth has not missed one day of school because of illness in years. But, Seth's situation is complicated, nonetheless, of which more later.

Haya is ill more frequently now that she is a teenager. She sees Dr. Masiello sometimes and likes to consult him for all that ails her. More and more I have been leaving it to her to talk to the doctor and describe her own symptoms. Haya is getting to be very good at choosing her own remedies too, which is something Dr. Masiello encouraged. Getting to know our symptoms is a way to know ourselves better. As I observe Haya in her adolescence and I myself pass through menopause, I can see how women's issues influence wellness. Our immune systems are affected by our menstruation, making us more susceptible in the best and most challenging sense of the word.

Haya misses school about one week a year. Recently, she brought my attention to something. She was sick with the flu for five or six days.

"Mom," she said, "do you know I was sick this same week last year. I remember because you and Dad were away." I remembered that what she said was true. We thought she was sick because we were away.

"And," she went on, "I am sure that if I looked back the same was true the year before. I always get the flu the same week every January."

This observation coincided with her growing ability to know how to remedy herself. Her sensitivity to her body and her rhythms is a sign she is attuned to herself. I am confident Haya is acquiring tools to stay in charge of herself. At the very least, she will know how she is feeling. The children shy away from medication and are skeptical about invasive remedies. They are comfortable with their homeopathic and osteopathic care.

I remember the morning after Haya's seventh birthday. Four of her friends slept over as part of the celebration. All four girls came with medication, and all of it had to be refrigerated. The bottles of pink liquid lined up like soldiers in our fridge were quite the unusual sight. It was up to me to dispense the girls' medication at breakfast.

The potions were bubble gum colored, offensively sticky, fluids that require pouring measured amounts on to spoons and then into the girls' open mouths. I administered this duty as Haya sat by, mouth agape. The four girls were hacking away with terrible coughs and noses running. One of them had already been taking the antibiotic for three weeks. What made their doctors, their mothers, anyone believe that this course of treatment was reaching the infections?

⌒

There is nothing "kooky" about the path I chose for us. As I have written, Osteopaths are fully qualified physicians, licensed to practice in all fifty states. They enjoy tremendous respect in Europe. Like M.D.s, Osteopaths diagnose diseases, prescribe drugs, refer patients to hospitals, and perform surgery. D.O.s are represented in all the practice specialties. There are osteopathic hospitals, some of which include large academic centers and seventeen schools of osteopathic medicine in the United States.

Unfortunately, the sad truth is that only a small number of D.O.s continue to explore the foundations of Osteopathy. Dr. Jim Jealous says that Osteopathy in its conception contained a philosophy as well as a science. Osteopaths were asked to consider the question of the soul, death, transcendence, and use only their hands in healing. He writes that traditional Osteopathy is not about episodic healthcare. It is about a long-term relationship with patients.

In our case, the fact that Dr. Masiello is also a classic Homeopath and Dr. Pelkey is studying Homeopathy, adds another dimension to our health care, which is for the most part, drug free—so far. The remedies are easy to administer (no annoying "child-proof" bottle tops, no gooey masses of offensively colored syrup) and are cheap. A few dollars often buys a lifetime supply of a remedy.

We have known Dr. Masiello over a long period of time, and one anxiety is he is not affiliated with a major New York City hospital. In Dr. Pelkey's care, she is at St. Barnabas, but in pediatrics. My children are young adults now. This means if any one of us gets seriously ill and requires hospitalization or treatments, we are without an advocate within the primary medical establishment.

We are presently trying to remedy this predicament by looking for a New York City internist who will include Seth in his practice. Seth is a young man and needs a doctor to monitor him. Such a person will have to accept us as a family and be sensitive to how we have been taking care of ourselves until now. We also think it will be a good idea for Seth to have a doctor in the Philadelphia area, close to the University of Pennsylvania, or maybe on campus, who knows him. We have the name of a Cranial Osteopath in Philadelphia. We are thinking about how to establish a network of support for the future.

◦

We had a terrible scare with Seth when he was eleven, however. On the day of his birthday party he was listless, without good color, and generally not looking well. We proceeded with our plans because of his insistence. By nightfall he was running a very high fever of 103 degrees. I consulted with Dr Masiello throughout the evening, reporting Seth's symptoms as well as I could. The overriding symptom was a severe, unrelenting headache, so that he could not bear any light or even open his eyes. The doctor prescribed one remedy and then another and even another.

The cycle continued for four days, his fever climbing or staying the same, the violent headache persisting. He had no appetite. I was beside myself with anxiety. I was fatigued from the all-night vigils. I constantly had to sponge him down with cold water in an effort to keep his fever from rising and to help make him more comfortable. I was applying cold packs to his head and around one of his ears, which was aching. Dr. Masiello was on the phone with me constantly.

Seth seemed to be fading away before my eyes. Never one to gain a lot of weight, although he can eat as much as the biggest man (especially these days), he was eating nothing. He was so thin I could carry him easily back and forth to the bathtub for his sponge baths. I rubbed him down with oil. He was dehydrated from the fever. I just about force-fed him liquids.

After Dr. Masiello first examined Seth, we consulted him incessantly, trying to decide what to do. We considered talking Seth to an emergency room, although there was nothing that could be done there. He didn't have a strep throat or an ear infection. Finally on the fifth day his fever began to diminish, his interest in fluids returned, and his headache subsided. By then I was a wreck.

As soon as his temperature returned to normal, I took Seth to see Dr. Masiello again. The doctor examined him thoroughly and gave him a cranial treatment. He also prescribed a course of homeopathic remedies to administer over the following two months. Two weeks later we left for California to see Dr. Frymann. At the same time we noticed a remarkable change in Seth.

Up until then Seth's one absolute personal characteristic was his lack of stamina. He was intelligent, enthusiastic, sociable, irascible, but he fatigued rapidly. He always required twelve hours of sleep every night. Suddenly, that changed. Not only was he more energetic than ever before, he was vigorous. He no longer slept as much. He stopped complaining about being tired. During the summer following his illness, he went to Science School, sailed, played tennis, trained with a local athlete, and had energy left over. We were amazed. (In adolescence, sleep again seemed to be his favorite pastime.)

Dr. Frymann examined Seth and told us that she believed he had "shed an old skin" during the terrible illness that had gripped him only weeks earlier. She remarked that children often experience an extreme malady prior to a significant neurological and/or physiological and/or emotional transformation. She also suggested that it was possible that Seth had suffered some degree of meningeal infection.

I flew to the dictionary to learn that anything "meningeal" refers to an inflammation in the brain usually caused by a bacterial or viral infection. I was shaken. I asked myself if I was just being stubborn about changing. I reviewed all the care Dr. Masiello offered during Seth's trauma. On reflection, I decided that administering an antibiotic probably would not have made much of a difference. Viruses have to run their course. But I faltered in my faith and momentarily thought I might reconsider some of my choices. It was momentary.

In the fall of 1993, after a wonderful summer during which Seth demonstrated this phenomenal surge of energy, we began another journey. It inaugurated big changes. Dr. Frymann had always encouraged me to think of Seth's speech and articulation difficulties as mainly a problem of proper breathing.

After all my years of study with Carola and all I had seen from working on Seth myself I agreed. I was already seriously studying and practicing Iyengar Yoga and had met a fellow student who was working with a breath coach, Carl Stough, known as "Dr. Breath."

Carl Stough acquired his sobriquet during the Olympics in Mexico City when he prepared the United States Olympic track team. Mexico City's high altitude alters breathing, making more demands on a runner's lungpower. Carl Stough came to the rescue, coaching the team in breathing techniques that helped them to win many gold medals.

Opera singers, trumpeters, pop vocalists, musicians, bodyworkers, many others were students of Carl Stough. His students also included people suffering from serious emphysema. Getting an appointment with "Dr." Stough was the equivalent of getting the first appointment with Dr. Frymann. It took time and persistence. I engaged everyone I knew who knew Carl Stough to help me. My efforts finally paid off, and Dr. Stough agreed to meet Seth. Once Carl agreed to take Seth on as a student, I let the speech therapist go.

Much of the work Carl Stough did with Seth relates to what I learned in Carola's studio years ago. The work was all centered in the breath. The lessons revitalized Seth, changed his carriage, his voice, and his alignment. Seth saw Dr. Stough once a week for years. I never heard him complain once about going. Of course, Carl had many celebrity clients who Seth saw coming and going. I think their presence and their commitment to the breathing work helped Seth recognize its worth. It is not easy for a young boy and then an adolescent young man to do this kind of work consistently and comprehend its value.

Unfortunately, Dr. Stough became ill very suddenly in the summer of 2000 and died a few months later. He saw Seth in June just before Seth left to live in Mexico for the summer. The town Seth went to was very high, and Dr. Stough helped him prepare for living there. Dr. Stough called several times over the summer to ask how Seth was faring. We were deeply touched by his concern especially because he was so ill himself. His devotion to Seth was profound.

Seth grieved deeply when he learned Carl died. But Carl Stough taught Seth for almost ten years. I believe that Seth was a good student during this time and learned what he can do for himself. Carl's dying was another reminder that it is up to us to be good students. Anat Baniel taught Seth for only nine months. When she refused to teach Seth anymore, we took over that summer, and a lot happened. A few months later Seth was walking.

The teacher student relationship has to go beyond the room and beyond the moment. There is always the possibility of loss. We have to accept the responsibility of being taught. Dr. Jealous has spoken about the need to become aware of something greater than ourselves. And there is also the need to remember our *originality*. We need to understand what is happening in the moment, to be awake to that breath of life and that stillness within.

⁓

We usually feel content with the course of "treatment" Seth receives. Right now everything is in flux because Seth needs to be treated as an adult man with cerebral palsy. And as Jay and I go into our "third age," I think it would be good to have a doctor who knows us and is affiliated with a City hospital.

Seth is doing a little Yoga with one of my teachers, although not nearly as much as I would like. It seems to relax him and help him open his chest; it relieves his patterns and habits. But it requires work and concentration and energy that a high school senior doesn't seem to have; at least not Seth. Dr. Frymann and Dr. Pelkey oversee his primary care, augmented by the annual trips to the pediatrician soon to be replaced by an internist. We do not know the consequences of Seth's cerebral palsy. Like life, it is still unfolding.

Now that Dr. Stough is dead, it is up to Seth to replace that weekly experience on his own with everything he learned. It is up to him to decide when to do this for himself. I can not influence the timetable though I remain convinced that since is my child, he will do it. Seth swims when he can, mostly in the summer and in California, but more in the City now too. He learned to play tennis and plays a little in the summer. He finished Science School, kept up his sailing and fishing and now has had summers away.

He will graduate from Friends Seminary in June. When he graduated from the Stephen Gaynor School six years ago, the director of physical education made a special presentation to Seth for "courage and persistence on the playing fields." He said that he had learned as much from Seth as he ever could teach anyone. At the Friends Seminary where Seth is a senior, there are no special awards or citations. It is antithetical to Quaker values to make any one individual "exceptional" because all are considered exceptional. And it is the wellness of the whole community that is central. The Quaker philosophy is holistic which has made the school's atmosphere very comfortable for Seth and for us.

When people dispute our choices, and some think that Seth needs a rigorous, orthodox physical therapy program, it makes me wonder whether I'm doing everything I can to help my son. Four or five years ago, for example, Seth twisted his ankle, and Dr. Masiello wanted X-rays. The pictures showed no broken bones, but there were bony spurs growing on his anklebones.

We consulted a highly recommended mainstream pediatric orthopedist, but not Dr. Grant who had examined Seth years earlier. The doctor faulted us for not having Seth enrolled in a more strenuous program of physical and occupational therapy pronouncing Seth far from his potential. He recommended a program that he supervised in the hospital. At first it upset me, but after I looked into the program and discussed it with Dr. Masiello, I saw its limitations and decided to proceed on the course we elected.

As we continue on our voyage parenting Seth, there are doubts and moments of faith. There is also great pride. There are tears of joy and tears of sorrow. And then there are the hard facts of my relationship to my son's condition. The biggest question I face each day is who I am and where I am in all of this. Sometimes the answers are terrifying. Most of the time I thank the power greater than I for sending me Seth. My hope for Seth is he feel good about himself, about what he has accomplished, about what he can look forward to in his life, and about how much we love him and believe in him.

In his Foreword Seth writes that he knows having cerebral palsy makes him special. I know being the mother of a child with cerebral palsy makes me special. We all use what life offers to help define us and give us purpose. I think knowing this and admitting it makes it richer and more blessed.

CHAPTER FIFTEEN

pathways

SINCE I WROTE *Uncommon Voyage* five years ago, many things have happened. The summer of 1997 was the last summer Seth spent entirely in Woods Hole. He attended the Children's School of Science. In the afternoons after Science School, he worked at the Marine Biology Lab (the MBL) for a neuroscientist, Dr. George Augustine, who was also Chairman of the Department of Neuroscience at Duke University.

The project was a study in the synapses of squid. Graduate fellows from universities around the world assisted Dr. Augustine. Seth's job was to interpret their data through a complex computer program. Suddenly, he found himself thrust into a world of intellectual rigor and scholarship. More importantly, and perhaps ironically, Seth was studying something very personal. Cerebral palsy effects the brain synapses. By studying squid brains, one of the most easily observable brains, he was learning how his own body functioned.

After that summer on the Cape, Seth went to other programs in July and August. The next summer he joined a Steven Spielberg funded program of art, Jewish studies and community building at Brandeis University. It was called the "Genesis Program." During the four weeks of the program Seth lived on the Brandeis campus in a dormitory with sixty other teenagers from all over the country. Everyone was Jewish, but they all came from diverse Jewish backgrounds. Seth seemed to have made life long friends during this program. And he shot his first movie.

Because the Genesis program lasted only four weeks, we needed to augment it so that he would not be on the Cape in August without anything to do. We inquired about Sail Caribbean at the suggestion of friends. It made sense, given Seth's love and knowledge of the ocean and his experience sailing on the Cape. The three-week program seemed a good segue from the Brandeis program.

The personnel at Sail Caribbean were appropriately concerned that Seth would be safe sailing on their boats in the Leeward Islands of the Caribbean. For the first time in many years we, Seth included, had to advocate vigorously. Dr. Masiello and Dr. Frymann had to provide letters of support. Seth and Jay drove out to a site on Long Island to meet with Sail Caribbean directors for an interview. The experience was very good for all of us. I was forced to reconsider Seth's circumstances when I thought about him being on a boat in the middle of the ocean. Difficult as that was, I think it was important to do.

Many of the questions the Sail Caribbean people asked were ones I needed answers for too. And I was glad they considered Seth's situation as thoroughly as they did. I would have been very suspicious had they not fully examined all the safety and health issues at stake. I would not have sent him sailing across the ocean without knowing if he would be safe. At the same time, I never doubted Seth could do it. My intuition told me he could. I left it to them to confirm it.

The three-week Sail Caribbean program was challenging. And Seth met those challenges. There were storms. There were days without wind. He visited many islands in many countries. He worked as a member of a crew. He grew strong. He learned to sleep on a boat. He cooked for himself and others. He inspired those around him to be compassionate and helpful. He was the only sailor on the trip to complete his Captain's qualifications. He got a tan. And because I forgot to include a "loofah," he came back with skin that needed a good scrub.

○~

When Seth returned from Sail Caribbean that fall, Dr. Masiello told me about a treatment known as Flexyx. He described it as a holistic, synergistic approach to biofeedback and recommended that Seth try it. Dr. Masiello thought Flexyx would be good for someone with cerebral palsy. His insight proved brilliant. And it appears to be excellent for many, many brain injuries, although the research is not yet complete.

Since 1990, Len Ochs, Ph.D., has been developing a form of EEG Biofeedback, which utilizes both light and electromagnetic stimulation to reduce the brainwave dysregulation underlying many neurological, psychological and physical conditions. His method is called the Flexyx Neurotherapy System. We were open to whatever would help Seth and were excited to learn of the availability of this program here in New York City. After reading the literature and meeting with Dr. Steven Larsen at Stone Mountain Counseling Center, we were convinced we should try Flexyx.

Trauma of any kind (physical, infectious, toxic or emotional) causes brainwaves to become fixated or "stuck" in a pattern of predominantly slow brainwave activity called "EEG slowing'. Researches believe EEG slowing is the way in which the brain protects itself from seizures and stimulation overload by releasing neurochemicals that protect it from any further danger. Unfortunately, this protective reaction also interferes with efficient neurological communications and causes the person to lose functional abilities in the areas of energy regulation, cognitive processing and mood modulation.

Dr. Ochs discovered that brains considered physically damaged beyond repair can be partially or totally rehabilitated, sometimes years after the initial injury, by treatment with this method. Research with light and sound stimulation had already proved useful in helping children with autism and learning disabilities. Dr. Ochs was asked to design a system that combined both EEG biofeedback and Light/Sound technology and therapy based on this research.

Basically, the Flexyx Neurofeedback System (FNS) is an advanced form of EEG biofeedback, which uses imperceptible light (from tiny LEDs) or infinitesimally weak electromagnetic pulses as the feedback signal. The system, in general, operates by monitoring patients' brainwaves.

People sit in a chair, eyes closed, wearing dark glasses that have a set of tiny lights mounted in the lenses. They are exposed to various amounts of the stimulation depending on their levels of sensitivity and responsiveness. With the help of sophisticated computer technology, the patient's dominant, or strongest, frequency brainwave is monitored and used to control the frequency rate at which the stimulation is delivered.

The length of the session and intensity of the stimulation are carefully adjusted to balance clinical effectiveness and patient comfort. The lights are programmed to pulsate at a slightly different frequency rate from the momentary dominant frequency in the patient's brain.

The basic premise is to interrupt the brain's rigid defensive pattern and stimulate it to develop a wider and more flexible range of responsiveness on the bioelectrical and neurochemical level. These brainwave changes eventually translate into a greater "flexibility" both neurologically and behaviorally.

Use of Flexyx therapy has resulted in rather significant alleviation of symptoms in conditions as varied as attention deficit disorder and post traumatic stress, to stroke and spinal cord injury, depression, headache, speech and fine motor skill and other problems.

⌒

In October 1998 Seth began the course of treatments, and there were immediate observable results. He was a sophomore in high school then and suffered from stress. There was so much work, and his stamina once again became an issue. He experienced difficulty sleeping and the combination of physical exhaustion and sleep depravation caused more spasticity and involuntary movement and even very dramatic mood swings. He frequently lost his temper, which was something new.

From the very beginning of his Flexyx therapy, he became calmer and slept more easily. His speech was clearer and his gross and fine motor skills seemed smoother. His work in school improved. A general sense of optimism prevailed. We were concerned that he would not be able to sustain his focus and stamina. He wanted to go to a top college, and so he needed to get good grades and be calm and clear for the required testing. He put a lot of pressure on himself.

The word I used as soon as I saw Seth after his first treatment was "grounded." He seemed to have his feet on the ground with new attitude. I was reminded of that first grade boy I saw swinging from the gate of the Beth Israel Day School the day after his first treatment with Frymann.

Seth has not had any noticeable mood swings except during a hiatus in the treatments in the winter of 1999–2000. When we realized that Seth was restless, less focused and more fatigued, we quickly resumed the therapy in February 2000. We hope to create an environment where there is an easy unfolding of the nervous system; where the nervous system is opened and stimulated. Flexyx offers one opportunity.

◡

In the summer of 1999, Seth went to live in Paris, for six weeks as a student of the New York Film Academy. He was sixteen years old and going to be a junior in high school. His determination to make films had survived the intervening year since the Genesis program. The Film Academy understandably was concerned that Seth would be able to manage the program. The equipment was big and cumbersome.

We went to meet the people at the Film Academy to see for ourselves what was involved. The equipment was, in fact, heavy and awkward. We all wanted to be sure that Seth would be able to participate fully. I had the added concern about his being so far away.

In the end, we made an arrangement with the Academy so that one of the participating teachers would be available to help Seth at the appropriate times. What made the Academy acquiesce to this request? Partly, it was Seth's enthusiasm and determination. He made it very clear to the people he met how much he wanted this program and how hard he would work to make it work. In addition, we give the Academy lots of credit for being so open minded about Seth. It says much about the institution that it is.

Seth made three five-minute black and white films that summer that are poignant and professional. These short films are his calling cards today. He applied for and got a summer internship in production at MTV News. His qualifications were straight-forward. Again, it speaks for itself about the institution and its ethos.

The other important thing is that Seth negotiated living in a foreign country (even when the airline temporarily lost his luggage on the trip over!) He learned a new language, made new friends, traveled independently, and proved he was responsible and mature. The experience in France matured him and that helped us to meet the new challenges that greeted us upon his return.

How can I explain what happened that junior year without discussing how ridiculous the rat race and popular culture that we live in here actually is? In the junior year of high school the testing begins: SATs, SAT IIs, Advanced Placement exams. The tests are for kids who want to go to private universities and colleges. Boy, did Seth want college. By the spring of junior year, he knew he wanted to go to the University of Pennsylvania.

His competition was stiff. Grades counted more than ever. The kids were studying like crazy to keep up their grades; preparing for exams, visiting colleges, and trying to maintain extra-curricular activities that would be attractive to college admissions committees.

I kept asking myself how they could test Seth in a standard way? Each time he filled out his SAT application we had to also apply for a non-standard testing situation. Additionally, shading in the little circles to indicate the correct answer is very difficult for Seth. We had to arrange for him to indicate his answers in a different way.

Finally, the College Board, Services for Students with Disabilities (SSD) assigned us a personal SSD code Seth that used on his applications for College Board exams. Seth was approved for extended hours of testing time and a writer to record the SAT answers.

While it was great that Seth was granted extended time, you can imagine what it meant to endure close to five consecutive hours of testing. The anxiety that surrounded these tests came not only because of the pressure to perform well, but also from the dread of exhaustion.

Fortunately, we had followed through with the Board of Education at the time of Seth's initial evaluations years before. We had kept good records and retained copies of all the paper work involved in arranging transportation at the time Seth attended the Stephen Gaynor School. These files were even more important to have for the College Board when Seth arranged his testing as it turned out.

It never occurred to Seth—or to us for that matter—that he wasn't entitled to the test time adjustment. Of course, we got the advice and support of the college counselor and head of school at Friends Seminary. They were allies from the beginning. But the fact is Seth had to make sure that he got what he needed to be evaluated fairly, and he did so successfully.

Seth's entire junior year was filled to the brim with stress. While he was maintaining his grades and getting help from a tutor in preparation for the standardized tests, he also participated in several extracurricular activities. He was photo editor of the yearbook which meant he was often taking photos or going to meetings after school until after dinnertime. Hours and hours of homework followed. He was involved in the executive committee of the youth group at our synagogue and participated in several forums with Future Voters of America. All of these activities were in addition to his appointments with Dr. Stough, going to Stone Mountain Counseling for Flexyx, or going for other bodywork.

Many things helped Seth survive his junior year. One was the closeness of the family. The years had made me wiser and calmer too. The family meetings of earlier years evolved into relaxed dinners where catching up and conversation dominated. Jay and I learned to let the children have center stage. When they bickered at dinner, we tried to stay out of it. I saw their struggles with one another as rehearsals for how they would struggle with others in the world.

The Sabbath continues to be the centerpiece of our week. Either we are all together for Sabbath dinner on Friday night or we are together for Sabbath lunch on Saturday. Taking this time away from the humdrum, casual, workaday, school day, and sanctifying it has added meaning to all our lives.

The other factor that influenced the last five years is my own practice of Yoga, which has deepened dramatically since I first wrote *Uncommon Voyage*. While I began exploring and taking classes almost thirty years ago, when we began our forays to La Jolla, I became a serious student of the Iyengar method. I have taken classes, attended workshops and "Intensives," gone away on Yoga vacations, and ultimately developed my own practice. I almost never miss a day of practice and carry a "Yoga bag" when I travel so that I can practice no matter where I am. As with other disciplines, after I tried it myself and experienced the profound changes that occur on all levels, I knew it would be great for Seth—and for everyone. I have been blessed to have a gifted teacher for the last few years with whom I often practice. He has also taught Seth and Haya and Jay. We converted our bedroom into a small Yoga studio. I even built a rope wall.

Yoga is a Sanskrit word and means yoke or union. It is, as Eleanor Criswell has written so eloquently in her book *How Yoga Works: An Introduction to Somatic Yoga*, "...the discipline and training of the human's embodied being so that it evolves toward what it is capable of becoming." Criswell explains that Yoga seeks to provide physical and mental training experiences to further refine the soma (unified mind-body). Yoga has become a household word in the West. Millions of men and women attend classes and seminars and read books. There are many stereotypes about Yoga: that it is epitomized by the headstand, the lotus posture, or other pretzel like poses. Some think of it as a system of meditation or religion. All these stereotypes are misleading. Yoga is first and foremost the discipline of conscious living.

James Murphy, my teacher, is blessed with great insight and ability. Originally, an accomplished dancer, he began his study of Yoga with Mr. Iyengar and Iyengar's children in the medical classes in Mr. Iyengar's Institute in India. I sought James because one of my senior teachers thought he would be an exceptional teacher for Seth. But I am the one who has benefited the most from James' profound knowledge. While I have always had great reverence for the practice of Yoga, in the last few years my appreciation has grown deeper. Through the Iyengar method, James has helped me to realign myself; to find balance; to overcome anxiety as I approach more difficult poses; to heal old and challenging injuries; and to accept the days when simple things elude me.

James has worked with Seth through postures—some demanding, some restorative—that affect Seth in perceptible ways. Seth's chest opens and his groins relax. The pronation and "fixing" he has had to cope with all his life are relieved. A change comes over his face, his eyes, and his demeanor. He breathes deeply and fully.

During the past twenty years, psychophysical research findings and Yoga research per se have expanded rapidly. The research has resulted in a strong substantiation of Yoga's effectiveness and has supplied an impetus for Yoga's widening acceptance as a part of contemporary life. What has become apparent is that people can understand and self-regulate their bodies far more easily than they had dreamed possible.

The research shows how more integrated we are mentally and physically. It proves that we humans are immensely capable of growth, self-regulation, intelligence, and self-healing. Viola Frymann, Carola Speads, Moshe Feldenkrais, Milton Ericson, and others I have written about are saying this too.

Sonia Sumar, an internationally renowned Yoga therapist and author, has developed a therapeutic approach for infants and children with Down Syndrome, cerebral palsy, learning disabilities, and other special needs. She has a therapeutic program of adaptive Yoga techniques designed to enhance the natural development of such children. Her *Yoga for the Special Child* is a book I have strongly recommended to other parents.

The mission of *Yoga for the Special Child* is to provide these children with a holistic option to conventional medical treatment and to make this option available to parents, educators, Yoga teachers and health care professionals through training programs and the distribution of educational materials. I wish I had known about Sonia and her book and training when Seth was a baby. I urge parents of children with special needs to consult Sumar and her book. In my experience, Yoga proves to be one of the most powerful disciplines we have to help us realize our potential.

Perhaps the ways I heal myself are by empowering those I love. My love for my children, Seth and Haya, informs me, grants me opportunity, nourishes me. That is what I believe love does.

As I have written again and again Seth has led me on my path. His cerebral palsy made me become who I am today. It meant I was able to create something for myself out of myself. I wonder if I invented myself, invented Seth, invented it all. We all do this if we are lucky. We write our destinies with our imaginations. How much do we allow ourselves to dream and imagine? This is what it takes every day to grow.

It makes me think of a boy I know with special needs whose family ignored the problem for a long time. It tortured him and them just the same. The boy, now a young teenager, had a severe speech anomaly—he was very difficult to understand and did poorly in school so he felt bad about himself and was always fighting with his mother. He lacked athletic prowess, emphasizing his status as an outcast among his peers. My friend is divorced and her son was running back and forth between his father and her, pitting them against one another.

Speaking up, being the messenger, are difficult roles to assume. Because I love my friend dearly and felt truly compassionate toward the boy, and, frankly, I was always uncomfortable being around them, I finally spoke my mind. I was honest in my observations of the child's problems. I encouraged the mother to take him to Dr. Frymann.

Of course, to begin with, I met with resistance. While money is no problem in this family, my friend gave every reason not to go. It took weeks of my pushing her to get her to make the call.

Six months later an appointment was gotten, and the boy was examined. True to form, Dr. Frymann made a sharp diagnosis and many specific suggestions. One thing the doctor identified was that the boy's eyesight needed correction. The boy's mother remembered that six or seven years earlier the pediatrician had recommended glasses, which they got. But the boy had not worn them. The evaluation yielded many other profound insights.

For various reasons the family determined that getting care for the son was better done near home. With my help and Dr. Frymann's guidance we worked together to establish treatment close to Boston where the family lives. Osteopathic care is gotten two hours away in New Hampshire, but after several weekly sessions was cut down to once a month. I notice that my friend and her son are getting a lot out of the time it takes to get to this appointment. Other care—vision training, biofeedback, and swimming—is also done close to home.

The point I am trying to make is that this family was not doing what was in front of them to do. Their son and brother's problem was calling out to them from the dysfunction of their lives. They were always fighting. The child was miserable and barely living up to his potential. As soon as the family got together to help the boy, everything else followed. Not only has the boy metamorphosed, his new independence has left my friend able to date and live her own life in a much more fulfilling way.

My point is that we have to wake up in the morning and *re-invent* ourselves every day. This is creative energy. It is about how we live. Life floods us with circumstance. We must carve, etch, and navigate out of these circumstances with originality by utilizing our *originality.*

And we must do this everyday.

Seth's story and my story are stories of challenges and meeting them, though different. Seth who has cerebral palsy must cope in ways I can only imagine. It is painful to watch him struggle to come to terms with it, but I can not jump in and help him. He is leaving home and going to college, and needs to make his way in the world. The reality of it washes over us all like a wave once more.

While we were vacationing in California last winter we went shoe shopping, something our harried New York life doesn't seem to allow. First I watched Seth struggle to explain to the clerk at the store what he wanted. I watched the clerk's face as it dawned on him that Seth is not like you and me. He talks "funny."

I watched Seth deal with his shoes, lacing, unlacing, and bending over to take them off, putting the new ones on. I wanted to jump up and kneel down before him and save him from the effort. I die a little inside every time I see him pour from a big bottle to a small glass. I cry an ocean of tears for all he will never do with ease. And I pray someone will love him and be a companion to him and help him without ever compromising his dignity.

Today I think about Seth in new ways. He has said he would have loved to be a surgeon, but of course because of his fine motor coordination, this is not possible. He is handsome enough to be an actor or television announcer, but his speech will keep him from doing this or from becoming a litigator. Because of these circumstances, he will have to choose another career, a different path than he may have. And, as a result, he will become who he becomes because surgeon, performer or litigator was closed to him. What I know is it will unfold. And I will be practicing to live in a way that makes it possible to receive this unfolding and to encourage it in myself, in him, in everyone.

guides

How do you know if there is something wrong?

Trust your instincts.

We have to believe that what we know counts. Those wise voices inside are our most important guides. We are the experts when it comes to our health. Our sacred instinct—the magic part of us that speaks from faith rather than fear and helps us to discriminate between information and wisdom—this is what deserves awe and attention. There is more wisdom in our bodies than in the greatest philosophy.

Sucking, crying, laughing, sleeping, how does your baby seem to you? Is your baby "comfortable"? How is your child sleeping? Trust what you see; it's the truth.

How can you stay in charge?

Trust what you observe.

This is particularly difficult to do when you first get a sense that there might be something wrong, or you just get the diagnosis. It is natural to be nervous and anxious.

But observation is very important. We see our children more than anyone else, even if we are not with them all day. Trust what you observe. We observe things as parents, no one else can see. Believe in these observations. Record them.

Listen to your gut.

Be intuitive. Your intuition may say try allopathic medicine (everyday, conventional). Or you may want to try holistic, or alternative, medicine. You may like one doctor and not another. Question yourself. Ask why? Is the doctor looking right into your eyes? Is she listening? Are your own intuitions about what is going on in your child in sync with what she is telling you?

What are the causes of developmental delay?

In at least 80 percent of children with developmental delays, including attention deficits and autism, there is a history of traumatic birth. Problems during labor and delivery may compromise the structural areas of the brain. This is referred to as cerebral dysfunction. Any serious disturbance to the nervous system at that time can interfere with physiological development. This means the brain is not functioning as efficiently as it should

The brain is contained within the bony skull, which is designed to accept the impact of labor contractions. Problems of labor and delivery may compromise these structural areas, which, in turn, disturb the nervous system within. The result is the possibility—and likelihood—of interference with physiological development. This translates into developmental delays.

Ten Tried and True Basics

Touch your children.

Touch is the great sense. There is no substitute for good hands. It is important to know how to touch your children. Observe how your doctors and therapists touch—or do not touch—your children. You read in our story how much touch did and still does play a big part in what happened.

Make eye contact with your children.

The eyes are our active seekers of the essence of life; look into your child's eyes as often as you can. Visual function and academic success are inseparable. If vision changes, so does personality and behavior.

Encourage movement.

Movement is learning. Sensation and motor ability are vital to function. Moving allows the brain to know where the body is in relation to the world. Movement provides the opportunity to touch, see, and hear.

Talk with your children and listen to them.

Talking with them helps them to explore their own feeling life and to express it. For instance, if a child comes to you at the end of your exhausting day and says, "I'm tired," try not to answer, "Me too." Ask them instead, "What made you so tired?" Having to answer this question helps them to explore their inner life.

Do not criticize your children or their expression of feeling. For instance, if a child comes to you and says, "I don't feel like being in the school performance," do not respond, "That's ridiculous." Or "That is a mistake." Instead ask, "What is making you feel that way?" Learn to ask complex questions of them so they can not answer a simple "yes," or "no."

Feed your children well.

Dr. Frymann believes good nutrition is the best prevention. Proper nutrition is one of the best weapons in the prevention of asthmatic episodes. There is clear evidence of a relationship between poor nutrition and bronchial difficulties caused by asthma. What's more, eating right can lower your risk of developing a chronic disease.

And I believe it is just as important to sit and eat with your children. As they grow, dinner is a time of conversation, interaction, catching up. Besides, food is fun, and I believe in deriving pleasure from it.

Learn to practice and teach your children to practice.

Practice anything: piano, knitting, basketball, meditation, Yoga, swimming, flute, but do it every day, whatever it is. The habit of practice is nourishing. It gives feedback. Practice is useful. There comes a time in everyone's life when having the patience practice encourages is essential. It breeds strength and discipline.

Practice allows us to cultivate continuity and perseverance: traits that release us from old patterns and from silly mistakes.

Put your children center stage.

We get our time in the limelight when we are children; we must reciprocate by letting our children shine. Fade in to the background as much as possible when your children are interacting with others, adults or peers.

Get educated.

We need to investigate all our choices. Ask your doctors whatever you want to know. We must not hesitate to ask every question we think we must have an answer for.

Keep good records.

This is like marking a trail; it safeguards memory. Write everything down, save everything, and make files that are well labeled and organized. Taking time for this is protection.

Be open-minded.

It leaves the future wide open, removing all obstacles; it keeps us from the temptation to be self-limiting. Do not fear mistakes. There are none. Life shrinks and expands in proportion to one's courage.

⌒

What is clear from the work of Frymann is that simple measures can be profoundly effective. She outlines many of them on her website. She asks astute questions about acute episodes of fever, tonsillitis, digestive upsets, etc. She suggests that we look at these acute episodes as healing experiences; that it is the body's way of bringing about change. And the reason that simple measures can be so effective is that the healing process comes from within the body not from outside the body.

We all know that when parents are in conflict, this reflects on the child. Sometimes we have to look at ourselves through the eyes of our children. When we praise them and offer stimulation and encouragement, children thrive. And children thrive on stability and on security. There is a great need for consistency of rules and regulations. A child needs to know boundaries.

I write this, and at the same time I am aware of how more and more children are prescribed psychotropic drugs, even as preschoolers and toddlers. I mean such drugs as Ritalin, Prozac, etc. Many of these drugs are prescribed at the request of parents who ask for them by name and are hoping to get better behavior or school performances from their children. I have a friend who worried about her daughter's low self-esteem and labeled it a "depression." Her first act was to seek out a psychiatrist who could write a prescription for one of the psychotropic drugs in the Prozac family. A psychotherapist I greatly respect recently told me that the new medicine is about "good chemistry." I do not agree.

Even I know from simple psychology that depression is anger turned to the inside. Instead of drugs I would prescribe a Feldenkrais

ATM class and Yoga for this adolescent girl on the precipice of her womanhood. I imagine this young woman lying on the floor rolling from side to side, kicking her legs in the air, turning on her tummy to growl like a lion. I hope she would learn how to cry. I would encourage her to open her chest and let loose; and hope she would find quiet and stillness within too. I would send her swimming every other day after such classes.

Sometimes overworked pediatricians hand out drugs to get frenetic children out the door. The last time I was in the pediatrician's office was last year when I needed the annual school forms filled out. The place was a mad house. Not only was it bedlam in the waiting room, it was unsanitary. I was sure that Seth and Haya who came for a routine exam would leave there sick. I wondered about the other mothers and whether like me they arrived healthy and left carrying a germ.

There were three or four children of differing ages in the waiting room with accompanying adults as well as my two children and me. The room was not particularly well ventilated and two of the other children were coughing and sneezing away. In the meantime, all the furniture in the waiting room probably needed wiping down with antiseptic having been handled all the day by a parade of sick toddlers. The toys were shared among all the children. Who knew when they were last washed with soapy water and a clean rinse?

More than anything, it was noisy which made me want to scream myself. I am usually composed, but I could barely hear myself think. The children and I often have conversation when we are waiting somewhere together, but we couldn't hear each other above the cacophony.

How teachers endure in noisy, overcrowded classrooms—many of which are poorly equipped—is a mystery to me. Teachers are harried especially by the issue of accountability, which has placed additional demands on them. Teachers often want difficult students medicated into submission. Who can blame them? What has teaching and learning become? Do our children pause in the day long enough to know if they are breathing? Do we?

A wide gulf of uncertainty prevails among doctors and mental health professionals and parents over when to use psychotropic drugs and when to stop using them. To me that should be enough to make them stop altogether. We know medication dulls these children's intellectual awareness. It is a stopgap measure and doesn't do anything for the underlying causes themselves. In fact, as Frymann points out, the longer the child takes the drugs the more difficult it is to break the habit, because when the drug is stopped, the child becomes more hyperactive than when the drug was introduced in the first place.

⌒

Seizures may also occur at any stage in life from newborn to old age. But the etiology or underlying cause varies from patient to patient. A rare cause is organic brain diseases. There are many degrees and varieties of trauma that can occur during pregnancy or during the birth process. There are many manifestations of the microscopic injuries to areas of the brain such as sudden jerking, muscle spasms in parts of the body and even full seizures affecting the whole body. Some children vomit after feedings or are slow to suck like Seth. There are other signs that microscopic injury may have occurred during the birth process. The Osteopath is trained to identify these subtle disturbances in the musculoskeletal system and apply gentle manipulative skills to correct them.

When I think of these afflicted children, I feel profound pain. I feel compassion for the hyperactive, withdrawn and depressed child. I want to put my hands on these children myself or send them to Dr. Frymann. I want to put them in a room with James Murphy. I want them to know the possibility that they can heal without invasion, but with the power and force from within. I know these "methods" offer them the possibility of using their creativity, creativity they all possess. It is *originality,* originality that must be liberated again and again.

The child with Down Syndrome (Congenital Hypopituitarism) is a very special person who reveals a purity and simplicity of life that is unique. This child's difference is not pathological. Some of these children have special physical needs that require surgery. Osteopathic care of these children does not try to make them like other children, but it will enable them to achieve their optimal potential, to attain a high level of good health and to grow in to the unique and special people they are meant to be. This kind of care is about liberating, unleashing, our *originality*.

Conductive Education

I have no first hand experience with Conductive Education, but it is a unique system of special education for children with motor disorders such as cerebral palsy and spina bifida. Conductive Education was developed in Hungary in 1945 by Dr. Andras Peto at his Peto Institute.

The goal of Conductive Education is to teach challenged children to be functionally independent and self-sufficient. Conductive Education is not a medical treatment or therapy, and offers no cure. Children with motor disabilities are taught to find their own solutions to problems in daily life. The process of active learning to achieve these goals is known as Orthofunction.

A Conductor who is trained in all aspects of each child's physical, intellectual, social, and personal development oversees the child's program. Children from three to ten years old who have been diagnosed with cerebral palsy are the students.

Many Conductive Education centers exist in the country now. I recommend you consult my Resource Guide for some of them.

Euromed and the Adeli Suit

I heard about Euromed and the Adeli suit from a reader of *Uncommon Voyage* who got in touch with me in 1999, but I have no first hand experience of it, and I am not sure I would call it "holistic." Recently another mother of a child with cerebral palsy contacted me by email. She wrote to me about Euromed and the Adeli suit too. The program is based in Poland. You can visit their website to learn more about them: www.euromed.bptnet.pl.

The therapy was born out of the Russian Space program, and first applied to the Mir cosmonauts whose muscles were debilitated by months in zero gravity. Its centerpiece is the Adeli Suit—a strange looking contraption, covered with interconnecting elastic cords that are said to realign the muscles, teaching them how to move properly.

The suit acts as an external skeleton and all over Nautilus machine in one, guiding the body while strengthening it. The method results in a certain normalization of the pattern of locomotive and motor actions of the patient's body, trunk, and lower limbs. Rather than go into great detail here, I recommend you consult the Resource Guide to find out how to contact them.

The Feldenkrais Method and the
Field Center for Children's Integrated Development

Many parents who read *Uncommon Voyage* and called me went on to explore work with either Dr. Frymann or Anat Baniel. I have learned from these parents that many different opportunities have sprouted up around the country. While it is optimal to first go to San Diego to be treated by Dr. Frymann, or to the Bay area to see Anat, it is not always possible. What is possible is that there may be places closer where your special needs child can be treated outside the mainstream medical model. An example of this is the Field Center for Children's Integrated Development in Montclair, New Jersey, www.thefieldcenter.org.

The Field Center is a non-profit corporation dedicated to the rehabilitation of infants and small children who are physically challenged due to neurological problems that affect their motor skills, physical growth and learning potential. The therapeutic intervention used at the Field Center is based primarily on the Feldenkrais Method.

The Center's treatment addresses physical, cognitive and emotional processes simultaneously. The children are given an intensive neuromuscular education and encouraged to "swim" in the Center's Endless Pool. Sheryl Field, a Feldenkrais practitioner, who has twenty years experience working with children with serious neuro-motor impairments, like cerebral palsy, directs the Center.

Can you imagine what it might have meant to Seth and to me to have the Field Center as an option fifteen years ago when we were just beginning to test alternative waters? And the financial issues are different now. Scholarships are available at the Center, and the Insurance companies consider these treatments in a different light today.

Hearing Impairments

Not long ago I read a report in the *New York Times* about deafness in children that confirmed what I already knew. Dr. Frymann had discussed hearing loss in many of the lectures I attended more than ten years ago. Deafness is the most common disability present at birth. And a deaf newborn looks and acts like any other baby. Often allopathic doctors do not detect the deafness until the child is two or three. Such delays can permanently impair a child's ability to learn to speak intelligibly and can result in long lasting, social, emotional and academic difficulties.

Dr. Frymann taught us that "the ear is not something sitting out there in space. The ear is part of a total mechanism in the body." Many children get frequent ear infections. Only, if the infections recur a number of times do the doctors finally perform a hearing test.

It is not uncommon to hear mothers admit that their child has had ear infections over and over again. Perhaps the first ear infection occurred when he was six weeks of age. The child was treated with an antibiotic; he got over it; two months later there was another ear infection. He was treated with antibiotics, he got over it and six weeks later there was another ear infection, and so it goes on, perhaps for several years. I recently heard such a story from a mother whose son is experiencing very challenging social situations in school.

The boy appears not to know when to whisper and when to speak up. He is entering his teen years, and his cognitive skills are uneven, and he displays inappropriate behavior, often in the form of shouting. When I questioned this woman about her child, she told me he was diagnosed as deaf in one ear many years ago, but it was a substantial time after his deafness probably occurred. In other words, as an infant and toddler he probably had a lot of difficulty hearing. Some area of his central nervous system had been compromised. Hearing stimulation at the correct level helps organize the brain. Learning is accomplished through complex and interrelated processes, and being unable to hear is hugely detrimental.

The Challenged Athlete's Foundation

I am ignited by challenge it's true. I recently became acquainted with the Challenged Athlete's Foundation. The Challenged Athlete's Foundation believes that competitive athletics for physically disabled individuals can foster self-esteem and the ability to achieve goals in life. Their mission is to assist and promote these athletes in their competitive pursuits. The foundation is based in La Jolla, and in November 2000, they hosted their sixth annual San Diego Triathlon Challenge. Nearly sixty challenged athletes; a dozen celebrities and a handful of professional triathletes joined the 400 participants of the SDTC to celebrate the excellence of unique abilities. Visit their website at www.AthletesHelpingAthletes.org.

Resources for Children with Special Needs

The Challenged Athlete's Foundation grew out of someone's passion and circumstances. We find many examples of this in life. Great, good works can be born out of tragedy and challenge. We need tools and support to meet these challenges.

This is one of the reasons I have dedicated so much of my life to Resources for Children with Special Needs. "Resources" is an information, direct referral, advocacy, training, publications, non-profit agency in New York for any child, birth to twenty-one with any special need. Visit "Resources" website www.resourcesnyc.org.

The founders of "Resources" are three women who have children with special needs. Resources for Children with Special Needs now annually provides services to thousands of interested New York families. Two of the founders are Directors of the agency, which today employs twenty people on their full time staff.

Radical Healing

Rudolph Ballentine is an American physician and psychiatrist trained in many of the world's healing traditions. He uses the principles of holistic healing and develops an integrated system combining the awareness, tools, and practices taught by a variety of healing disciplines, including Ayurveda, Homeopathy, and herbal medicine. Ballentine bases his treatments on the principles of herbal traditions of china, India, Europe and Native America. He presents several self-assessment techniques, including body maps and mind/body types. He describes the use of exercise, nutrition and cleansing (detoxification), and holistic techniques for working with energy and consciousness. A list of his books can be found on the Internet.

In saving the best for last, I want to mention:
The Foundation for Osteopathic Research and Training (F.O.R.T.)
Dr. Jim Jealous, Dr. Joseph Grasso and Dr. Domenick Masiello along with several other osteopathic physicians are involved in creating a center on the East Coast to meet the growing needs of a population seeking true osteopathic care. The Foundation for Osteopathic Research and Training is dedicated to preserving the traditional osteopathic principles provided by Andrew Taylor Still and William Garner Sutherland. What is being planned is a teaching and research center and an Osteopathic Center for Children for the East Coast, modeled, in part, on The Osteopathic Center for Children, London, England.

Although in existence for over one hundred years, osteopathic medicine has greatly diminished as the modern age has increasingly come to rely on technology. These individuals, instead, are focused on providing training to medical students and graduates seeking to develop skills, abilities, and insight that reflect the considerable depth and power of Osteopathy. The founding of this Center means I will be working for the realization of a place that will serve my own good as well as the good of others.

❧

Not long ago, because of *Uncommon Voyage* and my visibility as chairperson of Resources for Children with Special Needs, I was invited to join a startup, dot-com company. That experience, coupled with the thousands of families with special needs children who I met during my travels, convinced me that it was time to update and rewrite my book.

The Internet is a powerful tool for connecting people to each other and to information. But there is also great fragmentation. There are Internet sites for people with spinal cord injuries and Internet sites for disease specific conditions. There are health sites and medical/e-commerce sites, places that purport to address "lifestyle" needs. There are medical portals and other content/information sites. There are health-related sites like Bean Sprouts where membership is required. There are medical supply catalog sites and drugstore sites, and non-profit organization sites. I do not find cohesion. And I am not sure where my story belongs, on which of these sites. But I know it takes time and thought and the right questions to use the Internet effectively.

At the same time, as Seth writes in his Foreword, technology makes the biggest difference for people with disabilities. It has given Seth access, clarity, speed. To some extent, it leveled the playing field for him. The Internet can provide information about everything and it offers technical assistance, and I suggest using it for that. The world is open to technology. We already see how the University of Pennsylvania has employed technology and the Internet to integrate Seth into the community. With the aid of technology, there are fewer obstacles for people like Seth.

о⁓

I think about many things when I consider having to leave off. The question of the mainstream versus the alternative is only part of my story. There is continuing tension. In both areas the responsibility is actually on us, but that role is not as clear in the orthodox world. Maybe it is those white coats. No matter which world we are in it is imperative to question the practitioner, to know his/her qualifications, to ask all the right questions, and to get answers for what we need to know.

Individuals who present themselves as healers, Homeopaths, naturopaths, nutrition counselors, Feldenkrais teachers, and so on should be questioned closely as to their qualifications and training. We must be aware that in some of these areas standards are different in different states too.

When we are being treated in the orthodox world of medicine, we tend to accept the license of our doctors as a sanction for almost anything. In England, where there is no regulation or licensing, it is up to the patient to ask physicians what they are qualified to administer. That would be a good skill for all of us to acquire. We need to be sure that our doctors are really listening to us, answering our questions, and practicing their medicine responsibly.

At the heart of things, though, we must learn not to look for quick fixes; not to make gods out of our doctors. And we must forgive ourselves our mistakes. Remember that parents go through developmental stages just as children do. I had a lot to learn and continue to learn as I parent Seth. Now I am facing for the first time being a parent of a child leaving home for college.

We must recreate a partnership between our bodies and ourselves, trusting the body's exquisite capacity to heal itself. To stay well, we have to be self-aware.

A nursery school teacher of Haya's called me recently. We had not spoken in years, but he remembered that I was interested in "alternative" health. He wanted referrals, because for more than a year he had been suffering from a condition that the doctors could not help him cure.

He talked for a long time describing the history of his ailment, the tests, doctors, drugs, he had consulted and taken. I asked him many questions. Then I asked if any of the doctors and specialists had ever asked him what he thought was wrong. He replied, "no." He went on to say, in fact, that he had just begun to be bothered about not being asked. Then I asked him, "And what do you think is wrong?"

In his answer we both knew he had found the path to better health. He knew and I knew that he was getting in touch with himself through this experience, and there is no other path to be on.

where to turn

THE FOLLOWING ARE RESOURCES I referred to in *Uncommon Voyage* as well as some others. However, I suggest, begin by contacting your local Parent Training and Information Center. There is one in every state. *Exceptional Parent* publishes this list in their January issue every year. They also list early intervention centers, organizations by disability, and other major organizations. It is important to learn to search. Use the yellow pages, your local newspaper. Look for what is in your neighborhood. Talk to your professionals: your child's teacher, the doctor, occupational therapist, or your local clergy.

The National Organization for Rare Disorders (800-999-6673) is also an excellent resource. It can help put you in touch with other parents who are always the best guides. It is important to contact national organizations, but, more important, to uncover what is accessible: I suggest think national and use what is local. Use libraries and the Internet to search for specific programs and services.

Gary Shulman, a Program Director for Resources for Children with Special Needs, told me that he advises all parents: "Sticks and stones will break your bones, but words will get you money." Learn how to advocate, to frame what you need, and to get what you are entitled to.

Associations and Organizations

AMERICAN ACADEMY OF OSTEOPATHY
  3500 De Pauw Blvd., Suite 1080
  Indianapolis, IN 46268-1139
  Tel: 317-879-1881

AMERICAN ASSOCIATION OF
UNIVERSITY AFFILIATED PROGRAMS
FOR PERSONS WITH DEVELOPMENTAL
DISABILITIES
  8605 Cameron Street, Suite 406
  Silver Springs, MD 20910
  Tel: 301-588-8252
  Fax: 301-588-2842

AMERICAN OSTEOPATHIC ASSOCIATION
(A.O.A.)
  300 5th Street NE
  Washington, DC 20002
  Tel: 800-962-9008
  Tel: 800-560-6229
  (legislative hotline)

  142 East Ontario Street
  Chicago, IL 60611
  Tel: 800-621-1773

AYURVEDIC MEDICINE OF NEW YORK
Scott Gerson, M.D., Director
  13 West 9th Street
  New York, NY 10011
  Tel: 212-505-8971

THE CHALLENGED ATHLETE'S
FOUNDATION
  2148 Jimmy Durante Blvd, Suite B
  Del Mar, CA 92014
  Tel: 858-793-9293
  www.challengedathletes.org

CHILDREN'S DEFENSE FUND
  122 C. Street NW
  Washington, DC 20001
  Tel: 202-628-8787

THE CRANIAL ACADEMY
  8606 Allisonville Road, Suite 130
  Indianapolis, IN 46250
  Tel: 317-594-0411

DISABILITIES RIGHTS EDUCATION
AND DEFENSE FUND (DREDF)
  2212 Sixth Street
  Berkeley, CA 94710
  Tel: 510-644-2555 (Voice/TDD)
  Fax: 510-841-8645

EXCEPTIONAL PARENT
  209 Harvard Street, Suite 303
  Brookline, MA 02146
  Tel: 201-634-6550
  Fax: 617-730-8742
  TDD: 617-730-9856

EUROMED
THE REHABILITATION CENTER EUROMED
  76-032 Mielno,
  Aleja Plastow 10, Os
  Syrena, Poland
  Tel: 011-48-94 189-213
  www.euromed.bptnet.pl.
  Email: euromed @telbank.pl

NOVEL PRODUCTS
  P.O. Box 408
  Rockton, IL 61072-0408
  Tel: 800-323-5143
  Tel: 800-624-4866
  Exer-Cor (exercise and coordination
  equipment)

THE FELDENKRAIS GUILD
  524 Ellsworth Street SW
  P.O. Box 489
  Albany, OR 97321
  Tel: 800-775-2118

THE FIELD CENTER FOR CHILDREN'S
INTEGRATED DEVELOPMENT
  83 Park Street
  Montclair, NJ 07042
  Tel: 973-655-0385
  www.thefieldcenter.org

THE FOUNDATION FOR OSTEOPATHIC
RESEARCH AND TRAINING (F.O.R.T.)
Terry Sargent, Executive Director
   196 Weeks Mills Road
   Farmington, ME 04938
   Tel: 207-778-9847
   www.geocities.com/fortosteopathy
   /homepage.html

THE FUND FOR
CONDUCTIVE EDUCATION
   8 Jason Lane
   Mamaroneck, NY 10443
   Tel: 914-834-8707
*(Unique special education for children
with motor disorders. Developed by Dr.
Andras Peto at his Peto Institute in
Hungary)*

HOMEOPATHIC EDUCATION SERVICE
   2124 Kittredge Street
   Berkeley, CA 94704
   Tel: 800-359-9051

IYENGAR YOGA
IYNAUS NEWS
   P.O. Box 583
   Austin, TX 78767

LEARNING DISABILITY ASSOCIATION
OF AMERICA
   4156 Library Road
   Pittsburgh, PA 15234
   Tel: 412-341-1515

MANHATTAN MOTHERS & OTHERS
Susan W. Williams, Founder
   160 East 65th Street
   New York, NY 10021
   Tel: 212-570-6860

NATIONAL CENTER FOR HOMEOPATHY
   801 North Fairfax Street,
   Suite 306
   Alexandria, VA 22314
   Tel: 703-548-7790

NATIONAL INFORMATION CENTER
FOR CHILDREN AND YOUTH WITH
HANDICAPS (NICHY)
   P.O. Box 1492
   Washington, DC 20013
   Tel: 703-893-6061
   Tel: 800-999-5599

NATIONAL VACCINE INFORMATION
CENTER/DISSATISFIED PARENTS
TOGETHER (NVIC/DPT)
   512 W. Maple Avenue, Suite 206
   Vienna, VA 22180
   Tel: 800-909-SHOT
   Tel: 703-938-DPT3
   Fax: 703-938-5768

NEURO-DEVELOPMENTAL TREATMENT
ASSOCIATION (NDTA)
   P.O. Box 14613
   Chicago, IL 60614
   (Berta Bobath Method)

THE NEW YORK LEAGUE
FOR THE HARD OF HEARING
   71 West 23rd Street, 18th Floor
   New York, NY 10010
   Tel: 212-741-7650
   Fax: 212-255-4413

OFFICE OF SPECIAL EDUCATION AND
REHABILITATIVE SERVICES (OSERS)
   U.S. Dept. of Education
   Room 3132, Shwitzer Bldg.
   Washington, DC 20202-2524
   Tel: 202-708-5366
   *(clearing house on disability
   information)*

PAUL'S WHEELS
   P.O. Box 380784
   Cambridge, MA 02238
   Tel: 617-628-7955
   Fax: 617-628-6546
   *(manufacturers of custom-built sport
   wheelchairs for specific sports)*

RESOURCES FOR CHILDREN
WITH SPECIAL NEEDS, INC.
  200 Park Avenue South, Suite 816
  New York, NY 10003
  Tel: 212-677-4650
  Fax: 212-254-4070
  www.resourcesnyc.org

SIBLING INFORMATION NETWORK
CT UNIVERSITY AFFILIATED PROGRAM
  991 Main Street, Suite 3A
  East Hartford, CT 06108
  Tel: 203-282-7050

THE SOMATICS SOCIETY
& THE NOVATO INSTITUTE
  1516 Grant Avenue, Suite 212
  Novato, CA 94945
  Tel: 415-892-0617
  Fax: 415-892-4380

STONE MOUNTAIN
COUNSELING CENTER
  310 River Road Extension
  New Paltz, NY 12561
  Tel: 914-658-8083
  Fax: 914-658-8374
  Email: smcc@ulster.net

  130 West 42nd Street
  New York, NY 10036
  Tel: 212-840-8449
  Fax: 212-944-0738

Professionals and Expert Individuals

Viola Frymann, D.O.
OSTEOPATHIC CENTER FOR CHILDREN
5135 54th Place
San Diego, CA 92105
Tel: 619-583-7611
www.osteopathiccenter.org

Jim Giorgi, M.S.Ed.,
Flexyx Certified Research Associate
PATHWAYS/BIOFEEDBACK CONSULTANTS
50 Rockwood Circle, 2C
Middletown, NY 10941
Tel: 845-695-1256

Alfred Grant, M.D.
301 East 17th Street
New York, NY 10003
Tel: 212-598-6605

Joseph S. Grasso, D.O.
P.O. Box 743
Franconia, NH 03580
Tel: 603-823-4099

Sarah Harber, AIBT
STONE MOUNTAIN
COUNSELING CENTER
130 West 42nd Street
New York, NY 10036
Tel: 212-840-8449
Fax: 212-944-0738
Email: franeknyc@aolcom

James S. Jealous, D.O.
P.O. Box 844
Franconia, NH 03580
Tel: 603-823-7733

Marion Katzive
230 Park Avenue
New York, NY 10017
Tel: 212-557-0040
(advocate for special education)

Richard Kavner, O.D., F.A.A.O.
245 East 54th Street
New York, NY 10022
Tel: 212-752-6930
(behavioral optometry)

James Murphy,
Certified Iyengar Teacher
IYENGAR INSTITUTE OF NEW YORK
27 West 24th Street
New York, NY 10010
Tel: 212-691-9642
Fax: 212-255-1773
www.yoga.ny.org

Rueven "Robbie" Ofir, Ph.D., P.T.,
Feldenkrais Practitioner
159 West 53rd Street
New York, NY 10019
Tel: 212-265-6591
Fax: 212-765-7352
Email: robofir@aol.com

Zinaida Pelkey, D.O.
32 West 96th Street
New York, NY 10025
Tel: 212-662-6560

Susan Scheer, P.T.
173 Riverside Drive
New York, NY 10024
Tel: 212-799-8221

Dr. Joseph Shapiro
CENTER FOR UNLIMITED VISION
80 5th Avenue, Suite 1105
New York, NY 10011
Tel: 212-255-2240

Elizabeth Sharpless, Ph.D.,
Licensed Psychologist
24 West 12th Street
New York, NY 10003
Tel: 212-727-8131

Carola H. Speads
MISS SPEADS' STUDIO OF PHYSICAL
RE-EDUCATION
  251 Central Park West
  New York, NY 10023
  Tel: 212-787-6610

Sonia Sumar, Yoga Instructor
Jeffrey Volk, Programs Director
YOGA FOR THE SPECIAL CHILD
  Route 1, Box 1559
  Buckingham, VA 23921
  Tel: 804-969-2668

Peter Springall, M.D.
C/O THE OSTEOPATHIC CENTER FOR
CHILDREN
  5135 54th Place
  San Diego, CA 92105
  Tel: 619-583-7611

bibliography

Bateson, Gregory. *Mind and Nature: A Necessary Unity.* New York: E. P. Dutton Publishing, 1979.

Batshaw, Mark L. and Yvonne M. Perret. *Children with Disabilities: A Medical Primer,* 3rd ed. Baltimore: Paul H. Brookes Publishing, 1992.

Buck, Pearl S. *The Child Who Never Grew.* Maryland: Woodbine House, 1992.

Capra, Fritjof. *The Tao of Physics: The Bestseller That Reconciles Eastern Philosophy and Western Science in a Brilliant Humanistic Vision of the Universe.* Boulder: Bantam Books, 1975.

Cassileth, Barrie R., *The Alternative Medicine Handbook.* New York: W. W. Norton & Company.

Cohen, Sherry Suib. *The Magic of Touch: Revolutionary Ways to Use Your Most Powerful Sense.* New York: Harper & Row, 1987.

Coulter, Harris L. and Barbara Loe Fisher. *A Shot in the Dark: Why the P in the DPT Vaccination May Be Hazardous to Your Child's Health.* New York: Avery Publishing Group, Inc., 1991

Coulter, Harris L. *Vaccination, Social Violence, and Criminality.* Berkeley, CA: North Atlantic Books, 1990.

Criswell, Eleanor. *How Yoga Works: An Introduction to Somatic Yoga.* Novato, CA: Freeperson Press, 1989.

Doman, Glenn. *What to Do about Your Brain-Injured Child.* Philadelphia: Better Baby Press, 1974.

Dossey, Larry. *Space, Time and Medicine.* Boulder: New Science Library, 1982.

Eisenberg, Arlene. *What to Expect When You're Expecting.* New York: Workman Publishing, 1984.

Epstein, Gerald. *Healing Into Immortality: A New Spiritual Medicine of Healing Stories and Imagery.* New York: Bantam Books, 1994.

Feldenkrais, Moshe. *The Case of Nora.* New York: Harper & Row, 1977.

Feuerstein, George and Stephan Bodian. *Living Yoga: A Comprehensive Guide For Daily Life.* Los Angeles: Jeremy P. Tarcher, 1993.

Geralis, Elaine, ed. *Children with Cerebral Palsy: A Parents' Guide.* Maryland: Woodbine House, 1991.

Guinness, Alma E., ed. *Family Guide to Natural Medicine: How to Stay Healthy the Natural Way.* New York: Reader's Digest, 1993.

Hahnemann, Samuel. *Organon of Medicine.* New York: St. Martins Press, 1980.

Hanna, Thomas, ed. *Explorers of Humankind.* New York: Harper & Row, 1979.

Horrigan, Bonnie. *Healing and the Natural World: An Interview with Jim Jealous.* Aliso Viejo, CA: InnoVision Communications, 1996.

Kavner, Richard S. and Lorraine Dusky. *Total Vision.* New York: Kavner Books, 1978.

King, Hollis Heaton, ed. *Collected Papers of Viola M. Frymann: Legacy of Osteopathy to Children.* Indiannapolis: American Academy of Osteopathy, 1998.

Koetzsch, Ronald E. *The Parent's Guide to Alternatives in Education: The First In-depth Guide to the Full Range of Choices in Alternative Schooling, with all the Information you need to Decide what kind of Education is Right for Your Child.* Boston: Shambhala Publications, 1997.

Levine, Mel. *Keeping Ahead In School: A Student's Book about Learning Abilities and Learning Disorders.* Cambridge, MA: Educators Publishing Service, 1990.

Lobato, Debra L. *Brothers, Sisters, and Special Needs.* Baltimore: Paul H. Brookes Publishing Co., 1990.

Montagu, Ashley. *Touching: The Human Significance of the Skin,* 2nd ed. New York: Harper & Row, 1978.

Moore, Cory. *A Reader's Guide for Parent's of Children with Mental, Physical or Emotional Disabilities.* Rockville, MD: Woodbine House, 1990.

Pueschel, Siegfried M., et al. *The Special Child: A Source Book for Parents of Children with Developmental Disabilities,* 2nd ed. Baltimore: Paul H. Brookes Publishing, 1995.

Sandler, Stephen. *Osteopathy: The Illustrated Guide.* New York: Harmony Books, 1989.

Somatics Society, *Somatics Magazine,* 5 No. 3, "Journal of the Bodily Parts and Sciences." Novato, CA: The Somatics Society, 1985.

Speads, Carola H. *Ways to Better Breathing,* 1st ed. Rochester, VT: Healing Arts Press, 1978.

Weil, Andrew. *Health and Healing: A New Look at Medical Practices from Herbal Remedies to Biotechnology and What They Tell us About.* Boston: Houghton Mifflin, 1983.

Zeig, Jeffrey K., ed. *A Teaching Seminar with Milton H. Erickson.* New York: Brunner/Mazel, 1980.

index

A

Adeli suit, 239

Alexander method, 86, 99

allopathic medicine, 52

alternative medicine. *See also individual treatments*
  definition of, xxvii-xxviii
  fear of, 52

Amaya, Mayra, 16, 19, 20, 27, 29, 41, 46, 47, 57, 67, 70, 74, 77, 81, 82, 83, 92, 104

amniocentesis, 4

associations, list of, 248–50

athetosis, 96

athletes, challenged, 242

Augustine, George, 221

Awareness through Movement (ATM), 61, 69, 113

Ayurvedic medicine, 51–52

B

back arching, 29, 33

Bacon, Kevin, 3

Ballentine, Rudolph, 242–43

Baniel, Anat, x, 59, 61–62, 66, 69, 74, 75–88, 97–98, 143, 240

Bateson, Gregory, 99, 105

Batshaw, Mark L., 71

Berkshire Theater Festival, 2–3

Beth Israel Day School (BIDS), 127, 136, 143, 167–68, 177, 182–84

biofeedback, 181–82, 211, 222–23

birth trauma
  developmental delay and, 234

seizures and, 238
structural problems in babies and, 112

Black, Annie, 24, 40, 45, 48, 59, 75

Bobath, Karl and Berta, 26. *See also* NDT method

Bonner, Charles, 45, 48–50, 54, 59, 66, 74, 81, 83, 88, 92–93, 96, 98, 100, 106, 143

braces, 44, 45, 55

brain
  injuries to, 138, 185
  traumatic birth's effects on, 234, 238
  of young children, 176

Brandeis University, 221

Brazelton, T. Berry, 48

breathing, 67–69, 89–90, 157, 216

Bresnan, Michael, 27, 40, 49, 107, 128

Brook, Peter, 59

Brothers, Sisters, and Special Needs, 197

Buck, Pearl S., 53

Burke, Stoney, 162–63

Burrano, Michael, 171

C

Campbell, Worthington and Dorothy, 161

Capra, Fritjof, 105

The Case of Nora, 61

central nervous system dysfunction, 32

cerebral palsy
  Adeli suit and, 239–40

cerebral palsy *(continued)*
  causes of, 32
  Conductive Education and, 239
  definition of, 30, 31–32
  NDT method and, 26
  reactions to, 153
  selective posterior rhizotomy and, 95
  vision impairment and, 179–80
  Yoga and, 228
Challenged Athlete's Foundation, 242
Charles, Prince, 143
childhood organic learning, 60
children
  listening and talking to, 234–35
  putting on center stage, 235
Children's School of Science, 104–5, 160, 184–85, 186, 221
Children with Cerebral Palsy: A Parents' Guide, 32, 179
Children with Disabilities, 71
Chinese medicine, 52
chiropractors, 175–76
Churchill School, 153
Chutorian, Dr. (neurologist), 19, 23, 30, 40, 107, 128
Cohen, Cindy, 182
Cohen, Sherry Suib, 59
College Board, 226
Conductive Education, 239
Coulter, Harris L., 50
Cranial Osteopathy, 14, 124–25, 176
Criswell, Eleanor, 227
cruising, 63

D

deafness, 241. *See also* hearing impairments
DeBear, Kirsten, 209
denial, 34, 147
depression, 236–37
developmental delay, causes of, 234
diabetes, gestational, 3

doctors
  asking questions of, 235, 244
  not elevating, 44, 245
Doman, Glenn, 99, 105, 126, 137–39, 140
Down's Syndrome, 35, 228, 238–39
DPT vaccine, 50–51
drugs, psychotropic, 236–38
dystonia, 95–96

E

ear infections, 165–66, 241
EEG slowing, 222–23
episiotomy, 4, 8
Erickson, Milton, 98–99, 105
Euromed, 239–40
Exceptional Parent, 247
Exer-Cor, 157, 161
experts
  depending on, 26–27, 34
  list of, 251–52
eye contact, making, 234

F

Fabricant, Phyllis, 30, 40, 41–42, 54, 79
falling, 49, 65–66, 108–9, 136
Falmouth Commodores, 161–62
family meetings, 199–200
Feldenkrais, Moshe, 60, 61–62, 76, 77, 85, 97, 105, 106, 113, 137, 138
Feldenkrais Guild, 62, 84–85
Feldenkrais work, 25, 40, 45, 48, 59–62, 66–69, 73, 78, 83–88, 98, 106, 112–13, 140
Fernald School for the Handicapped, 35
Field, Sheryl, 240
Field Center for Children's Integrated Development, 240
Fisher, Barbara Loe, 50
fist clenching, 15, 29

Flexyx Neurotherapy System (FNS), xv, 211, 222–24
floppiness, 33
Forem, Sandra, 95–96
Foundation for Osteopathic Research and Training, 243
Friends Seminary, xii, 207
frustration, 55, 64, 81
Frymann, Viola, xiii, xiv, 81, 124, 125–28, 135, 136, 137, 141, 143–45, 157–58, 171, 176, 177–78, 186, 187, 215, 222, 229–30, 236, 240, 241
functional integration, 60–61, 62
functional skills, 26

G
Gateway School, 153
Genesis program, 221
Gifford, Jennifer, 164
Gindler, Elsa, 67
Grant, Alfred, 29, 31–34, 40, 43, 45, 54–55, 64
grasping, 16
Grasso, Joseph, 243
Green, Jill, 167

H
Hahnemann, Samuel, 122–23
"handicapped," use of, xxviii–xxix, 36
Hanna, Thomas, 42, 175
Harber, Sarah, xv–xvi
Haya, 100–101, 103, 114, 141–42, 165, 172, 178, 185, 187, 189–203
headgear, protective, 49, 108–9
hearing impairments, 47, 241
herpes, vaginal, 101
Heschel School, 100, 107, 116, 141
high tone, 33
"holistic medicine," definition of, xxviii
Homeopathy, 121–23, 143–45

Horowitz, Betsy, 117–18, 129
hypertonia, 33
hypnotherapy, 98
hypotonia, 33

I
immunizations, 50–51
inhibitory casts, 44, 45, 46, 54–55, 57, 62–63, 76
instincts, trusting your, 29, 233
Internet, using effectively, 243–44
intuition, listening to your, 233
Irving, Julius, 60
Iyengar, B. K. S., 99, 115
Iyengar system, 115, 228

J
Jealous, Jim, 213, 243

K
Kahn, Madeline, 3
Katz, Amy, 18–19, 26, 30
Katzive, Marion, 149, 150, 153
Kavner, Richard, 180–82
Keller, Helen, 36
Kessler, Daniel, 46, 47–48, 54, 55, 57, 63, 117
Kilmer, Val, 3

L
language disorders, 71
Larsen, Steven, 223
Law of Chronic Disease, 123
Law of Infinitesimals, 123
Law of Similars, 123
learning
    childhood organic, 60
    frustration and, 55, 56, 81
    unconscious mind and, 98
learning disabilities, 152–53, 183, 185, 228

Lee, Dr. (pediatrician), 9, 18, 19, 23, 29, 32, 39–40, 42, 44, 54, 73, 84, 158, 165, 209–10
listening
  to your children, 234–35
  to your gut, 233
Lobato, Debra, 197, 201
Lowen, Alexander, 99, 105
low tone, 33

M

Madell, Jane, 30, 47, 56
The Magic of Touch, 59
Manhattan Mothers and Others, xxvi
Masiello, Domenick, xv, xvi, 121–24, 144, 166, 171, 210–16, 218, 222, 243
massage, 13
McDowell Learning Center, 153–54
Mead, Margaret, 59, 105
meconium, 6, 8, 10, 19
Melnick, Virginia, 206–7
Menuhin, Yehudi, 59
"mongoloid," use of, 36
Montagu, Ashley, 99, 105
Morisco, Jackie, 165, 167, 173
motor delay, 32
motor disorders, 32, 239
movement, encouraging, 234
MTV News, 225
Murphy, James, 228
muscle tone, 33–34
music therapy, 136

N

National Childhood Encephalopathy Study, 50–51
National Organization for Rare Disorders, 247
natural childbirth, 4
NDT (neurodevelopmental treatment) method, 26

neuromotor dysfunction, 32
New York Film Academy, 225
New York League for the Hard of Hearing, 30–31, 47
nutrition, importance of, 235

O

observation, importance of, 233
Ochs, Len, 222–23
Ofir, Robbie, 59, 61, 62, 63–64, 67–68, 73, 75, 83
Oldberg, Phyllis and Julian, 146–47, 149, 150–51, 156–57, 158, 159, 166, 173, 208–9
open-minded, being, 236
organizations, list of, 248–50
originality, liberating, 238
orthotic devices, 43, 44, 45
Osteopathic Center for Children, 125, 129, 243
Osteopathic Manipulative Therapy (OMT), 122, 175
Osteopathy, 122, 123–24, 174–77, 213, 238, 243
Osteopathy: The Illustrated Guide, 176

P

Parent Training and Information Center, 247
patterning, 138–39
Pelkey, Zinaida, 210–12
Penn, Sean, 3
Pennsylvania, University of, xiv, 225
perceptual deficit, 56
Perls, Fritz, 67, 99
Perret, Yvonne M., 71
pertussis vaccine, 50–51
Peto, Andras, 239
physical therapy, 14–15, 18. *See also* NDT
Pitocin, 7
practice, 235

pressure experiments, 90–91

Pribram, Karl, 60, 105

Price, Larry, 43, 44, 57

professionals, list of, 251–52

Prozac, 236

Q

questions, asking, 235, 244

R

reactions, of others, xi-xii, 53–54

Reader's Digest Family Guide to Natural Medicine, 51–52, 122

reading, whole-language vs. phonetics approaches to, 140, 141

receptive language disorder, 71

record keeping, importance of, xxiv, 31, 236

resources, 247–52

Resources for Children with Special Needs, 150, 242, 243

"retarded," use of, 36

Rhogam, 3, 4

Ritalin, 236

Rodeph Sholom, 116–19, 141, 154–55, 157

Rolf, Ida, 99

S

Sail Caribbean, 221–22

San Diego Triathlon Challenge, 242

Sandler, Stephen, 176

SATs, 225–26

Scheer, Susan, 24, 25–27, 29, 34, 40, 42, 43, 49, 54, 64, 71–72, 78

scissoring, 33

Segal, Mia, 83, 84–87, 88, 92, 96–97, 112, 114

seizures, xxvi, 238

selective posterior rhizotomy, 95

self-esteem, 198–99

sensory experience, importance of, 44–45

sensory reeducation, 60

Seth

pregnancy with, 2–5

birth of, 2, 5–11

first ten months, 13–19

diagnosis of cerebral palsy, 2, 19–21

first birthday, 1–2

further consultations and therapy, 27–34, 39–51, 54–58

Anat Baniel and, 75–88

summer of 1986, 89–92, 98

Charles Bonner and, 92–93, 96, 98, 100

on birth of sister, 103

first summer at Woods Hole, 104–5

on horseback, 107

at Heschel School, 107–10, 116

walks, 111

Dr. Frymann and, 124–29, 135, 136, 137, 143–45, 167–69, 171, 177–78, 186, 187, 215

first grade, 116–19, 133, 136, 140–43, 145–46, 154–55, 157–58

special education and, 146–47, 149–54

first summer at CSS, 160–64

second grade, 164–69, 171–72, 177–84

Dr. Kavner and, 180–82

second summer at CSS, 184–85, 186

third grade, 186–89

fourth grade, 205–7, 208

in Team, 207–8

Dr. Masiello and Dr. Pelkey and, 210–16

Carl Stough and, 216–17, 218

at Friends Seminary, xiv, 207, 218

last summer at Woods Hole, 221

at Genesis program, 221

at Sail Caribbean, 221–22

begins Flexyx, 221–22

at Film Academy, 225

junior year, 225–27

in Yoga, 217, 228

A Shot in the Dark, 50

Shulman, Gary, 247
siblings, of special needs children,
    141–42, 165, 191–203
Siblings Information Network, 197
Siegel, Yvette, 159
sign language, 42, 54, 56, 63
sitting up, 16, 33
skin-fold experiments, 89–90
Slab Boys, 3
Smith, Peggy, 40–41, 43, 56, 64–65,
    66, 78
Solomon, Ellen, 136, 140, 143,
    151–52, 157–58, 167
spasticity, 33, 95
Speads, Carola, xii, 66–70, 73, 74,
    83, 88, 89–90, 97
special education, 146–47, 149–54,
    165
"special needs," definition of, xvi,
    186, 190
speech therapy, 40–41, 165, 167
Spielberg, Steven, 221
spina bifida, 239
Spitz, Eugene, 40, 126, 128–29
Springall, Peter, 126, 129, 137,
    139–40, 141, 145, 157–58, 162,
    167, 177
static encephalopathy, 32
Stephen Gaynor School, 152, 153,
    159, 164–67, 182–84, 188, 205–7
Still, Andrew Taylor, 243
Stone Mountain Counseling Center,
    xiii, 211, 223, 227
Stough, Carl, xiii, xiv, 216–17, 218,
    227
Studio Elementary School, 79, 100
sucking, importance of, 17, 112
Sumar, Sonia, 228–29
Sutherland, William Garner, 124,
    243
swallowing, 112
sympathetic nervous system, 42

T
talking, 234–35
Tay-Sachs, 3
tests, standardized, 117, 151, 187–88,
    193–94, 225–26
toe, big, 114–15, 140
tongue, 42, 80
touch, importance of, 234
Trager, Milton, 87
Trager Psycho Physical Integration,
    87
trauma, 223. *See also* birth trauma

U
unconscious mind, 98–99
United Cerebral Palsy, 31, 34, 53

V
vaccinations, 50–51
vision training, 180–82
visual impairments, 179–80

W
walkers, 43–44
Ways to Better Breathing, 67, 89
Weeks, Carolyn, 106
*What to Do about Your Brain-Injured
    Child*, 126, 137
What to Expect When You're Expecting,
    3
Woods Hole, 104–5, 160, 184–85,
    221

Y
Yoga, 52, 115, 227–29

Z
Zukav, Gary, 105